'This is a book that belongs on the bookshelf ... ... interested in contemporary British theatre, black performance studies, or the terrain that exists between these dynamic fields.' — Harvey Young, Northwestern University, USA

'A timely contribution to the field of theatre and performance studies, this important book expands the critical conversation relating to Black British Drama and helps to establish this area as a significant genre worthy of study.' — Colin Chambers, University of Kingston, UK

As a refashioning of British theatre history, this edited collection spans seven decades of distinctive playwriting from black-centred perspectives. Interweaving social and cultural context with close critical analysis of key dramatists' plays from the 1950s to the present day, leading scholars explore how these dramatists have created an enduring, transformative and diverse cultural presence.

The essays establish a clear critical and creative trajectory while also recognising the diverse aesthetic legacies and cultural continuities that characterise the work of black dramatists in Britain. Playwrights examined include Barry Reckord, debbie tucker green Kwame Kwei-Armah, and Oladipo Agboluaje.

Mary F. Brewer is Senior Lecturer in English and Drama at the University of Loughborough, UK.

Lynette Goddard is Senior Lecturer in Drama and Theatre at Royal Holloway, University of London, UK.

Deirdre Osborne is Senior Lecturer in Drama and Theatre Arts at Goldsmiths, University of London, UK.

Modern and Contemporary Black British Drama

Edited by

Mary F. Brewer

Lynette Goddard

Deirdre Osborne

 palgrave

First published 2015 by
PALGRAVE

Palgrave in the UK is an imprint of Macmillan Publishers Limited, registered
in England, company number 785998, 4 Crinan Street, London N1 9XW

Palgrave Macmillan in the US is a division of St Martin's Press LLC,
175 Fifth Avenue, New York, NY 10010.

Palgrave is a global imprint of the above companies and is represented
throughout the world.

Palgrave® and Macmillan® are registered trademarks in the United States,
the United Kingdom, Europe and other countries.

ISBN: 978–0–230–30319–5   hardback
ISBN: 978–0–230–30320–1   paperback

This book is printed on paper suitable for recycling and made from fully managed
and sustained forest sources. Logging, pulping and manufacturing processes are
expected to conform to the environmental regulations of the country of origin.

A catalogue record for this book is available from the British Library.

Library of Congress Cataloging-in-Publication Data

Modern and contemporary Black British drama / [edited by] Mary Brewer,
Lynette Goddard and Deirdre Osborne.
    pages cm
    ISBN 978–0–230–30320–1 (pbk.)
    1. English literature – Black authors – History and criticism. 2. English drama –
20th century – History and criticism. 3. English drama – 21st century – History
and criticism. I. Brewer, Mary, 1968– II. Goddard, Lynette, 1966- editor. III.
Osborne, Deirdre.

PR120.B55M63 2015
822'.91409896041—dc23   2014037827

Printed in China.

Contents

Part III Neo-Millennial

Acknowledgements

The contributors and editors would like to acknowledge the following people and organisations, who kindly provided them with information for the publication of this collection of essays: Bola Agbaje, Oladipo Agboluaje, The Black Plays Archive at the National Theatre, London, Theatre and Performance Collections of the Victoria and Albert Museum, London, and the British Library Sound Archive, London. We would like to extend special thanks to Kate Haines, Jenni Burnell and Felicity Noble for their unstinting help in guiding this book through the commissioning and publication process. We also acknowledge with thanks the support and encouragement of our colleagues and students at Loughborough University, Royal Holloway, University of London and Goldsmiths College, University of London. Thanks also to Richard H. Smith for kindly providing us with a fitting cover image from a classic black play. Lastly, the editors would like to thank our contributors for their commitment, patience, and timeliness throughout the process of completing this book.

Cover Image

Shango Baku (right) and Okezie Morro in Mustapha Matura's *Rum and Coca Cola*. Co-produced by English Touring Theatre, Talawa Theatre Company and West Yorkshire Playhouse, 2010; directed by Don Warrington. Photo by Richard H. Smith: http://www.richardhs.com.

Notes on Contributors

Nicola Abram is Lecturer in Literatures in English at the University of Reading. She is interested in post-colonial and feminist writings, non-naturalistic aesthetics and archival methodologies. Her recent research sees these interests converge in black British women's theatre; she has published on contemporary playwright debbie tucker green, and is currently preparing a monograph. As Widening Participation Officer in the School of Literature and Languages, Nicola works to promote equitable admissions processes, diverse curricula and inclusive pedagogies. Nicola is also Associate Fellow of the Higher Education Academy, and Vice Chair of the Postcolonial Studies Association.

Mary F. Brewer is Senior Lecturer in English and Drama at the University of Loughborough. She has a D.Phil. in English and American studies from Sussex University, where her research focused on women playwrights. One of her principal areas of specialisation is the representation of race and gender in modern and contemporary British and American drama. She is the author of two monographs, *Race, Sex and Gender in Contemporary Women's Theatre* (1999) and *Staging Whiteness* (2006). Her edited collections include *Exclusions in Feminist Thought: Challenging the Boundaries of Womanhood* (2002) and *Harold Pinter's The Dumb Waiter* (2009).

Brian Crow recently retired from the Department of Drama and Theatre Arts at the University of Birmingham. He continues to research and write in his specialist areas and is currently working on a monograph on African literary theatre in English and French. He has taught at universities in Nigeria and Australia, as well as in Scotland and England.

Ekua Ekumah is a PhD candidate at Goldsmiths, University of London attached to an AHRC funded research project, in the Theatre and Performance Department. Ekua holds an MFA in Theatre Arts, from the School of Performing Arts, University of Ghana, Legon, where she lectures in the Department of Theatre Arts. She is a trained actor, earning a BA (Hons) in Theatre Arts from Rose Bruford College of Speech and Drama.

Lynette Goddard is Senior Lecturer in the Department of Drama and Theatre, Royal Holloway, University of London. Her research focuses on contemporary black British theatre, looking in particular at new writing by black playwrights and black directed adaptations of Shakespeare and other canonical plays. Her publications include the monographs *Staging Black Feminisms: Identity, Politics, Performance* (2007) and *Contemporary Black British Playwrights: Margins to Mainstream* (2015), which examines the mainstream profile and social politics in plays by Kwame Kwei-Armah, debbie tucker green, Roy Williams and Bola Agbaje.

Deirdre Osborne is Senior Lecturer in the Department of Theatre and Performance at Goldsmiths, University of London, where she convenes the MA *Black British Writing*. In addition to her research in late-Victorian women's writing, maternity and colonial ideology, she has published on many aspects of Black British poetry, fiction and drama, as well as editing the black British play anthologies *Hidden Gems Vol. I and II* (2008; 2012). A current project includes the editing of *The Cambridge Companion to British Black and Asian Literature 1945–2010*. She is Associate Editor of the literary journal *Women's Writing 1558–1915*.

D. Keith Peacock is a retired Senior Lecturer in Drama of the University of Hull where he specialised in Modern British Theatre. He has lectured and directed in the USA, the West Indies and Europe. Among his many publications are the books *Radical Stages: Alternative History in Modern British Drama* (1991), *Harold Pinter and the New British Theatre* (1997), *Thatcher's Theatre* (1999) and *Changing Performance: Culture and Performance in the British Theatre since 1945* (2007).

Michael Pearce completed his PhD titled 'Black British Theatre: A Transnational Perspective' at the University of Exeter in 2013. His research focuses on tracing influences from Africa, the Caribbean and the USA on black theatre in Britain. Michael has recently finished working with the National Theatre on their 'Black Plays Archive' project, for which he conducted filmed interviews with theatre practitioners as part of the project's catalogue of oral testimonies for their website. Michael is also a theatre producer and director and works between the UK and his native Zimbabwe.

Meenakshi Ponnuswami teaches dramatic literature and theatre history at Bucknell University, where she is Associate Professor of English. Her research focuses on racial and sexual politics in contemporary British theatre. Her publications include critical studies of plays by Caryl Churchill and Winsome Pinnock, as well as wide-ranging surveys of British feminist theatre, New Left historical drama and black British theatre. She is currently researching British Asian stand-up comedy and African American drama.

Suzanne Scafe is Reader in Caribbean and Postcolonial Literatures at London South Bank University. She has published several essays on Black British writing and culture and Caribbean women's fiction. Her recent work includes essays on Black British women's autobiographical writing which were published in the journals *Changing English* (17:2), *Women: A Cultural Review* (20:4) and *Life Writing* (10:2). She is the co-editor of a collection of essays, *I Am Black/White/Yellow: The Black Body in Europe* (2007) and 'Affects and Creolisation', *Feminist Review* (104), and she is currently co-editing a special issue on 'Black British Feminisms' for the same journal.

Helen Thomas is Principal Lecturer in English and Writing at Falmouth University, UK. Her research interests include black British writing, C18th slave narratives and narratives of illness and disease. Her publications include two monographs, *Romanticism and Slave Narratives* (2000) and *Caryl Phillips* (2006), a co-edited volume, *The Nose Book: Representations of the Nose in Art and Literature* (2000), a chapter entitled 'Slave Narratives and Transatlantic Literature' in *The Oxford Handbook of the African American Slave Narrative*, ed. John Ernest (2013) and a chapter on 'Breast Cancer Autopathographies' in *Nothing Normal*, ed. Jennifer Cooke (2013).

Victor Ukaegbu is Principal Lecturer in Theatre at the University of Bedfordshire. He is a theatre and performance academic, practitioner and critic with interests in African and Western theatre and performances, including Black British and Diaspora theatres, applied theatre, theatre adaptations, intercultural theatre, post-colonial performances and ethnodrama. His latest publications include *Reverberations: 'Britishness', Aesthetics and Small-Scale Theatres* (2013); *Intercultural to Cross-Cultural Theatre: Tara Arts and the Development of British Asian Theatre* (2013); *Re-Contextualising Space Use in Indigenous African Communal Performance* (2013); *African Funeral Rites: Sites for Performing, Participating and Witnessing of Trauma; Performance Research: On Trauma* (2011); and *Anansegoro: Modern Storytelling as Narrative Trope in Contemporary Ghanaian Literary Theatre* (2010).

Framing Black British Drama: Past to Present

Mary F. Brewer, Lynette Goddard, Deirdre Osborne

This book aims to trace the evolution of post-war drama in Britain from the 1950s to the first decade of the 2000s in a selection of key plays by black writers. In giving critical attention to this work, *Modern and Contemporary Black British Drama* centralises perspectives and play-writing that are often positioned beyond the sightlines of Britain's conduits to theatrical and cultural longevity. The book observes the dynamic of cultural reinvention articulated by R. Victoria Arana and Lauri Ramey (2004) in relation to literature, charted via the post-colo-nial theorising that has flourished within the late twentieth- and early twenty-first-century academy. It extricates the work from a traditional discursive positioning, as cleaved to discussions including British Asian or African American drama, to make the case for a black dramatic canon, addressing the question mark around this idea posed by Gail Low and Marion Wynne-Davies (2006). Whereas canon formation can suggest the replication of the hegemonic critical apparatus and its dominant rhet-oric, an aesthetic focus can also function to retrieve works, to reformu-late the parameters of canonicity. In this spirit, *Modern and Contemporary Black British Drama* explores the aesthetics of the plays and their distinc-tive contribution to modern and contemporary British culture. For as Kobena Mercer has argued, there exists a 'relative neglect of the aesthetic dimension that has contributed to the current state of play whereby black artists in Britain may be recognised, acknowledged, and tolerated in the art world, but the work itself often seems to be taken less seriously as an enriching site of aesthetic experience' (Mercer, 2007, p. 71).

In this volume, post-war British theatre historiography is thus re-viewed through a lens focused exclusively upon black British drama-tists, and contributes a unique angle to the critical mass forming around this emergent scholarly field. The essays explore how modern and

1

contemporary black British dramatists' work coincides with discourses of race and gender, and particularly the role that New Writing has played in articulating contemporary experiences *vis à vis* debates about race, nation and Britishness.[1] Playwrights such as Kwame Kwei-Armah and Roy Williams were often placed under the umbrella of 'new', when each had been writing plays since the mid-1990s.

This volume seeks to acknowledge the continuity of black British play-writing within frameworks of cultural knowledge. As a relatively new area of dedicated study within contemporary British theatre scholarship, its essays also constitute tests of different methodological approaches to analysing contemporary black British plays and productions. The application of a range of critical approaches is fundamental to this project including literary-based textual analysis, some performance analysis and approaches that draw from interdisciplinary links to social theory and cultural studies. Recognition of these various approaches reflects the diversity of scholarly training and contributors' research interests, which in all their variety play an important part in consolidating and further developing the field.

Past – present

The increased profile of British-born black playwrights in Britain from the 1990s, and the publication of their play texts to accompany productions in London and regional venues coincide with a growth in scholarly interest in their work. One feature of such scholarship has been to restore the contributions of writers from earlier periods whose heritage has paved the way for the substantial neo-millennial presence. In particular, this scholarship features the post-war migratory, first-generation playwrights who have not yet had the widespread critical attention that their legacy deserves. As the essays by Helen Thomas, Mary F. Brewer and Brian Crow show, male playwrights such as Errol John, Barry Reckord and Mustapha Matura (in keeping with the dominance of men in British theatre at this time) premiered work during periods in Britain's history where multiculturalism and diversity initiatives had not yet influenced and altered artistic access points for representing Britain's multi-ethnic experiences. The essays in this volume provide a bridge between post-war historical periods and cultural responses to these social and theatrical circumstances. They recognise the inheritances bequeathed across a body of drama spanning 60 years from the early plays of Reckord in the 1950s to more recent ones by debbie tucker green and Bola Agbaje. This approach foregrounds continuity and acts as a counter-stance to marginalisation, and the critical amnesia that has too often characterised the history of plays by writers who are black, in British theatre historiography.[2] Black British writers have played a crucial role in the formation of modern British theatre, and have provoked a revolution in dramatic language and form that is equitable with the impact attributed to the Angry Young Men in (re)defining theatre history. The collection explores the meanings and interpretations of this impact.

To recalibrate the positioning of Britain's modern and contemporary black playwrights' work necessitates the acknowledgement too of the heft of determiners which have traditionally constrained the creative autonomy, production opportunities, and the cultural sustainability of this work. As Maryrose Casey notes in writing about Indigenous Australian performance, 'These frames provide a basis for understanding and constructing collective narratives about events that become social memory' (Casey, 2004, p. xvii). The defining frames that have surrounded black British playwrights' production include a range of issues emanating from: venues – their programming and commissioning trends, the politics of arts subsidy, the problematics of archiving, uneven critical reception, absence from drama school training and other educational curricula, the lack of non-stereotyping casting opportunities and niche marketing by Britain's theatre complexes in terms of audience diversification.[3] Moreover, as Claire Cochrane notes, the seeding of black heritage in theatre historiography has also been 'further complicated by the fragmented and inadequately published record, itself a product of marginalisation within the academy' (2011, p. 224). As shall become apparent in the essays that follow, the matrix of commissioning, programming, reception and the establishment of a critical mass in some cases, continues to contribute to the difficulty that black dramatists in Britain face, in obtaining a secure cultural foothold. This volume represents a timely intervention into redressing this dynamic.

Proportional representation

Although well preceding the periodisation of this volume, the legacy of racism must be acknowledged in any account concerning the evolution of modern and contemporary British theatre, and the positioning of black writers' plays.[4] From the early modern period onwards, overt racial ideology took shape, as an underpinning of imperialist territorial acquisition. It became the rationale for the capture and commodification of African people in trans-Atlantic enslavement, through to the subjugations enacted in the maintenance of the British Empire. The origin of its performance theatrically begins with mediaeval and renaissance stages where visual and verbal metaphors of blackness equated black people with increasingly negative and debased representations. These evolved across theatre history as informed by, and contingent upon, surrounding social behaviours and power relations. The development of theatrical practices of prosthetic blackness, whereby white actors employed costuming and skin colouring techniques, established a long-standing performance semiotics that was still evident in the 1980s.[5] In their contextualising chapters, Helen Thomas, Meenakshi Ponnuswami and Keith Peacock indicate the parameters around the social, political and economic frameworks in which cultural expression operates, to suggest how the plays by black writers affirm, resist and rewrite the terms and impact of this legacy.

The post-war era is arguably the moment that might be claimed as the beginning of a sustained black theatre movement of actors and practitioners in Britain. The sizeable presence of black artists within the British theatre complex is ostensibly a late-twentieth-century occurrence following on from the seismic alterations to Britain's demographic composition via migration after World War II. Unsurprisingly then, the post-war and subsequent years have become the most significant in terms of the representation of black British experiences in plays written by black British playwrights. In this respect, drama constitutes a barometer of socio-cultural shifts qualified by class, economic and social access that defines elite and popular contexts, and the divisions between professional and mainstream, and amateur and community spheres. As W. B. Worthen writes:

> Stage production operates in both a material and an ideological register: the theatre works with (and against) emerging (and residual) social, political, legal, economic, and religious institutions not only to represent social reality – a vision of what is (and isn't), of what is (im-)possible – but to fashion human beings as subjects of/in ideology. (1994, p. 3)

The decades in which black British theatre flourished relative to its usual marginality means that the impact and significance of these creative and receptive peaks must be viewed in relation to periods in which other more inhibitory factors feature. As Low and Wynne-Davies highlight in relation to literature, 'the 1980s represents a kind of creative watershed in black expressive cultures [...] which has certainly led to the current eminent stature of some black artists and to an intense critical interest in their work' (2006, p. 1). It is also important to recognise that many of the plays discussed in this book were performed within black-led and women's theatre companies that were prominent in the 1970s and 1980s. In the 1950s, the director Joan Clarke (a Unity Theatre activist) claimed new territory in being a rarity as both a woman director and in pro-actively staging plays with black actors. Although the director–writer relationship is an area that falls outside the scope of this volume, it should be noted that women like Clarke paved the trail for the possibility of Joan-Ann Maynard, Yvonne Brewster, Paulette Randall, Josette Bushell-Mingo, Dawn Walton and Karena Johnson to follow in later decades.

Developments since the 1970s-era can be linked to how government funding initiatives affected the presence of black-authored plays on the British stage. As Thomas' chapter suggests, the racialised politics of subsidised theatre saw more casualties than recipients as the twentieth century drew to a close. Although socio-political factors of economic recession impinge periodically upon subsidised arts sectors (which are overwhelmingly, the primary funding contexts for theatres in Britain and in particular, black artists' work), these have again in recent times been further enforced by the Conservative-led Coalition government's proposed austerity budgets.[6]

In opening the book's final section, Peacock's chapter outlines how black playwrights in the new millennium reaped the benefits of New Writing initiatives that characterised the subsidised theatre sector. Much of this was also impelled by this sector's attempt to attract a younger and more diverse audience composition, which better reflected contemporary society – the audiences of the future. The 2005 transfer of the first play by a black British writer, Kwei-Armah's *Elmina's Kitchen* (2003), to the West End was greeted optimistically by many artists and critics as heralding something of a sea change. In celebrating the achievements and retrieving the merits of these neo-millennial black dramatists, it should be questioned, too, why the proliferation of plays that characterises the first decade appears to be diminishing? Whereas numerous productions typified a single season (such as 2007/8), there are fewer plays in total across an aggregate of the first three years of the second decade. This could suggest retrospectively, the prematurity of claims for a cultural renaissance (as was expressed by a number of writers and directors themselves at the time), that it was in fact an anomaly to the traditional normative, which has been the low representation of black artists' work across all of Britain's cultural institutions.[7]

Standpoints and vantage points

As Bruce King notes, the beginnings of West Indian drama in England 'is intertwined with the beginnings of the new West Indian theatre in the Caribbean' (King, 2004, p. 71). The diasporic routes followed by black writers have been both geographical and via acts of the imaginary. When *Black Pieces* by Matura was staged at the Ambience and for the *Black and White Power* season at the ICA 1970, it marked the beginning of a new direction of first-wave, first-generation, black male playwrights following Reckord, Wole Soyinka and Derek Walcott. As Foco Novo's Founding Artistic Director Roland Rees describes, they 'allowed an English audience to experience a world hidden from their view' (1992, p. 25). Together with Michael Abbensetts, Matura represents West Indian dramatists who wrote from a colonial educational background and anti-colonial politics. As Crow's chapter shows in relation to Matura's work, West Indian male dramatists produced male-dominated, Caribbean-centred worlds where white characters are marginal and frequently one-dimensional. Their work begins a tradition whereby black dramatists have persistently and successfully exploited the gaps in representations of Britishness via the stage, drawing connections between language, race and power, in order to generate alternative and at times, oppositional conceptions of modern and contemporary British identity with all its variegations. This includes reconfiguring perspectives on white British identities, where the white majority culture is represented invariably from a black person's viewpoint.

To understand precisely how black British playwrights have exploited such gaps, it is necessary to consider the origins of the term British as a descriptor of national and cultural identity, the range of racial identity categories that may be encompassed within it, as well as how it differs from Englishness in dominant racial discourse. As mentioned earlier, the notion of race was formalised as a concept in English language in the Early Modern period, and within the context of the sixteenth-century slave trade, at which time English was understood to refer to descendants of the Anglo-Saxon race. The economic imperative that underlay the creation of distinctions between the lighter-skinned colonisers and those whom they enslaved was overwritten by a narrative in which race became naturalised; in other words, historically, one could not become English – one could only be born English.

British identity, in contrast, is the outcome of a different kind of historical struggle – one rooted mainly in the direct conquest and maintenance of a global empire. Linda Colley's study of how the British nation was established reveals the connection between imperial wars and how these created porous borders of Britishness, compared to Englishness, as a concept of national and racial identity, for the defence of empire could not afford a concept of Britishness based on birth (Colley, 2009, pp. 376–7). A mass consciousness of patriotism was required to sustain the British Empire, and this could be generated only by defining a wide range of people as members of the British nation. Thus, for instance, Welsh and Scottish people are included as British. Given the history of English colonialism within the British Isles this is of course problematic – as devolution and the referendum over Scottish independence reveals.

However, as so many of the plays treated in this volume illustrate, black people have rarely been viewed as legitimate claimants either to Englishness or to Britishness, despite the greater permeability of the latter. Amina Mama recognises the deep structural tension between blackness and Britishness, when she describes how the black British subject is 'born out of an imposed contradiction between blackness and British-ness, British-ness being equated with whiteness in the dominant symbolic order' (Mama, 1995, p. 114). The terrain for modern and contemporary black British writers is in part shaped by the presence of a racial 'other' – whiteness – and this intersection means that Black-defined Britishness involves not only the representation of a more authentic black identity, but also the deconstruction and refashioning of hegemonic whiteness in Britain.[8] The connection between Britishness and whiteness has led many black British playwrights to offer reconfigurations of white British identities, and to foreground a black person's viewpoint on the white majority culture. Although first-generation immigrant plays and later plays by black British-born writers may indeed other the English in different ways, and defamiliarise expectations, both strands constitute a vital dimension to the aesthetic development of playwriting heritage, what Jamaican dub poet Louise Bennett (a RADA graduate) was to observe with a satirical eye, 'But me wonderin' how dem gwine stan'/ Colonizin in reverse' (1966, p. 180).

The discursive negotiation of remaining forever defined in relation to whiteness, while gaining agency through constructing a more authentic role in one's cultural expression and representational possibilities is navigated in differing degrees throughout the volume. Heidi Safia Mirza points to the challenges of creating this authentic agency when she writes,

> To be black and British is to be unnamed in official discourse. The construction of a national British identity is built upon a notion of a racial belonging, upon a hegemonic white ethnicity that never speaks its presence. We are told that you can be either one or the other, black or British, but not both. (1997, p. 3)

Black identity in all its variety rather than as essentialised remains the subject of much black British writing. Nicola Abram's essay on Winsome

Pinnock, Michael Pearce's essay on Kwei-Armah and Lynette Goddard's chapter on Williams foreground how its significance to modern drama and theatre lies as much in its relation to traditional representations of Britishness as it does to the development and transmission of a self-defined black British identity. British theatre, like British identity, may be defined as much by what it does not represent as by what it does present. As Nirmal Puwar argues, the projections of neutrality of social and cultural spaces is highly questionable; rather they are as racialised and gendered in power relations as the bodies who enter into them – or who do not. Black British dramatists in the UK demonstrably constitute what Puwar has termed 'space invaders'. There have been – and are – entry points for their work, but what their presence means or how it alters British theatre is open to question (Puwar, 2004, p. 1).

The sense of belonging *or not* differs significantly among first-, second- and third-generation black British people, and, as Suzanne Scafe's discussion of Caryl Phillips' work demonstrates, this has been an important theme for black British dramatists. The inter-textuality that can be located in the work of playwrights across the 1980s and 1990s reveals acts of repetition and transformation of textual structures as well as themes. Today's young creative artists are much more comfortable in asserting their right to occupy a part of the British cultural landscape than were their parents' and grandparents' generations whose birth-lands were generally outside Britain. In this respect, chapters by Deirdre Osborne, Ekua Ekumah and Victor Ukaegbu evince particular negotiations with a theatricalised voice, one that is poly-vocal in its dismantling of the standard registers of English as an aesthetic as well as communicative strategy. The new millennial prominence of British Nigerian cultural presences on the stage has reshaped Caribbean heritage as the predominant trope and, as Pearce's chapter addresses, the larger diaspora. Key creative figures from transnational contexts in Africa, the Caribbean, and the US, continue to be a formative influence upon some contemporary black British dramatists.

Moreover, how the black British community is politically configured has also altered over time. In the immediate post-war era through to the mid-1980s, when Caribbean and South-East Asian immigrants faced particularly virulent forms of racism, activism under an inclusive banner of blackness drew together many diverse groups where the term Black signified anyone who was not white. The use of capital 'B' still signals this political dimension today for many people, referring to a range of ethnicities and nationalities from the regions spanning the Caribbean to South-East Asia, to the continent of Africa. Black, when employed by black British playwrights, tends to be more delimited in scope to refer to people of Caribbean or African antecedence and their descendants. In Ponnuswami's chapter, this tapering of Black as a political category is charted to pave the way for its nuances in the plays discussed. Although black British dramatists may increasingly treat race as a metaphor today, this does not mean that they ignore the reality of racism or neglect to illustrate and challenge its continuing impact on black people's lives. It is important to realise that the meaning of British identity foregrounded in their work is not bounded solely by concerns with race, but the intersectional exploration of a range of social identities: class, gender, sexuality and religion among others.

The artistic inroads made by the dramatists in this book cannot be considered without acknowledging the back cloth of a historical legacy that is characterised by neglect and even erasure. In a trajectory that can be traced from Reckord's experiences in the 1950s, through to Puwar's theorisation of the allowable spaces of occupation (and production) that contour contemporary writers' work, there is a shifting insider/outsider dynamic that pervades black playwrights' membership of this cultural institution. Issues surrounding longevity and its tenuousness have always tracked the progress of black writers in Britain along the road to cultural legitimation. Modern theatre bears the hallmark of the politics of exclusion imprinted from the surrounding society in which it operates, one which has exerted and continues to exert contributory negligence in respect of black playwrights and their work.

As first-generation migrants focused upon gaining the security of food, shelter and employment to sustain family life in a hostile surrounding environment, there is little documented evidence that theatre-going was either a priority or even possible. It should be remembered that in the context of migration and racism, the audiences and attendees were overwhelmingly white. In the West End, the staging of black plays was dominated by the work of African American writers, namely, Langston Hughes's musical *Simply Heavenly* directed by Laurence Harvey at the Adelphi in 1958, followed by Lorraine Hansberry's *A Raisin in the Sun* at the same theatre in 1959. Although no archival study has yet been conducted to explore the ethnic–demographic composition of audiences attending plays by black writers, the glimpse possible of this time, is achieved in the reviews of these plays in the West End; as Cochrane concludes, 'there was an audience in London for plays about the black experience, but as something that happened at a safe distance, somewhere else and certainly not to be mediated by Black British actors' (2011, p. 143). This elicits questions about the split between the imagined, the ideal and the anticipated audiences for black playwrights. As Cochrane refers to 'the black experience', this demonstrates another restrictive factor for black writers in the context of cultural opportunities. Although unity is a key element in refusing a 'divide and rule' dynamic, reduction to a single term also conflates actual diversity into homogeneity, rather than evoking the possible nuances of national, historical and cultural variety that accompanies artistic creativity and its reception.

Although claiming diasporic roots from Africa and the Caribbean, the survival of these influences has become more mediated by second-generation writers as they meld the context of a British-located upbringing with the cultures of their parents and grandparents. A significant transformative aspect lies in what audiences could hear on stage from the mid-twentieth century, where plays by black playwrights enabled the articulation of vernaculars, accents, dialects and creolised languages from black cultural heritages. During the 1950s when Trinidadian writer Errol John's *Moon on a Rainbow Shawl* (1956) was staged at the Royal Court (and won *The Observer* play competition), his use of what Kamau Brathwaite was to term 'nation language' (1984, p. 5) challenged Standard English as the expected and inevitable sound on stage. The influences of spoken-word poetry further endowed weight and recognition to the fluidity of English as a powerful political, cultural and linguistic public voice for black writers on the pin wheel of influences from oral and print cultures. As any focus on textuality – its in/de/scribing, re/en/coding – exposes language to prevailing or understood structural principles and the resistances to them, the linguistic assertions of such forms and polyphonic experimentation characterise many of the plays from Matura to tucker green.

One area in which major critical work still remains to be achieved is in Afro-Queer theatre history in Britain, and plays by writers who identify under Black Lesbian Gay Bisexual Transgender (BLGBT). Whereas the visual arts, literature and performance media have received limited critical attention in this respect, the area of playwriting and theatre has suffered from neglect.[9] Work by BLGBT playwrights regrettably falls beyond the discursive scope of *Modern and Contemporary Black British Drama*, but it signals rather than condones this absence. Although progress has been made by the black community in terms of achieving recognition of a legitimate presence in British society, there remains a clear need for still greater inclusiveness of Britain's diverse communities on British stages. The prominence enjoyed today by writers of Caribbean descent such as tucker green, Williams and Kwei-Armah, and the presence of the post-1990s British Nigerian writers from Biyi Bandele-Thomas (not included in this volume) and Oladipo Agboluaje to Agbaje suggests that black dramatists are playing a more equal role in establishing creative contributions to the collective understanding of what it means to be British, and helping to make theatre a leading space for its cultural redefinition at least.

Trajectory

The book is divided into three parts, clustered by decades. Part one focuses on plays that respond to the experience of black post-war migration to Britain. Part two features the work of second-generation black British playwrights, whereas Part three addresses drama produced in the New Millennium. The chronologically ordered sections offer a view of the field as it has developed in Britain's post-war theatre complex, attuned to the surrounding socio-cultural and political climates alongside aesthetic developments. Each of the book's three sections begins with an essay that contextually maps the period, thereby helping to locate textual analyses of the plays within relevant historical, political and theoretical paradigms. Thomas writes about the social and political conditions for producing black British drama from the 1950s through to the early 1980s. Ponnuswami addresses these issues in the 1980s through to the 1990s, and Peacock focuses on black British theatre since 2000. These prefacing chapters also offer theatrical contextualisations, which then segue into discussions of selected key plays in the chapters that follow.

The essays that treat individual black playwrights provide a rich analysis of the intersection of race and theatre in modern and contemporary Britain and a wide range of their attendant socio-cultural and political issues. Brewer charts the racism that surrounded the positioning of high and low culture in Reckord's playwriting context in Britain where, as the working-class white male playwrights achieved perpetuity, Reckord's work, acclaimed at the time of its premiere, sank into relative obscurity until its recognition and revival through publication in the past few years. Crow concentrates on Matura's dramatic treatments of the issue of identity, which he deems central to Matura's writing from his earliest plays in the 1960s. The chapter addresses Matura's approach to the pervasive sense of rootlessness that is common to the post-colonial condition, as well as how the plays explore both the subjective and social effects of colonialism upon black migrants to Britain. Scafe's chapter on Phillips maps the relationship between contemporary British identities and the notions of shared histories between overlapping and conflicting cultures, as revealed throughout his body of plays, including early works and later intertextual material when he had departed from drama as his preferred genre. In particular, Scafe analyses how Phillips' writing for the stage is informed by an understanding of shared experiences within and between national and cultural borders.

This relationality becomes further complicated by the next generation of dramatists who, as Abram, Goddard and Pearce's chapters identify, are British-born and raised writers of Caribbean descent. They introduce both thematic innovations and shape stage idiom in ways distinctive from the legacies of colonial English employed by the previous playwriting generation. Abram explores the female-centred heritage created by Pinnock's matrilineal focus, where the dramatising of first-generation experiences is a vital developmental route to negotiating these cultural inheritances – as tailored to the material and social realities of an English context. The duality of holding onto and valuing cultural inheritances, and yet divesting oneself of generationally inflected legacies is apparent. As Abram configures women's roles in Pinnock's dramas, Goddard centralises the contestations of masculinity in Williams' works. A number of overlapping arenas of performance are identified by Goddard's discussion of sport as a motif in Williams' work, and its compelling display as both dismantling and consolidating expected social roles and aspirations. Goddard considers the power of media representations in a dialogic relation to the theatre, and its use as a site of sociological debate in Williams' plays. For Pearce, the influence of August Wilson upon Kwei-Armah features as an abiding framework in which to encounter his work with its emphasis on the universal aspects of black people's histories and experiences. He foregrounds how Kwei-Armah's plays frequently dramatise correctives to past oppressions, richly referenced by polemic and spiritual sources which are woven into the dramaturgy.

As the anticipated audiences in mainstream settings are more apparently heterogeneous by the 2000s, not only inter-racially or ethnically, but also in terms of the various communities of black people who live in Britain, this becomes reflected in production semiotics. Exploring the work of Nigerian heritage playwrights Agbaje and Agboluaje, chapters by Ekumah and Ukaegbu identify the changing sense of diasporic aesthetics in conjunction with the audiences for their work. Both chapters are careful to underscore the influences of African-inherited traditions in staging techniques and forms which are not dependant upon Caribbean-derived or Western–European conventions and yet are conversant with the heritages of both. Ukaegbu frames his interpretations through applying dialogic centrism to capture this occupation of centre and periphery in Agboluaje's work, not only in its trans-generic compass but also receptively through Martin Orkin's concept of witnessing drama. For Ekumah, Agbaje's West African heritage may be titrated through her distinctly British oeuvre, but it is certainly not diluted by it. The chapter employs Stuart Hall's concept of the unchanging frame of reference to recognise the challenge to hegemonic readings of unified or singular black experience. As Ekumah illustrates, Agbaje's characters inhabit multi-heritage perspectives, where a use of un-glossed Yoruba can simultaneously point to belonging and unbelonging for black audience members who can or cannot speak the language. As their dramatist forebears changed forever the kinds of English heard on British stages, so too as Osborne explores, does tucker green's dramatic poetics enter a territory of linguistic experimentation from which has evolved a truly unique stage idiom. In considering her work in terms of Julia Kristeva's theory of abjection and the impasse of language, Osborne analyses the ways in which tucker green's plays embody distinct performativity both in their live enactment, and on the page where they evoke the poetic traditions of literary texts. As one of two women featured in this final section, it is significant to remember how women, absent from accounts of the 1950s and 1960s, constitute a noted presence today. Whereas the work of black playwrights has been sidelined and critically neglected, the formidable contribution of women has been doubly so despite the pioneering work of many women editors.[10]

The project of restitution and recognition that this book claims is illustrated comprehensively in its diversity of both scholarly voices and approaches to plays by black writers in Britain. It offers a refreshing refashioning of British drama and theatre history, to show how these writers have created an enduring and transformative cultural presence, indispensible to any account of modern and contemporary British drama.

Notes

1. This term is here understood to characterise the new plays commissioned by subsidised theatres (in London and regionally from the late 1990s). Aleks Sierz connects New Writing to articulations of nation, 'work which is often difficult, sometimes intractable, but it usually has something urgent to say about Britain today' (Sierz, 2011, p. 5).
2. Indicative scholarship includes: Brewer (1999) who analyses black British work alongside African American women playwrights, and Griffin (2003) who produced the first book exploring black British women playwrights (in conjunction with British Asian work). Goddard (2007) is the first to offer sole focus on contemporary black British women's theatre. Essays in edited collections and scholarly journals include Aston (1997; 2011); Joseph (1998); Pinnock (1999; 2012); McMillan (2000; 2006; 2007); Ponnuswami (2000; 2007); King (2004); Goddard (2005; 2007; 2009); Peacock (2006a; 2006b; 2008) chapters in Godiwala (2006; 2010), chapters in Davis and Fuchs (2006) and Osborne (2006a; 2006b; 2007a; 2007b; 2010).

3. For indicative reports and studies in these areas see: Khan (1976); Runnymede Trust (2000); Arts Council (2002; 2006b); Cochrane (2011).
4. To map earlier eras preceding the post-war period but vital to developing a sense of continuity in theatre and drama historiography as it intersects and represents race, see an indicative range of scholarship. For an overview: Croft, Bourne and Terraciano (2003), Chambers (2011) and Osborne (2006a; 2011c). For Early Modern – 1800: Jones (1965), Tokson (1982), Barthelemy (1987), Macdonald (1997), Lhamon (1998), Hutner (2001), Mason (2005), Thompson (2008). On minstrelsy and Empire: Reynolds (1928), Noble (1946), Gainor (1995), Choudhury (2000), Orr (2001), Waters (2007) and Worrell (2007).
5. Jonathan Miller cast Anthony Hopkins as Othello in response to the British Equity Union's refusal to allow an African American actor James Earl Jones to play the role. *Evening Standard* (Anon, 1987, n.p). *The Black and White Minstrel Show* was removed *eleven years* after a petition was lodged by the Campaign Against Racial Discrimination. Malik (2002) observes that its removal was more to do with the declining popularity of the variety genre on British television rather than in response to the offence its racism caused.
6. Culture Secretary Maria Miller made the case that the arts must prove that they benefit the economy or they will lose funding. (www.politics.co.uk 2013).
7. For debate on the concept of a cultural renaissance for black drama and theatre, see Transcript 3, 'Debate: State of Black Theatre' (2004) and Kwei-Armah in Davis and Fuchs (2006).
8. For a more detailed exploration of whiteness and British theatre, see Brewer (2005).
9. For an indication of some initiatory work see: Mason-John and Khambatta (1993); Mason-John (1995; 1999); Griffin (2003); Goddard (2007; 2008); Osborne (2009).
10. Wandor (1985); Considine and Slovo (1987); Brewster (1987; 1989; 1995; 2010); George (1993); Gray (1990); Griffin and Aston (1991); Mason-John (1999); Osborne (2008; 2012); Goddard (2011a).

Part I
Post-War Migration

1
The Social and Political Context of Black British Theatre: 1950s–80s

Helen Thomas

The arrival of the *SS Empire Windrush* on 22 June 1948 at Tilbury Docks marked one of the most significant turning points in the history of race relations, black historiography and the development of black theatre within twentieth-century Britain. The disembarkation of the ship's 492 West Indian emigrants, and those who followed on board the *Orbita*, the *Reina del Pacifico* and the *Georgic*, was interpreted as a national media event and signalled the beginning of one of the most important phases of black immigration into Britain since the eighteenth century.[1] The *Evening Standard* of 21 June 1948 greeted these black British subjects from the colonies with the words, 'WELCOME HOME', and celebrated their return to the post-war 'Motherland' (Qtd. in Procter, 2000, p. 1). By 1950, the number of black people arriving from the West Indies had increased to 1,000; by 1956, this figure had escalated to 26,000.

However, many of these new arrivants experienced widespread prejudice as the 'host' population refused them entry into their homes as lodgers, avoided communication with them and condemned mixed-race marriages (Fryer, 1984, pp. 372–3). Within ten years of the *Empire Windrush*'s high-profile disembarkation, Britain's black community had reached 125,000 persons, many of whom had been educated under the British colonial system and were actively recruited by industries such as London Transport in order to satisfy the huge demand for labour created by Britain's post-war regeneration schemes. This highly visible community was to have both a vexed experience of and make a creative impact on British culture during the period (1950–80), as can be seen in artistic responses to racism in the development of black British drama and theatre. Indeed, as Colin Chambers has argued, black

Asian presences in British theatre transformed and reinvigorated traditional repertoires and introduced new verbal and visual vocabularies
into performance aesthetics (2011, p. 1). Efforts to chart black people's
position in Britain thus attempt to recover a history that has often been
'downgraded, ignored or suppressed', but also make visible a 'history of a
struggle for self-definition' in an often hostile 'host' culture (Chambers,
2011, pp. 1–2).

The significance of 1948 as an extraordinary turning point in British
cultural history, and the development of black theatre can be understood
more clearly in relation to the political events and changing attitudes
towards immigration and race which framed the *SS Windrush*'s arrival in
Tilbury. India's long-awaited achievement of independence from Britain
had occurred a year earlier, in 1947, as a culmination of Gandhi's leader-
ship in the struggle against colonial rule, a struggle which was to prove
a catalyst in the political process of dissolution of the British Empire
and its colonies. Moreover, the Universal Declaration of Human Rights,
decreed at the General Assembly of the United Nations in December
1948, had pronounced that 'the equal and inalienable rights of all
members of the human family' were 'the foundation of freedom, justice
and peace in the world'.[2] Britain's legal response to this upheaval in
world politics found its manifestation in the *Nationality Act* of 1948, an
act that granted UK citizenship to black subjects of the former British
colonies and officially sanctioned immigration into Britain. In 1962, a
significant revision was made to this in the form of the *Commonwealth
Immigration Bill* to strategically *regulate* the entry of Commonwealth
citizens into Britain. By distinguishing between skilled and unskilled
workers and British passport holders born in the UK and those born
in the colonies, the *Commonwealth Immigration Act* – which was rushed
through Parliament within three days – restricted the entry of Kenyan
Africans holding British passports into Britain, but allowed that of white
ex-colonials, and thus manifested the first comprehensive legislative
attempt to racially *control* immigration into Britain. Such contradictory
and ambivalent legislation, combined with the British public's changing
attitudes towards black subjects stamped its mark on both the practical
and political development of black theatre in the UK and the themes
and concerns that engaged black playwrights.

Although the Unity Theatre had a significant activist history in casting
black actors in roles (notably, Paul Robeson), and staging anti-colonial
plays, up until the late 1940s, any sense of black theatre in Britain had
mainly been represented by African American theatre, such as the American
Negro Theatre's production of Philip Yourdan's *Anna Lucasta* (1947) and

Arnaud d'Ussea and James Gow's *Deep Are the Roots* (1947).[3] Black parts were usually given to black Americans rather than black British subjects. Excuses for this ranged from black Britons' lack of training, their perceived lower professional calibre and ungainly accents. As a consequence, access to the British stage by black Britons was often restricted (Chambers, 2011, p. 111). Moreover, as Claire Cochrane has observed, the focus upon the *black American* experience in American drama further marginalised the narratives of black British colonial subjects (2011, p. 143).

However, several factors contributed to a critical transformation of this situation in the late 1940s and 1950s. The BBC's broadcasting of influential radio programmes such as *Caribbean Voices* (which had evolved from *Calling the West Indies* and was directed at West Indian soldiers in the British army), between 1943 and 1958, together with other radio broadcasts such as *Caribbean Carnival, African Theatre* and *Caribbean Theatre*, made a significant contribution to the development of black theatre in Britain (Chambers, 2011, p. 111). Hired by the BBC in London in 1941, feminist Jamaican writer Una Marson had transformed *Caribbean Voices* into a platform for Caribbean literary work and interviews. Likewise, the establishment of the Negro Theatre Company, London, in 1947 by Jamaican-born Pauline Henriques began what Henriques, Earl Cameron and Errol John believed to be the 'nucleus' of the Black British Theatre Movement (Cochrane, 2012, p. 143). Henriques's efforts strategically endeavoured to redefine black British actors as more than just understudies to black American parts.

Although freedom from colonial restraints had been gained, black subjects in 1950s Britain found themselves subjected to both covert and overt racism and discrimination. As a consequence, the majority of the plays that emerged during the 1950s–80s reflected and grappled with the disillusionment of black subjects within the imperial centre, but also 'staged' and interrogated its racist regimes of discourse and representation. Theatrical productions by black dramatists pivoted around central themes of exodus and exile, as well as 'strategies for survival' in an often 'hostile environment' (Maynard, 1996, p. 55). This body of work presented unprecedented reflections of, and strategic confrontations with, the challenges presented by cultural racism. It also engaged with – and thus participated within – the fluid discourse of race relations and changing attitudes towards assimilation, British identity and black subjectivity, and miscegenation.

As the plays produced across the period suggest, race relations within the UK were often tense, despite pervading beliefs in equality and democracy.

Although John Osborne's revolutionary kitchen sink drama, *Look Back in Anger* (1956), signalled an oblique reference to race and black gospel via its inclusion of jazz music and the protagonist's trumpet playing, Shelagh Delaney's play *A Taste of Honey* (1958) was one of the first plays by a white playwright in Britain to foreground an interracial relationship – between a working-class girl and a black sailor. The subject matter recalls the histories of many of Britain's port cities such as Liverpool, Cardiff and Bristol where racial mixing between black sailors and white women over centuries had established long-standing multi-racial and ethnic communities, such as the area formerly known as Tiger Bay in Cardiff.[4]

For those blacks who had arrived in England during the 1950s, the imperial centre had manifested a powerful dream predicated on wealth, culture and readily available work. In his semi-autobiographical essay, 'Finding Piccadilly Circus', the Trinidadian-born author, Sam Selvon described the mother country not as a place, or a people, 'but as a promise and an expectation' (Qtd in Procter, 2000, p. 57). Yet, prejudice against blacks in the UK was widespread and for many black arrivants, Britain was a disappointment. As Kenyan-born, Indian writer, G. V. Desani commented in *All About H. Hatter* (1948), 'Things are not what I thought they were, what they seemed they were, [or] what I might-have...wish[ed] they were!...Liverpool...was as unexpected a hole as I ever unexpected!' (2007, pp. 51–2). Moreover, concepts of racial inferiority persisted: according to Peter Fryer, 'over two-thirds of Britain's white population' considered black people 'uncivilized, backward...inherently inferior to Europeans...and suffering from unpleasant diseases' (1984, p. 5). In his text, *Colour Bar* (1954), the Trinidadian cricketer and barrister, Learie Constantine complained that while 'legal slavery' had been abolished in Europe, equality between black and white citizens in European cities was non-existent and blacks in Britain were forced into 'ghettos' amidst industrial areas of economic decline:

> Let us take Cardiff for instance. A city of about 250,000 people, it has fine shopping streets, parks, every civilized amenity. But let us turn towards the Adamstown area, and there, shut off by a compact barrier of docks, water, rails, fences and machinery, is a coloured population of about 7,000 people, mainly Arabs, Africans and West Indians...Coloured residents in Britain...find themselves virtually obliged to reside in a recognized 'black area' which is often a slum area. (Constantine, 1954, pp. 64–5)

Despite the existence historically of an ethnically mixed population, racism was directed towards any mixing. Constantine observed, not only

would few Englishmen 'sit at a restaurant tabl[e]
woman' but that *'interracial marriage* is considere[d]
be out of the question' (1954, p. 67). A statement o[f]
Society in London bears out its racist underpinnin[g]
good *inborn* qualities and decreasing the bad in the
tions of peoples' (1958).[5] As the plays of Jamaican-bor[n]
who came to Britain via a scholarship to study English a[t]
1950, Trinadian-born Mustapha Matura, who came to the[   ]⁄61
and Caryl Phillips, who was brought as a four-month-old ..oy from
St Kitts to England in 1958 represent, unofficial segregation, prejudice
and high unemployment challenged the assimilation of black communities into its host culture – a situation further exasperated by stringent
racial barriers and fears of intercultural contact. Linked by their colonial
heritage and their racial marginalization amid this culture, the works of
these playwrights reveal a sophisticated understanding of the 'inevitable
economic, social, political – and *even erotic'* [my emphasis] consequences
of racial identification and corresponding fears of racial miscegenation
(Constantine, 1954, p. 23).

Writing by black playwrights in the 1950s and early 1960s, such as:
Errol John's *Moon on a Rainbow Shawl* (Royal Court Theatre, 1958);
Reckord's *Flesh to a Tiger* (Royal Court Theatre, 1958); Wole Soyinka's
The Invention (Royal Court Theatre, 1959); *The Lion and the Jewel* (1962);
Reckord's *You in Your Small Corner* (1960; 1962); *Skyvers* (1963) registered
some of the experiences of black British colonials, hopeful migrants and
the young black community in Britain, but also included their disappointment, dislocation and disillusion. Such works functioned as effective critiques of blacks' bleak and alienated positions within post-war
British society.[6] In *Moon on a Rainbow Shawl,* for example, the disjunc-
ture between ideals about the imperial centre and its harsh realities
were played out. Edric Connor's cabaret, *Caribbean,* was staged at the
Irving Theatre in 1952 (owned by D. P. Chaudhuri, who considered
himself an agent for 'coloured artists'), as was Tagore's *Red Oleanders*
and *Black Napoleon,* a play about the slave rebel, Toussaint L'Ouverture
(Chambers, 2011, p. 109). In *You in Your Small Corner,* first produced at
the Cheltenham Theatre in 1960 and then transferred to the Royal Court
in 1962, Reckord dramatised the racial and class prejudice experienced
by a young middle-class West Indian and his white, working-class girlfriend.[7] As Eleni Liarou notes, the play's 'frank sexuality' concerning
the protagonist, Dave, 'embodies the dilemmas and disillusions of the
first post-war generation of black intellectuals'.[8] Jamaican-born Clifto[n]
Jones's *La Mere* and *The S Bend* (1960) were performed as a double bil[l]
the Theatre Royal, Stratford East London. Derek Walcott's *Sea at Dat[n]*

Malcochan: Or, Six in the Rain (1966) were staged as double ... at the Royal Court Theatre Royal, whereas Trinidadian-born Errol Hill, who travelled to England in 1949, produced the three-act play, *Man Better Man* (first performed in vernacular prose in Jamaica in 1957) which was then revised as a calypso-inspired piece that used rhymed verse and traditional chants and performed in 1960 at the Scala Theatre, London.

Not all of these black productions were well attended. In 1950, for example, *Hali*, a poetic play about a prophet by Kenyan-born Govindas Vishnoodas Desani was staged at the Watergate Theatre Club in London, but drew a small audience (Chambers, 2011, p. 109). Conversely, in Liverpool, Guyanan-born Norman Beaton produced the hit musical, *Jack of Spades* (1965), which centred upon the doomed relationship between a black man and a white woman. Works such as these, by Reckord and Beaton, reflected the exasperation of black arrivants as they found themselves the targets of both overt and indirect forms of racism never previously imagined, including anti-black marches, racist attacks, open-air fascist meetings and 'Let's Get a Wog' chants. In the years that followed, the *Kenyan Asian Act* of 1968,[9] together with Enoch Powell's infamously racist 'Rivers of Blood' speech[10] sensationalised racial antagonisms via images of impending national disaster and overcrowded maternity units, and brought interracial relations within Britain to an unprecedented level of confrontation. Blacks faced unfair discrimination in the crucial areas of education, housing and employment: they were 'more vulnerable' to unemployment than whites, were concentrated amidst lower job levels or shift work despite their academic or job qualifications and received 'lower earnings than whites' (Fryer, 1984, p. 387; Smith, 1977, p. 104). Between 1973 and 1976, 40% of blacks lived in overcrowded conditions compared to 11% of whites; 50% of Pakistanis had no baths, hot water or inside toilet, compared to 17% of whites and at school non-whites were often treated as 'uneducable' or deemed to have 'unrealistic [career] aspirations' (Sivanandan, 1982, p. 30).

In terms of theatrical developments, very few plays, as Lynette Goddard comments, produced during the 1950s–80s at establishments such as the Royal Court Theatre were by black (or other non-white) playwrights (Goddard, 2007, pp. 17–18).[11] Moreover, very few plays were by black women, and those that were produced 'tended to be by American-American playwrights' or about 'heterosexual black women' (Goddard, 2007, p. 18; p. 1). However, those plays that were produced by black male playwrights demonstrated the frustrations and disappointments of the post-war black experience as well as the various modes of survival and cultural and political resistance. As a response, therefore, to racist regimes of discourse and representation, black theatrical production in the 1960s and early 1970s Britain endeavoured not only to alleviate black 'second-class citizenship' and connect with anti-apartheid and anti-imperialist struggles across the world (such as Civil Rights in America and anti-apartheid in South Africa), but to 'challenge, resist and where possible transform' negative, objectified and/or fetishised representation of black subjects (Jones, 1964, p. 68). Community activism and professional theatre interacted and combined to instigate projects such as the instrumental Negro Theatre Workshop at London's Lyric Theatre in 1960; the Dark and Light Theatre Company established by Jamaican-born Frank Cousins in 1969 (which later transferred to Longfield Hall between Brixton and Camberwell and became the Black Theatre of Brixton) in order to reflect the local community's more radical stance (Chambers, 2011, pp. 141–3).[12]

The period spanning 1950s–80s which witnessed two high-profile race uprisings in Britain (Notting Hill 1958 and Brixton 1981) also ushered in a significant phase in the *physical* development, the *infrastructure* and visibility of black theatre within the UK. In 1970, the Guyanese architect, Oscar Abrams, founded the Keskidee Centre in Islington as a major platform for African and Caribbean culture including theatre, political forums, and educational and housing and welfare workshops. The Keskidee Theatre Workshop opened in 1971 with a production of *Sighs of a Slave Dream* (1972) by Lindsay Barrett who arrived from Jamaica in 1962. Three important contributions to black theatre history in this period were in the founding of: Carib, Temba (from the Zulu word 'hope') by Alton Kumalo (1970) to focus on new black writing from the UK and South Africa; the Black Theatre Co-operative (now Nitro) by Matura and Charlie Hanson (1978), in order to address the fact that plays by Asian, African and Caribbean playwrights – or indeed with central black protagonists – had been consigned to the fringes of British theatre (Shank, 1996, p. 7) and the publication of Naseem Khan's *The Arts Britain Ignores: The Arts of Ethnic Minorities in Britain* (1976), a watershed report which highlighted the cultural contributions made by Britain's ethnic minorities in spite of marginalisation. Commissioned by the Arts Council, the Gulbenkian Foundation and the Community Race Relations Commission, Khan's document – itself a re-examination of 'legitimate' English culture – made a significant contribution to the development of funding for theatrical groups. Khan, born in London and with German and Indian ancestry, argued that support of ethnic minorities' arts, together with the provision of buildings and training, ought to be considered a 'right' rather than a privilege (Chambers, 2011,

p. 142, pp. 154–5). Similarly, in response to the violence of the Brixton riots, the *Scarman Report* (1981) highlighted the problems of racial disadvantage and urban decline and stressed the need of 'a positive effort' by those in responsible positions to tackle racial discrimination including investment in both people and material surroundings.[13]

Although the terms 'black' and 'white', 'margin' and 'imperial centre' tend to operate as polarities, black and Asian migrants to Britain did not, as Gabriele Griffin argues, 'constitute a homogenous group of people, even if they were treated as such' (2003, p. 8). Despite their shared historical experience of colonialism, enforced transportation and sometimes, slavery, such 'diasporic communities' were also separated from each other on account of their diverse backgrounds, languages, customs, religions and practices (Griffin, 2003, p. 4). During the 1950s–80s, such dichotomies were further complicated by tensions between first-generation arrivants to Britain and their second-generation children who were born in the UK. This inter-generational tension is seen in Matura's *As Time Goes By* through the relationship between a West Indian migrant, Albert, and his teenage skinhead son. Albert grapples with raising a second-generation child who embraces working-class white male youth identity (his name is Skinhead)[14] over any West Indian-derived one. The non-communicative impasse is evident on many fronts, as played out through cultural and linguistic differences:

> ALBERT: Me ask him what is a skin head. Him say him don't know, so me ask him why him is a skin head. Him say him don't know so what we go do? (*Thump*). [...]
> SKINHEAD: Don't know do I.
> ALBERT: (*thump*). What's dis, 'do I' business? (*Thump*). Answer properly.
> [...]
> ALBERT: What dat have ter do wit' what yer go do wit' yerself.
> SKINHEAD: Nofink. It don't have nofink ter do wifit, nofink. I don't know what yer getting so excited about.
> ALBERT: (*thump*). Don't answer me back. What's all dis about yer carn't even talk properly. (Matura, 1992a, pp. 44–6)

This exchange illustrates an important dynamic played out on the stage during the 1970s and 1980s, that of language – most especially in relation to authority and representation and the class/cultural dynamics of standard/Queen's English, vernacular and patois forms (McMillan, 2009, p. 300). The confident posturing of 'black' vernacular and style within black British culture of this time fulfills Brathwaite's identification of a new aesthetics which fuses the music and language of Africa and the Caribbean (Brathwaite, 1971). This corresponds with Sivanandan's call to black writers and artists in Britain to *transform* and thereby liberate themselves from a language that had historically defined their inequality:

> White language, white education, white systems of thought... alienate
> him [the no-good nigger] from himself... He must blacken his language,
> suffuse it with his own darkness, and liberate it from the presence of
> the oppressor. In the process, he changes radically the use of words,
> word-order – sounds, rhythm, imagery – even grammar... In effect he
> brings to the language the authority of his particular experience and
> alters thereby the experience of language itself. He frees it of its racial
> oppressiveness (black is beautiful), invests it with 'the universality
> inherent in the human condition'. (Sivanandan, 1982, pp. 83–92).

As Keir Elam suggests, the shift away from the 'above-standard rhetoric' of noble Moors such as Othello and towards the use of black vernacular on stage marked a significant departure from the appropriation of, and assimilation with, the colonialist's language and values as defined by Frantz Fanon in 'On National Culture' (Elam, 1995, pp. 173–7). The emergence of Black British English on the stage not only signalled a struggle 'for freedom from European hegemony' but also 'cultural self-consciousness', alongside an endeavour to achieve postcolonial cultural 'validation and authentication', as manifested via the Caribbean topography ('the yard') (Elam, 1995, p. 184). And yet, such markers of culture – the grammar, syntax and pronunciation – were also, as Elam contends, 'diluted' and further mixed so as to be accessible to a non-Caribbean audience (Elam, 1995, p. 177).

Dedicated to Fanon, Matura's *Play Mas* (1974, Royal Court Theatre) made explicit the politics of linguistic registers and 'mas' (masquerade, performance, creativity) within a postcolonial setting, highlighting the ambivalence/carnivalesque/conflictual aspect of language as determined by Mikhail Bakhtin (1981) and the 'signifying' characteristic of black English as discussed by Gates (1988). As Elam notes, 'Playing mas offers no guarantees against the dangers of playing the colonialist game... Matura's dramaturgy is in this sense knowingly self-critical, exposing the myths behind the very discursive modes it embodies' (Elam, 1995, p. 187). The potentially liberating yet also potentially problematic aspects of 'black language' (such as Rasta talk) and its variable correspondence with trans-global black consciousness, pan-Africanism and black Zionism were further explored in plays such as Matura's *Welcome Home Jacko* (1979) and Caryl Phillips' *Strange Fruit* (1980). Both plays explored and critiqued the dangers of 'not inherited but invented' linguistic/mythical indoctrination (Elam, 1995, p. 190) and voluntary racial segregation and black apartheid in the context of neocolonialism, global economics, cross cultural creativity and feminist liberationist politics in post-war Britain (Thomas, 2006, pp. 11–13).

As Deirdre Osborne notes, black dramatists often 'face the familiar conundrum of representation vs. artistic individualism', a factor that 'their white counterparts simply do not have to face' (2007b, p. 224). Moreover, as their work suggests, despite the significant historical and cultural differences between black Asian, Caribbean and Indian communities, the term 'black' gained increasing political and cultural dynamism over the 1950s–80s period via its usage as a shared signifier for all groups of the 'common experience of racism and marginalization in Britain' (Hall, 2003a, p. 223). Reckord, Matura and Phillips responded to – and thereby transformed – black migrants' positioning as the invisible 'others' of predominant white aesthetic and cultural discourses. Matura's *Black Pieces* presented not only the black experience of racism within England, but also white middle-class fascination with black culture. These playwrights' works inscribe unique testimonies of the vibrant synthesis between artistic production and the emergence of sociopolitical understanding within the context of post-war, decolonizing and postcolonial consciousness, as their representations of black experiences within Britain corresponded with the experiences of other subordinated and marginalised groups across the globe. By envisaging the links between struggles for survival in their new environment and international struggles for freedom, they engaged with the ideological and practical merits and problematics of full integration with British life and/or segregation based upon racial and cultural identities.

Clashes 'between the black community and the state' together with the reduction in arts funding which began in the 1970s and peaked in the mid-1980s contributed to the continuing siting of black theatre on the margins of British culture (Ramdin, 1999, p. 340; Chambers, 2011, p. 137). Whereas black identity was frequently configured as a 'migrant' or 'marginal' identity, new arrivals had begun to realise that migration was usually a 'one-way trip', that there was never any real 'home to go back to' and that the black/colonised subject was always 'somewhere else', always 'doubly marginalized or displaced', always *other* than where he or she was able to speak from (Hall, 1996a, p. 115). As Chambers notes, the language of plays by this generation differed significantly from the work of previous playwrights, a departure that 'helped black theatre in Britain find a new confidence and character' (Chambers, 2011, p. 138). The emergence of those playwrights representing mixed-race origins such as Tunde Ikoli (born of a Cornish mother and Nigerian father) who wrote *Short Sleeves* (Theatre Royal, 1977), *On the Out* (Bush Theatre, 1977) and *Scrape off the Black* (Dir. Peter Gill, Riverside Studios, 1980) which was set in London's East End of the 1970s further nuanced the spectrum of representational possibilities housed under the umbrella term (as it was) of Black.

By the 1980s, over 40% of all blacks in Britain had been born within its borders. Many of them had never visited their 'ancestral homes' and many, like Phillips, having been educated and raised in Britain, were closer to the idiosyncracies of British culture than their parents were. Yet for most members of white society, these people were still 'immigrants', 'Pakis' and 'coloureds', located on the margins of power and culture, rather than equal British citizens. Racial prejudice continued to be 'both everywhere and nowhere' at all (Malik, 1996, p. 1). In addition, the emergence of increasingly stringent policing strategies in the late 1970s which targeted 'black' inner city areas in Britain, together with the creation of Special Patrol Groups (SPGs) and (re) introduction of SUS ('Stop and Search') laws from the 1824 Vagrancy Act, signalled both the increasingly deteriorating relations between police and blacks, and indeed, between blacks and predominantly white communities, as immortalised in Linton Kwesi Johnson's dub poems of the time, 'Five Nights of Bleeding' (1974) and 'Sonny's Lettah: An Anti-Sus Poem' (1979) (Ramdin, 1999, pp. 249–51; Procter, 2000, p. 95).

In an issue of *Platform* (1981) dedicated to black theatre, Mike Phillips argued that 'black theatre' had yet to emerge in Britain (Shepherd, 2009, pp. 205–6; Phillips, 1981, pp. 3–6). For Phillips, the term 'black theatre' implied both a fundamental concern with black culture as well as the 'emotional relevance' of material to its audience. However, despite this claim, during the 1980s black theatre in Britain burgeoned, and provocatively and successfully addressed questions of black identity and subjectivity in the postcolonial world. Plays by Phillips and Matura both responded to and critiqued institutionalised and cultural racism and portrayed central concerns with the experience and consequences of migration, displacement, alienation and racial tension. Matura's *Meetings* (1982, Hampstead Theatre) exposed the effects of consumerist culture on a middle-class Trinidadian couple and formed part of a collection of multi-voiced narratives that raised 'questions about decolonization and personal identity by constantly juxtaposing the past and the present, Trinidad and England' in an effort to recover and confront both personal and social history (Joseph, 1999, p. 97). Similarly, the plays by Michael Abbensetts, *In the Mood* (1981, Hampstead Theatre), and Caryl Phillips' *Where There Is Darkness* (1982, Hammersmith Lyric Theatre) interrogated concepts of race, gender and family life amidst the context of the post-war diaspora.

Plays produced in the early 1980s continued to explore issues concerning migration, belonging and racism as well as the tensions between those blacks born in the UK and their African Caribbean parents who 'wanted their children to be seen and not heard'. Caryl Phillips's play *Strange Fruit*, performed at the Sheffield Crucible in 1980 and the following year in London, highlighted the inter-generational tensions within a black British family in the 1970s and their differing attitudes towards concepts of 'home', homeland and transatlantic identities. Matura's *Welcome Home Jacko* (1979, The Factory, London), which focused upon the lives of four young Rastafarian youths, also highlighted some of the problematics of black cultural nationalism, the political and aesthetical ideologies of the Black Power movement and Rastafarianism. Although works by black female playwrights were few and far between (a situation which paralleled the late emergence of publications by black female novelists in Britain), plays by black women did reach the stage during the 1980s. Born in London to Trinidadian parents, Peggy Bennette Hume's, *The Girl Who Wished* (1985, Carib Theatre) highlighted the longings of a girl who wants to be someone other than herself, while Jamaican-born Grace Daley's plays, *Rose's Story* (1984) and *Grace's Story* (1986) premiered at South Bank Polytechnic and The Cockpit, London. Jenny McLeod's *Island Life* was first performed at the Nottingham Playhouse in 1988 and presented the narratives of three women in an old people's home. Paulette Randall's *Fixed Deal* (1986) performed at the Sphinx Theatre, centred upon the ways in which the lives of four women of different backgrounds and cultures are affected by legal and illegal drugs.

The emergence of work across the decades by Reckord (1950s), Matura (1970s) and Phillips (1980s) radically transformed and extended the parameters of British theatre of the period by highlighting questions of race, class, gender and sexual orientation from the perspective and experience of black immigrants. Theatrical productions of their plays – such as Reckord's *You in Your Small Corner, Skyvers* and *X* (1974); Matura's *Dialogue* (1970), *Indian* (1970), *Party* (1970), *My Enemy* (1970) and *As Time Goes By*; and Phillips' *Strange Fruit, Where There Is Darkness* (1982) and *The Shelter* (1982) – provocatively explored black people's experiences of social alienation, prejudice, frustration and anger in post-war Britain. Other important plays of the 1970s feature Yemi Ajibade's *Parcel Post* (1976);

Alfred Fagon's *11 Josephine House* (1972) and *Death of a Black Man* (1975); and Michael McMillan's *The School Leaver* (1978) which interrogated the tensions among race, tradition and identity experienced by these first-generation migrants. Plays such as these correspond with Hall's 1978 reading of blacks in Britain as 'the bearers, the signifiers of the crisis of British society' (Qtd. in Owusu, 2000, p. 4). Moreover, the increase in black productions and a theatrical infrastructure paid testimony to the fact that black artists had not only gained access to the 'dominant regimes of representation', thus allowing them to contest the marginality and objectification of black subjects, but had begun to explore and explode notions of essentialism in relation to subjectivity, identity and politics relevant to all (Hall, 2003b, p. 243). This trajectory corresponded to what Hall termed 'the end of innocence', or 'the end of the innocent notion of the black essential subject' in which 'blackness' could be grounded in a set of fixed cultural, racial or historical categories (2003b, p. 243).

The early 1980s also witnessed the emergence of a variety of black-run theatre companies. Talawa Theatre Company, founded by Yvonne Brewster, Carmen Munroe, Mona Hammond and Inigo Espejel in 1985, aimed to increase theatre audiences among the black community in Britain; to use black culture and experience to enhance British theatre; and to enable black actors to perform in European classic plays.[15] In addition to increasing the number of creative opportunities for actors from ethnic minority backgrounds, Talawa set out to counter the isolation of black imperatives from dominant cultural movements within Britain. Other black theatre companies which emerged during this period also included: Sahar Arts founded by Shakila Taranum Maan and the Black Mime Theatre, established in 1987 by Sarah Cahn and David Boxer, in order to encourage black performers in mime.[16]

The creative practice by black dramatists during the 1950s–80s focused specifically upon discrimination and/or individual, familial and cultural fragmentation within the context of postcolonial Britain. Many highlighted the difficulties of self-articulation and realisation at the margins and within the parameters defined by historical, cultural and racial discourse. This dynamic, between the past and new subjectivities of the present, was rigorously explored, re-created and transformed, both in terms of individual personalised narratives and those connected to larger groups and communities irrevocably altered by the effects of post-war migrations and relations. At times, and as is evidenced in the chapters that follow, the development of black drama and theatre proffered radical departures from the tangents prescribed by mainstream British cultural authorities and public discourse, and challenged the failed imperatives of educational and race and gender reform within Britain. Often adopting very different forms, the plays and publications produced during this period vigorously articulated a defiant stance against the racial discrimination and indignities experienced by blacks throughout Britain, and in so doing made a significant contribution to the developing understanding of black shared historical and cultural heritage within the UK (Jones, 1964, p. 70). Moreover, within these plays the relationship between black and white, coloniser and colonised, pre-war and post-war culture is rarely trivialised or oversimplified. Instead these plays bear witness to the complexities, ambiguities and anxieties of black subjectivities, alongside the possibilities of representation.

Notes

1. The increase in the black population in Britain at the end of the eighteenth century was related to Britain's defeat in the American War of Independence (which saw black soldiers escape to Britain) together with the relocation of households from West Indian plantations. The visibility of the black servant class is captured in paintings of the time and represented in the late-twentieth-century historical novels of S. I. Martin and David Dabydeen.
2. *The Universal Declaration of Human Rights*, http://www.un.org/en/documents/udhr/index.shtml.
3. See Chambers (1989) on Unity Theatre's history.
4. White writer Colin McInnes's novels *City of Spades* (1957) and *Absolute Beginners* (1959) also represented black immigrant culture in 1950s England, most especially the poor and racially mixed area of Notting Hill. Roy Williams adapted the latter for the stage in 2008.
5. 'Statement and Aims', *The Eugenics Review*, April 1958 50(1), 23–30, http://www.ncbi.nlm.nih.gov/pmc/articles/PMC2974469/?page=1.
6. See Nasta (1995) in R. Lee (ed.) pp. 48–68.
7. http://historicalgeographies.blogspot.co.uk/2011/09/biography-barry-reckord.html.
8. See Liarou, 'You in Your Small Corner',http://www.screenonline.org.uk/tv/id/537722/index.html.
9. http://www.runnymedetrust.org/histories/race-equality/38/commonwealth-immigration-act-1968.html.
10. http://www.telegraph.co.uk/comment/3643823/Enoch-Powells-Rivers-of-Blood-speech.html.
11. For further details see Croft, Bourne and Terracciano (2003).
12. The Caribbean Artists Movement (CAM) was established in 1965 with aims to increase the visibility of black literature, arts, academia and theatrical performance in the context of racial discrimination and immigration. Britain's first black publisher and bookshop, New Beacon Books, was established in 1966 by John La Rose together with new periodicals such as *Race and Class* (a journal for Black and Third World Liberation) and the *West Indian Gazette*.

13. The Scarman Report, www.peoplecan.org.uk/media/ ... /1981scarman-report_ summary.pdf.
14. At the time Matura was writing, the term *skin head* carried a slightly different connotation than the neo-Nazi associations it has today. The skin head subculture that developed in Britain was in part influenced by West Indian traditions, in music especially, and many second-generation black men were involved in the movement.
15. http://historicalgeographies.blogspot.co.uk/2011/09/biography-yvonne-brewster.html.
16. http://www.talawa.com/downloads/resourcepacks/retrace/retrace_general_ resources.pdf; http://www.movinghere.org.uk/galleries/histories/caribbean/ culture/theatre4.htm.

2
Identity Politics in the Plays of Mustapha Matura

Brian Crow

Alongside Edgar White and Michael Abbensetts, Mustapha Matura has been a pioneering figure in the development of Black British drama since the 1970s, not only as a playwright, director and writer for television, but also as a co-founder with Charlie Hanson of the Black Theatre Co-operative (renamed Nitro in 1999). For all his years in Britain where he has set many of his plays, Matura seems to have personally retained a very strong sense of his Caribbean, and specifically Trinidadian identity. In an interview just before the premiere of one of his later plays, *The Coup* (Royal National Theatre, London, 1991), Matura told Kate Kellaway that he would describe himself as a Trinidadian writer and indicated the continuing centrality of his Caribbean roots for his oeuvre, 'The theme that runs through my work is the discovery of Caribbean sensibilities and culture – starting with unawareness, arriving at awareness' (Kellaway, 1991, p. 55). Two aspects of this abiding concern with Caribbean culture and sensibility have given Matura's work its distinctive quality: his achievement in exploring and rendering West Indian experience, in the Caribbean or in Britain, through sharply observed relationships and in richly textured speech; and more specifically his exploration of the disappointments and failures, personal and national, of post-colonial Trinidad.

As a dramatist, then, he has sought to chronicle not only Black English experience over two generations but also the lives of Trinidadians both before and since independence. In the process, he has dramatised in a variety of genres a wide range of social and personal issues embracing both the migrant experience and the post-colonial Caribbean complexities of race, class, generation and gender. The scope of Matura's oeuvre over several decades dictates the approach taken in this chapter, which is to address his key concerns with reference to a wide range of his writing, rather than to concentrate attention on a small number of plays. This seems particularly appropriate because, despite his significance in the development of Black British theatre as well as a playwright writing on urgent Caribbean themes, Matura's work as a whole has not received the amount of critical attention that his status would seem to justify. What emerges from a consideration of his otherwise varied oeuvre, when approached as a whole, is the centrality of the linked themes of change, identity and authenticity. Matura's characters, whether they are young or old, male or female, poor or affluent, living in London or Trinidad, struggle with the pressures of changing times and places and their concomitant challenges to personal identity and its anchorage in something that feels like cultural authenticity. For all the humour and compassion with which Matura depicts his characters, the overall picture that emerges is far from optimistic. The underlying bleakness of Matura's portrayals of modern Black experience is perhaps most tellingly indicated by the wording of his dedication of *Play Mas* (Royal Court, London, 1974) to Frantz Fanon, where he writes of the latter's commitment to the struggle 'to understand and overcome black misery'.[1]

As Ania Loomba identifies, this misery, for Fanon, was associated with the psychic trauma that results 'when the colonised subject realises that he can never attain the whiteness he has been taught to desire, or shed the blackness he has learnt to devalue' (Loomba, 1998, p. 176). She makes the point, in her useful discussion of colonial and post-colonial identities, that 'the experience of migration or of exile has become, in the Western academy, emblematic of the fissured identities and hybridities generated by colonial dislocations' (1998, p. 180). While we certainly encounter depictions of fissured identity in Matura's work, it is important not to confuse his explorations of post-colonial identity, in Trinidad or England, with the 'problem' of identity as a deeply debilitating loss or absence of a culture, as a way of life in which the subject meaningfully engages and with which he or she spontaneously identifies him or herself. Whatever the problematic relations many of his characters have with it, there is always – or almost always – present in Matura's plays the rich and vigorous presence of Trinidadian culture. A collective sense of what it is to be Trinidadian is as implicit in the displaced Batee's experience in Matura's first substantial play, *As Time Goes By* (Traverse Theatre, Edinburgh, 1971) as it is for the deposed, corrupt president of a fictional Trinidad in *The Coup*.[2] This identity is, of course, about those deeply embedded Trinidadian institutions of Carnival[3] (as in *Play Mas*) and calypso, which is explored in *Rum An' Coca Cola* (Royal Court, London, 1976), but this concept of identity is also, more pervasively, about ways of perceiving, thinking, behaving and speaking that Matura consistently delights in rendering through his dramatic characterisation and language. In only one play, *Welcome Home Jacko* (Riverside Studios, London, 1979) does Matura present characters (in the persons of the young, unemployed Black youths), who have no genuine relationship to their Caribbean roots, or even to the cultural environment that the first generation of immigrants had established for themselves in England. The youths' Rastafarianism, in Matura's eyes, is only a pathetic refuge given their lack of a genuine identity in contemporary British society.

Though the playwright has lived in England since the early 1960s, the majority of Matura's plays are set in Trinidad. However, *As Time Goes By*, which won Matura both the George Devine and John Whiting Awards when it was first produced, is about West Indians living in London. Ram, the Indo-Trinidadian who presides over the action, gets stoned with his ridiculously 'cool' white visitors Lucille and Mark, engages in sporadic verbal warfare with his wife Batee, who wants only to be back in Trinidad, and in his role as fake swami receives other Trinidadians who come for his help and advice. For the presumably largely white, middle-class audiences of the early 1970s who witnessed the play on the Edinburgh Fringe and subsequently at the ICA in London, there must have been some novelty in witnessing West Indian characters living a life in London without, in many ways, having (psychologically) really left the West Indies. Ram's black visitors – Arnold and his brother Bertram, as well as Alfred and Albert with the troublesome son – remain thoroughly Trinidadian in their attitudes, behaviour and language, and this provides much of the comic charm of the play. Another vein of the comedy is the fact that, although he spends much of his time dealing with others' marital issues, Ram and his wife Batee are forever at logger-heads. Batee is unashamedly nostalgic for the island and hates her life in England with a passion. She has no patience with Ram's pretensions as a 'cool' would-be 'holy man'. As we learn from another visitor, Thelma, Ram is really only a failed law student, and Batee loses no opportunity to remind him about his lack of success at conning people out of their money. The main comic contrast in *As Time Goes By* is between those – like Ram, his white visitors and Una – who are in one way or another attuned to the zeitgeist of changing times, and those – like Batee and the other Trinidadian male characters – whose migrant experience has not noticeably affected their behaviour or sense of identity. Arnold complains that his wife Una, who has left him for his brother Bertram, is not the woman he knew back in Trinidad – whereas Ram makes the opposite complaint about his wife to his white friends Mark and Lucille. The immigrant Trinidadians of *As Time Goes By* are divided between those who adapt and seek to belong in their new environment and those whose Trinidadian sensibilities remain largely untouched by their experience in the 'mother' country. Overall, the comic balance of sympathy lies with those characters that have remained resolutely Trinidadian in their ways and sense of identity.

Though not a dramatist noted for his explorations of the lives of black urban youth in contemporary Britain, Matura made one of British drama's earliest sorties into this area in *Welcome Home Jacko*, his other full-length play set in England. It focuses on four unemployed black youths who hang out in a youth club run by a benevolent white woman, Sandy. The boys are juxtaposed with Jacko, a former regular at the club whose five years in prison have made him articulately disillusioned about the failures of black resistance to the oppressions of white society.

> I was in prison, but me en know whey all yer was. I read all de time I in dey, everyting, I read about how de National Front an dem terrorising black people an nobody en doing notting, an how dis Rastaman ting saying peace and love an smoking dope an dreaming bout Africa an de Bible, an de National Front attacking people. I car understand all yer. Wha happen, all yer car see, all yer blind? I say wen I come out I go meet de youth fighting back, because de paper en go print dem ting, an I go join dem. But de paper right. Wen I went in people eye was opening, now I come out it close. Wha happen, wha happen ter all yer? We fight de racist in prison. All yer outside, wha all yer do? (Matura, 1992c, p. 292)

When the action culminates in Marcus pulling a knife on his taunting antagonist, only for Jacko to disarm and humiliate him, Matura seems to indicate the ineffectuality of Rastafarianism as a spiritually based form of black activism and resistance and, at the same time, to suggest the violence that may underlie its rhetoric. (Marcus has already committed a sexual assault on Gail, the young middle-class black woman who works at the club). If in *As Time Goes By* Matura satirises one kind of fake spirituality, in *Welcome Home Jacko* he strips bare the pretensions of another, far more influential one, which had emerged as a source of identity for many black men in Britain, offering a sense of cultural worth and hope to counter their pervasive sense of disenfranchisement. In an interview with Michael McMillan, Matura says he thought Rasta was 'superficial and politically unhelpful' at the time he wrote *Welcome Home Jacko*, though he admits he later became much more sympathetic to it (McMillan, 2000, p. 261). By rejecting Rastafarianism as a spurious, fantasised sense of identity, Matura leaves *Welcome Home Jacko* bleakly open-ended about the problem of deracinated and disenfranchised black youth who are now out on the streets rather than in the relative security of a youth club. In response to Sandy's diagnosis of their fate, 'They haven't got a chance, the moment they walk on the street they're guilty' (Matura, 1992c, p. 291), the play seems to offer only Jacko's prison-hardened militancy, with its connotations of black power politics, as the way out of the impasse of black suffering.

Complex issues of race, nationality, class and identity explored in *Jacko* are also addressed in *Play Mas*, Matura's first play set in the West Indies after a return visit there in 1972, 12 years after his departure. *Play Mas* is rooted in the historical and political contexts that defined Trinidad's transition to at least nominal political independence – its political polarisation between the Indian-dominated Democratic Labour Party and the Afro-dominated People's National Movement and the subsequent rise of Black Power. Carnival – 'playing mas' – becomes a complex image of Trinidadian racial and socio-political tensions – less an authentic image of national belonging than of confused identities, duplicity and contending claims as to what and who is genuinely Trinidadian. Early in the play, the Indian tailor Ramjohn and his Black employee Samuel discuss the forthcoming Carnival. Ramjohn identifies himself as Trinidadian rather than Indian. Samuel denies this, asking Ramjohn why 'if you is a Trinidadian how come yer do' play Mas, eh how come?' (Matura, 1992b, p. 107). To Ramjohn's assertion that he can be a real Trinidadian without playing Mas, Samuel insists that this is impossible. Later in the same scene, they discuss politics. In Samuel's view, as Ramjohn is Indian he must support the DLP, as it is an Indian party. Ramjohn denies this, again insisting that 'I en' no Indian, I is a Trinidadian' (Matura, 1992b, p. 119). Their ensuing exchange reveals Samuel's confusions about identity, as he indignantly rejects Ramjohn's assertion that he is African and insists that he is Trinidadian but also English (Matura, 1992b, pp. 119–20). Although Ramjohn seems genuinely multicultural and inclusivist in his conception of Trinidadian identity, his mother uses Samuel as a skivvy and is blatantly racist, at one point upbraiding her son for not dealing appropriately with Samuel, 'You don' know how ter treat dem nigger yer know, you tink dey is human, dey en' human, dey is dog, feed dem and dey happy' (Matura, 1992b, p. 126). Her treatment of Samuel is simply the other side of the racial and racist coin already articulated by one of Ramjohn's black customers, Frank, who sees Dr Eric Williams as a redeemer of his Trinidadian people, who will change the situation in which 'all yer [meaning Indians] just want ter see black people foolish an working fer allyer, an Indian driving bout in big car...while we beg for shit' (Matura, 1992b, p. 116).

Power passes in the course of the action from the Indian employers to their former employee. Summarily sacked by Mrs Gookool for asking permission to attend one of Dr Williams' PNM meetings, Samuel becomes a PNM organiser – in effect a 'big man' running a protection racket extorting money for his party – and by the start of Act Two, some years later and after Independence, is in high office as Chief of Police. Now it is Samuel who can proudly display his 'Yankee' suit bought on a trip to New York, and it is Ramjohn who is condescended to and pressured into supplying information on what is happening 'up the Hill'. Enjoying the fruits of office, Samuel has adopted the sort of inclusivist rhetoric he rejected earlier, telling Ramjohn that '[a]lla we is Trinidadian now' and patronisingly suggesting that 'we have ter help one anodder' (Matura, 1992b, p. 152). But the idealised idea of Trinidad he appeals to is revealed by Matura to be in reality as fractured and insecure as it was before Independence. For what is happening 'up the Hill' is the advent of Black Power, which has brought riots in the streets and forced the government to impose a state of emergency – reflecting the actual Black Power disturbances of 1970 in Trinidad. Matura writes the scene in which Samuel receives a delegation of Trinidadians wishing to lift the state of emergency to demonstrate how post-colonial Trinidad is dominated by a power elite united only because their particular class interests happen to coincide. Further, he emphasises how Samuel as state functionary is no less confused about his identity than when he was poor and exploited by the Gookools before independence. His flash American suit has only been purchased courtesy of the regime's neo-colonial dependence on Washington, represented in the play by the sinister Chuck Reynolds. What Reynolds and therefore Samuel most want to know is how many guns and other supplies the disaffected of Trinidadian society have in their possession, and where they are coming from. On this depends not only Samuel's position of power but the future of American investment in the country and the kickbacks it will bring him. Matura's point is very clear: though the racial balance of power may have changed in Trinidad and a new post-colonial élite established in power, the supposedly independent nation is in neo-colonial thrall to the capitalist super-power, America.

Matura presents Carnival as deeply implicated in the issues of politics and cultural identity. He uses dramatic performance to point up how the artifice of Carnival can be the occasion for a representative failure to discriminate between real identities and the fantasised ones associated with 'playing mas'. Prefiguring his future political relationship with the

Americans, Samuel returns to the Gookools' shop after his sacking in his Carnival costume as a US Marine, brandishing what appears – at least to Ramjohn and his mother – to be a real sub-machine gun. Though it is only capable of squirting water, it is enough to give the old lady a fatal heart attack and to terrify Ramjohn. Samuel is delighted with himself at having got one up on his former Indian employers and, significantly, what he repeatedly emphasizes about this encounter is how 'real' he was in his Carnival outfit and role. 'I was a real marine, nobody en' tell me what ter say yer know, I just make it up' (Matura, 1992b, pp. 128–9). Later, when Ramjohn fetches someone to attend to his mother, the doctor is irritated that his Carnival role has been interrupted to examine someone who is already dead. He is more interested in eliciting admiration from Ramjohn for his exotic Mas garb than in offering sympathy for his dead mother, and like Samuel in his US Marines garb, he is keen to emphasise its 'realness' – 'is Ashanti, genuine Ashanti' modelled on 'a genuine photograph' (Matura, 1992b, p. 134). Compounding the grotesquerie, when two figures arrive dressed in the long black coats and hats of undertakers, intoning 'We come fer de body, accept our sympathies' they turn out not to be Carnival figures, as Matura has led us to imagine, but the real thing. Ramjohn, 'staggering' and shouting hysterically, tells them to get out of his shop and cries 'I is a Indian, I is a Indian' and dances out of his shop shouting 'Play Mas, PNM, PNM' with all the Mas characters gathering on stage chanting 'Play Mas, Indian, play Mas' (Matura, 1992b, p. 138). The temporary suspension of fixed identities associated with the carnivalesque is presented by Matura as a more permanent confusion, a limbo between the African heritage (the Ashanti costume) and the present and future of American power (the US marine outfit) in which fantasied appearance is mistaken for authenticity. If Carnival has been seen by a critic such as Denise Hughes-Tafen as a 'site of resistance' (Hughes-Tafen, 2006, p. 48) and by Errol Hill (1997) as the seedbed for a national drama, here it functions to grotesquely figure post-colonial rule in Trinidad; this is succinctly described by D. Keith Peacock as 'corrupt, oppressive, and willing to abandon Trinidad's cultural heritage in return for personal wealth and status' (Peacock, 2006a, p. 192).

The cultural confusion associated with playing Mas is transformed into a more sinister, political duplicity when it is repeated at the end of the play. Using Ramjohn as an intermediary, Samuel has done a deal with the boys 'up the Hill' whereby if he lifts the state of emergency and allows them to play Mas they will not cause any more trouble. Armed now not with a toy gun but with a genuine 357 Magnum, the Chief of Police and his men, dressed as German storm troopers, join in the Carnival but only to grab the 'terrorists' and 'hit de Hill wit a search party' (Matura, 1992b, pp. 169–70). The music and dancing of the Carnival crowd that forms the final stage image is interspersed with freezes during which we hear the machine gun fire as the dissidents are hunted down. Carnival has become a killing ground. The exuberant, celebratory theatricality that, as Samuel tells Chuck, 'make we a uniquely fantastic people' becomes the pretext for murderous political deception.

Socio-political and cultural change and their personal ramifications are once again at the heart of the other two Trinidad-based dramas written by Matura in the 1970s, *Rum An' Coca Cola* and *Independence* (Bush Theatre, London, 1979). The focus now is not so much on political and racial tensions, as in *Play Mas*, but on the shift in the cultural balance of power between the generations. In both plays, there are central characters who yearn nostalgically for what they regard as the glory days of yesteryear – that is, before Independence and the establishment of a ruling post-colonial elite in Trinidad. This nostalgia, and the recognition that there is no place for them in the present set-up, results in the protagonists engaging in violent acts of destruction – the murder of an innocent American tourist by Creator, the has-been calypsonian of *Rum An' Coca Cola*, and the deliberate arson of his workplace by Drakes, the barman of *Independence*. In both, Matura pairs the ageing protagonist with a young male character whose optimistic energy and hope for a better future has not – or at least not yet – been extinguished.

The sense of changing times as bringing decline for the older generation pervades *Independence* through the figure of the ageing barman Drakes. Matura evokes a post-independence island that still clings to the alleged splendours of colonial days without having succeeded in halting or reversing economic decline. Drakes has lost his eminence as the island's 'number one barman' – an accolade now enjoyed by his former apprentice – but even the hotel in which he works, once 'de best hotel in de whole a de West Indies' (Matura, 1992d, p. 174) grandly (and symbolically) named the Hotel Imperial, has been reduced to a mere poolside bar with no customers and not even the ingredients for Drakes to mix the cocktails – were any ever to be ordered. While the older man reminisces nostalgically about how 'it was happiness in dose days' (Matura, 1992d, p. 174), his young colleague Allen accuses him of having a slave mentality, and offers his entirely different view of the past and future. In place of serving the white man, as in the past, or the uselessness of his job now, he dreams of farming the land. His sense of vocation has the context of a political vision – of how it is time to overcome the heritage of slavery in the West Indies and remove the stigma of farming the land and the problem of self-esteem that goes with it. 'My vision what I see man, how we rob we self a tings man, how we rob we self a pride, because a we own false pride, man' (Matura, 1992d, p. 188). His sense of pride is such that he turns down Drakes' offer of putting in a word for him with their boss to get a transfer, since he so much despises the corruption he feels all around him, and he recognises in their boss Harper only a 'penpusher in he grade three suit, an he grade three brain' (Matura, 1992d, p. 189).

Allen's view of the calibre of those who are flourishing in the post-in-dependence order is borne out by Matura's characterisation of Harper – a hypocritical and vindictive apparatchik in a Mao jacket, wielding his brief-case and a command of the rhetoric of socialist fraternity. He announces that, given the absence of a clientele for the pool bar – otherwise known as the 'People's Recreation Centre' – his Government Committee has decided that 'if by tomorrow evening at sunset, this establishment has not had one or more patrons, it will be closed' (Matura, 1992d, p. 197). The two men react in opposite ways to Harper's edict: Allen can hardly wait, seeing the decision as a liberation that could allow him to fulfil his ambition of becoming a farmer; but for Drakes, the decision offers a bleak future as he has no pension and is unlikely to be redeployed. The closure of the pool bar is, ironically, forestalled by the brief return of the very symbols of the era in which Drakes is mentally stranded. However, it is the reminiscences of the elderly British couple, a former governor and his wife, who have been invited back to attend the Independence Day anniversary celebrations which reveal the history of exploitation and hypocrisy that underlay Drakes' memory of the beautifully dressed people 'just shining an talking' (Matura, 1992d, p. 174) in the Hotel Imperial. The wad of dollar bills the former governor's wife foists on Allen in payment for their drinks is an expression of her generalised sense of guilt about the colonial past, her awareness that '[w]e came here and caused things, we took things and left some, we made scars, deep scars, we can't pretend we didn't' (Matura, 1992d, p. 216). For Allen, as for Bird in *Rum An' Coca Cola*, the money offers the opportunity for genuine independence and for fulfilling his vocation as a farmer. But Drakes rejects the idea of partnership in a farm, unable to envisage a future so alien to what he has known and valued. Rebuffed and insulted by Harper, Drakes mixes his last cocktail, a Molotov, which burns down the hotel and presumably the old colonial couple who are still some-where within its perimeter.

Matura sets *Independence*'s last act a year later in the burnt out hotel's wrecked pool bar. He establishes a tone of ambivalent requiem, in which Drakes and Allen articulate their understandings of the place and their different ways of coming to terms with it. Though he has begun to realise his dream and become a successful young farmer, Allen still struggles to articulate its hold on him. As he tells his partner Yvonne, who is perplexed that she has been dragged here apparently to 'relive de good old days wen de white man was boss' (Matura, 1992d, p. 232), even though he says he hates the place.

> I needed dis place ter show we where we come from an where we going yes, we need places like dis dat is one a de jokes about it, we need de horror ter show we or else we could never know, my eyes open in dis place, ter what we was. (Matura, 1992d, p. 233).

If, for Allen, the hotel and its pool bar constitute a symbol of the colonial regime that still provides an essential compass bearing to situate Trinidadians historically – and crucially to imagine a genuinely independent future – for Drakes, when he emerges from the shadows, it represents something stranger and, for the reader or audience member, something more elusive. He is less a watchman than possessive custodian of – for him – a complex symbolic site.

> My job is ter watch over dis place, ter see dat notting ever move in dis place, ter see dat notting ever change in dis place, ter see it never rise up again, in no shape or form, no bulldozers or crane must come near dis place. (Matura, 1992d, p. 235)

As he built it, he says, he must be alone in pulling it down, accompanied only by the dogs who come there at night. Rejecting Allen's repeated offer of a future in farming, Drakes is left with the remains of the days of colonisation, a deeply internalised image of an idealised past now destroyed by his own hand, to which he is irretrievably tethered, even when offered his freedom.

Meetings (Phoenix Theatre, New York, 1981; Hampstead Theatre, London, 1982) is less interested in a complex colonial legacy than in the Trinidadian élite's collusion in the island's neo-colonial relationship with the US. More obviously a morality play, it does not have the tragicomic complexities of *Independence* or *Play Mas*. It satirically observes a 40-something couple, Hugh and Jean, who are the educated and affluent beneficiaries of Trinidad's oil boom and its economic relationship with its huge capitalist neighbour to the north. For all his privileges, Hugh cannot conceal his growing sense of disaffection with the round of meetings and convenience food that constitute their daily diet. Under the influence of their new live-in cook Elsa and her grandmother, Marie, Hugh returns to the authentic Trinidadian food he grew up on, is educated by the old woman through her stories about Trinidadian history and culture and eventually attends Shango meetings up in the hills.

Though Jean's strictures about modern Trinidadians simply renouncing their modernity and heading back to the bush are reasonable and arguably compelling, Matura chooses to weigh the scales entirely in Hugh's favour. As her latest business venture in partnership with Americans causes people to fall sick and die, Jean is deprived of moral credibility. The deaths in Elsa's and her grandmother's village are the turning point for Hugh. Summoned by Marie, he goes to the wake for the deceased and in the process, it seems, casts off his modernised self after he sees the dead. He decides that he is going back to the village for good, and asks Elsa to call him LeRoy – a reference back to an earlier conversation with her after his nocturnal visit to the Shango meeting, when she assured him that he could become a king selected by the people just as her grandmother and other relatives were royal in a tradition handed down from the days of the slave plantations.

It is hard to disagree with Nicholas de Jongh's complaint, when reviewing a revival of the play in London in 1991, that 'Hugh's ideological conversion is pure hokum' and that consequently the production 'cannot cope with the essential implausibility' (de Jongh, 1991). With its final image of the modern, educated Trinidadian woman, Jean, coughing blood – the victim of her entrepreneurial rapacity – Matura's play unambiguously endorses the idea that one can return to – or at least try to return to – an 'authentic' West Indian identity and experience, unsullied by Western modernism. The dramatist seems to have succumbed to what Edward Said called 'nativism', with its powerful emotional appeal to 'a native past, narrative or actuality that stands free from worldly time itself' (Said, 1993, p. 275). One need not doubt that Trinidadian villagers, or at least some of them, have a way of life and values associated with it that contrast sharply and that are perhaps in fundamental conflict with the Trinidadian modernity of the educated and commercial elite. There is also the possibility of finding in this traditional way of life and its values the moral and spiritual basis for a critique of that modernity, or some at least of its aspects. But the trouble is that a return to 'the metaphysics of essences' (Said, 1993, p. 276) tends to abandon history and the secular world, as Said sees it on the terms established or encouraged by imperialism through the colonial encounter. The dramatic potential of the modern Trinidadian troubled by a pervasive sense of the inauthentic and wishing to return to something simpler and more 'real' is compelling; but Matura chooses not to explore the kind of dilemmas such a situation is likely to give rise to, even though he allows Jean to at least hint at them.

In *The Coup*, Matura turns his attention to the exercise of power and power-seeking in a Caribbean island, its subject echoing both the Black Power coup in Trinidad in 1970 and more recent events of 1990, when members of a Muslim organisation stormed the Parliament building and television station in an attempted coup d'état. Though Matura has always deployed his talent as a comic writer to good effect, it is nevertheless striking, and significant, that he frames his 'play of revolutionary dreams' as a farce. The coup is initiated by a group of army officers whose Marxist rhetoric and supposed disgust at President Jones's corruption and decadent behaviour in fact only camouflages their personal ambition and desire for a slice of the cake. Driven only by self-interest, they are soon at each other's throats. Not only are they devoid of anything resembling ideology or a national vision, they are represented as bumbling fools with a penchant for accidentally shooting themselves and blowing each other up. The only sympathetic characters are Jones himself, whose corruption is at least genial, and his gaoler Mikey, with whom he gradually forms an alliance – and who, it turns out, may even be one of his evidently numerous illegitimate children.

The Coup, then, offers a picture of its Caribbean island as a place devoid of genuine history or politics. In their stead is nothing more than a repetitive cycle in which one form of corruption or violence merely replaces, for a while, another. Much of the play's farcical entertainment derives from the fact that events happen not by design or as part of an identifiable historical evolution, but by accident or stupidity, or a combination of the two. The apparently sinister Major Ferret, in trying to shoot the president with the revolutionary cry of 'power to the people', only succeeds in shooting himself. Similarly, Ferret and his enemy within the military, Lieutenant Chan, are blown to bits when they light up their cigars to celebrate their peace talks when the match ignites some leaking petrol tanks. If the content of the deposed president's dreams are anything to go by, Trinidadian history has from the first been determined more by farcical misadventure than purposeful design – just as Columbus, when meeting the island's indigenous inhabitants for the first time, picks up and waves a red flag, thus accidentally causing his men's cannons to open fire on them.

The final dream-like accident of the play seems to have put paid to Jones himself and his plan to defeat the attempted coup. We are left, in its closing moments, with two nuns exchanging their thoughts on the impressive size of the ex-president's penis, before they move off-stage to the sound of sirens that presumably presage yet another crisis – perhaps a coup or an attempt at one – but with no more purpose or rationale than anything that has gone before. In the comic world of *The Coup* at least, the late president's egregious sexual organ and the large number of offspring he produced with it has some kind of reality, and can be celebrated by the population. Whatever their politicians and elite may throw at them, the play infers, Trinidadians have a wayward, never-say-die vitality and love of life that cannot be defeated.

Between the premières of *Meetings* and *The Coup*, Matura wrote two adaptations of European classics, both of which have enjoyed considerable commercial and critical success. Both transpose the action and characters of their originals to colonial Trinidad, *The Playboy of the West Indies* (Oxford Playhouse, 1984) adapting J. M. Synge's Irish masterpiece *The Playboy of the Western World*, to village life in 1950, whereas *Three Sisters* (Donmar Warehouse, London, 1988) reworks Anton Chekhov's play in the context of war-time Port of Spain. Matura's artistic achievement in the two adaptations is to have kept closely to the original plays in plot, character and mood, but to have infused his versions with an entirely persuasive Trinidadian-ness. The folk lyricism of Synge's Irish idiom is successfully transposed into the richness of Matura's Trinidadian patois. The Irish pub becomes a rum shop and the villagers of County Mayo are transformed into a collection of entirely believable Trinidadian types. Ken, like his Irish original, the playboy Christy, grows into the hero that the villagers want him to be, in order to fulfil a yearning in their own lives. The tough and sceptical Peggy most of all responds to that yearning by falling in love with him, only to fail to take the one chance she will ever have of escaping from the drab mediocrity of village life. What makes Matura's adaptation so successful is not just his identification of the affinities in language and culture between rural Ireland in the early twentieth century, and rural Trinidad in the 1950s but, more specifically, a common structure of feeling in which a richly chaotic and potentially destructive energy is revealed as lying dormant beneath a stagnant social surface.

A more languorous, claustrophobic atmosphere pervades Matura's version of Chekhov. The upper class sisters – daughters of a headmaster – dream of their youthful days in Cambridge as they witness their present lives gradually deteriorating. As Trinidadians join up to fight for the Mother Country against Germany, there is already conflict within the colonial set-up as people protest against the imposition of increased water rates and the city burns. Even within the island's élite there is growing discord. Eddie and Lucas, once friends and fellow officers, fall out when Eddie resigns his commission on the grounds that he does not want to fight someone else's war. Apart from their personal animosity, there is evident political rancour between Eddie and Francis, the merchant–politician husband of Helen, who is flourishing economically through the war and opposes Eddie's belief in the need for independence from the British. By the end of *Three Sisters*, there is a melancholic sense that one era is coming to a close but that what may follow it remains deeply uncertain.

It is precisely for his success in evoking West Indian sensibilities and culture, both in the migrant community in London and on the island of Trinidad, that reviewers have consistently praised productions of Matura's plays, even when – justifiably – they have also indicated their occasional dramaturgical weaknesses. Comments such as 'it puts the authentic spirit of Trinidad onto the Court stage' (Michael Billington on *Play Mas*, 1974) and it 'trac[es] the national character to its very source' (Michael Coveney on *The Coup*, 1991a) are not uncommon, and are usually accompanied by praise of the rich texture of Matura's Trinidadian language. We might add that, to be discovered, Caribbean sensibilities and culture have to be approached and explored from a particular standpoint. Matura has been remarkably consistent in viewing West Indian experience from below, from a subaltern position that does seem to correspond with popular perceptions and behaviour. But if this has been his main dramatic and theatrical strength, it has also arguably been the source of his limitations as a playwright. For 'awareness' in Matura's understanding seems increasingly to have excluded a sense of politics and historical movement, in favour of an emphasis on the celebration of local identity and its alleged 'essence'. It may be that the issue of audience has been significant here. In concentrating mainly on Trinidadian themes in Trinidadian settings, while writing in Britain for mainly white audiences, has perhaps encouraged a tendency to essentialise and stereotype so evident in later work like *Meetings* and *The Coup*. Had Matura returned to Trinidad, his audience there might have dissuaded him from this tendency. In remembering Matura's dedication of *Play Mas* to Frantz Fanon, the understanding and overcoming of black misery that this great Caribbean theorist of decolonisation articulates, never excludes political and historical process, and always looks beyond the local.

Notes

1. Fanon was a doctor, writer and activist from Martinique who worked in Algeria and whose research in psychology studied the negative impact of colonialism on the black subject.
2. *The Coup* was the first West Indian play to be commissioned by the Royal National Theatre in London.
3. For a useful survey, see Riggio (2004).

3
Staging Social Change: Three Plays by Barry Reckord

Mary F. Brewer

Introduction

Barry Reckord represents one of the most extraordinary public voices of black experience in post-war Britain, whose dramatic output in the 1950s and 1960s, alongside that of Derek Walcott and Wole Soyinka, laid the foundation for the following generation of black playwrights in Britain. Reckord was a prolific writer, and more than a dozen of his dramas were produced in British and Jamaican theatres. This chapter addresses three of his plays that were produced in London: *Flesh to a Tiger* (1958, Royal Court), *Skyvers* (1963 and 1971, Royal Court), and *White Witch* (1985, Rehearsed reading, Tricycle Theatre). These plays comprise the only published copies of his work. My reading of them is organised around each one's thematic concerns, with reference also to their key historical, cultural and theatrical contexts. My overarching aim, though, is to investigate the role of the plays as part of the post-war public discourse on social identities, especially in light of the transition from British colonial to post-colonial relations. Further, because Reckord's work is equally attuned to the realities of gender and class privilege and how each intersects with race, I examine also the way in which the plays depict and challenge conventional gender and class hegemony.

Born in Kingston, Jamaica, in 1926, Reckord came to Britain in 1950 on a scholarship to Cambridge University. He settled in London, where he worked as a teacher in the state school system before establishing a career as a writer. In the immediate post-war era, Caribbean immigrants formed part of what Theodore Shank terms Britain's 'unofficial cultures': groups excluded by the social establishment because they possessed physical and cultural characteristics that were perceived as alien, and thus fundamentally incompatible with British identity (1996, p. 3). As a Jamaican,

47

Reckord constituted an unsanctioned cultural presence. In an interview with *The Jamaica Gleaner*, he reflects on how his 'unofficial status' affected his ability to feel at home in British theatre: 'One of the reasons I never succeeded as a playwright was I never mixed…I never knew any of the other playwrights, never went drinking with them or anything' (Reckord, 2003). Even had he wanted to fraternise, the extent to which a Caribbean playwright would have been welcomed into the networks of a white-dominated industry is open to question, for despite his Oxbridge education, and white-collar profession, he was not sheltered from the racism experienced by the first generation of black migrants to Britain. This hostility was indelibly imprinted upon his consciousness as soon as he arrived:

> I remember the first day I landed in England. The white man at the immigration desk saw the name on my passport slightly fudged and passed it to his chief who said, 'It's all right. Probably done by some bastard from the bush.' I scarcely registered what was said […] In the meantime I was cosmopolitan, a man of all worlds and of none. Too hostile to whites to identify with them. Too white-minded and well-behaved to fight them. A double alienation. (Reckord, 1971, p. 17)

Reckord's drama spans an era of British social history when racism could be expressed in blatantly crude terms because it formed part of official public discourse. Hence, his sense of 'double alienation' – from his indigenous and adopted cultures – was not an uncommon feeling among the growing black British community, because they shared what Reckord calls the 'stock-in-trade memories of every colonial' (1971, p. 84) as reinforced through Anglo-centric education and cultural traditions. In his non-fictional study of the Cuban revolution, *Does Fidel Eat More Than Your Father?* Reckord's reflections on his upbringing record his uncomfortable suspension between two points of psychological response to colonisation – identification and resistance. Gabriele Griffin describes a post-colonial life as involving an identity that is shaped by 'in-betweenness', a situation in which one's cultural self-image is not necessarily in sync with one's racial heritage (2003, p. 111). Reckord's memories reflect not only the degree of his social estrangement, but also, and more important in terms of his dramatic output, his intimate knowledge of the white 'other' contributes towards his ability to critically negotiate between the position of the colonised and the coloniser.

Notwithstanding, as Yvonne Brewster attests in her introduction to the sole collection of his work, Reckord's 'place in the history of black play-writing in the United Kingdom goes almost unrecognized' (2010, p. 11).

The fate of one of his most acclaimed plays, *You in Your Small Corner*, exemplifies his marginalisation. Based on the playwright's time at Cambridge University, this play looks at the experiences of first-generation immigrants attempting to settle in an unwelcoming environment, while exploring the intersection of class and race prejudice through the relationship between Dave, a middle-class West Indian, and the daughter of a white, working-class family. After its premiere at the Royal Court in 1961, the play transferred to the West End, and was later adapted for television and broadcast by Granada TV on 5 June 1962. Although, Brewster explains, in 1962 Reckord was doing what no white playwright was achieving at the time (Qtd. in Reckord, 2009) only a battered typescript has been preserved. [1] The fact that he receives scant mention in the critical record is not unique for a black British dramatist; rather, Reckord's absence reflects the lack of importance traditionally placed upon recording black people's contributions to British society by the cultural establishment. When discussing the impetus behind setting up the National Theatre's Black Plays Archive, Kwame Kwei-Armah, a foremost contemporary playwright, speaks of his disappointment at having 'nowhere else to go' after reading the handful of published plays he could find by black British playwrights (2009).[2] His experience demonstrates how the failure to preserve and disseminate earlier black theatre history has impacted on subsequent generations of writers. Acquiring knowledge about the many different black traditions informing British drama has been a significant struggle, and black playwrights have had little access to sources of inspiration derived from their communities.

British theatre in the 1950s and 1960s was dominated primarily by critical concern with the group of writers dubbed the 'Angry Young Men'.[3] On the one hand, playwrights such as John Osborne, Edward Bond and John Arden, who produced plays that challenged the conservative social values embedded in the commercially oriented drama dominating the West End, were hugely important. On the other hand, they shared a background that was rooted in what Shank calls the 'official' culture of Britain (1996, p. 3). They were white, English and male, and thus enjoyed the social privileges attendant upon their cultural centrality. Michael Billington notes that 'The stage did a lot to pin down social change in the 60s – but, if you were female or black, the chances were your voice went unheard' (2006, p. 18).

Contemporary work by white writers that was considered radical tended to ignore the social injustices women suffered as a result of entrenched sex-gender discrimination. Stephen Lacey draws a connection between the critique of class in Kitchen-Sink-Drama and male sexual insecurity. In *Look Back in Anger*, 'class resentment...is inseparable from an antagonism towards, and fear of, women' (Lacey, 1995, p. 31), he argues. To the contrary, Reckord showed unusual sensitivity to gender difference and the position of women within the colonial order as well as racial difference. Reckord's focus on complex women characters also marks him out as distinctive from other contemporary black male writers whose work was produced in Britain. Consider, for instance, Derek Walcott, whose ideology of gender Paul Breslin describes as 'distasteful' (2001, p. 268). Whereas Wole Soyinka admits that he sees no reason for even attempting to address femininity. When Mary David, in an interview with Soyinka, expressed disappointment with his depiction of women as unrealistic, being a combination of the bitch and the Madonna, he responded:

> But that's the role of women. It is the women who must realize them-
> selves in their writing. I can't enter into the mind and body of a
> woman. No, let women write about themselves. Why should they ask
> me to do that? (Qtd. in Jeyifo, 2004, p. 99)

Reckord explains his interest in relationships between men and women as rooted in his belief that the 'sexual plight of women reflects the polit-ical plight of society,' a society that is based on power; therefore, people either feel power or fear rather than a sense of commonality, commu-nity or respect (Benson and Conolly, 2005, n.p.). As Don Warrington expresses it, 'Reckord saw sex as crucial to the way we live and as that which can block us from communicating' ('Reckord Celebrations', 2012). This perspective reflects women's position in terms of colonial gender relations, but departs from the view of Jamaican society as matriarchal, which Brewster describes as follows:

> Coming from a West Indian background, the word 'feminism' had a
> really hollow ring. Simply, it's a matriarchal society. There, the women
> rule the roost without actually wearing the trousers. So, entering a
> European or British situation, one found the feminist hang-up a bit
> difficult to grasp. (Qtd. in Goodman with de Gay, 1996, p. 121)

Flesh to a Tiger, Reckord's first play to be produced in Britain, focuses on Della, a poor black woman in a shanty town. According to Brewster, 'to be feminist means to look at things from a woman's perspective' (Goodman with de Gay, 1996, p. 121), and if we accept this as a working definition, it is fair to say that Reckord creates two feminist characters – Della and Annie Palmer in *White Witch*. However, this unusual aspect of his work went unnoticed among contemporary critics, for whom it was more remarkable to see a black person of any gender on the British stage. Patrick Gibbs, in his *Daily Telegraph* review of *Flesh to a Tiger*, felt it necessary to remark that 'for the second night in London we have had a play about coloured [*sic*] people' (1958). Gibbs' comment reflects the fact that staging a black presence in this era was, in itself, a remarkable and political act.

Flesh To a Tiger and *White Witch*

Flesh to a Tiger takes place during the colonial era in Kingston. It explores the issues of colonial exploitation and the intersection of women's subordination and imperialism through a cross-racial relationship between Della and a physician known simply as the Doctor or the White Wolf. The narrative follows her struggle to break free from folk superstitions – symbolised by Shepherd, the leader of the local *obeah* cult,[4] while avoiding merely exchanging indigenous superstition for the colonial ideology that the Doctor represents; in other words, how may Della escape being reduced to mere black flesh to a white tiger?

The sexual rivalry between Shepherd and the Doctor serves as an analogy for larger colonial conflicts between West Indian practices and white values. That Della has internalised the colonial racist viewpoint is evidenced by her belief that Shepherd's behaviour is 'savagery' compared to the Doctor's 'gentlemanliness' (Reckord, 2010a, p. 22). In reality, the Doctor exploits Della to fulfil his sexual needs, comparing her to something he can draw around himself 'like a garment for my strength' (Reckord, 2010a, p. 37). This accounts for his violent reaction to Della's kiss, which symbolises her attempt to define the meaning of their relationship as one of genuine intimacy, thus defying the Doctor's need to remain the controlling subject over his colonial object. Ironically, the Doctor is willing to 'risk his privy', but only because he configures Della's mouth as the portal for contagion by the black male 'other' – the third figure in his nightmare vision of 'three in a bed' (Reckord, 2010a, p. 37). The grotesque imagery he uses to describe Della's putative black male lodger – a 'sweaty brute of a lecher', a 'flesh pot' with 'grease under his broken nail' and 'food hiding in his cavities' – exploits the stereotypical associations drawn in colonial discourse between black men and animalistic sexuality, but his attempt to maintain the illusion of superior difference serves to demonstrate his terror of 'going native' through his sexual association with a black woman (Reckord, 2010a, p. 36).

His rejection provokes an emotional crisis for Della that generates greater self- and political awareness. In breaking with the Doctor, she rejects the system of values that structure not only men and women into hierarchical roles, but also the colonial system that locates the occupier as superior to the indigenous person – female and male. The import of her rejection is emphasised by the striking language and imagery of her confession to Lal that when she had sex with the Doctor 'a slave hide came over my flesh, and back to a slave heart my free heart went', but henceforth, she vows to 'vomit all white flesh and cover it with dust' (Reckord, 2010a, p. 38).

The pace with which Reckord moves from incipient resistance to the restoration of the colonial order in Act Two is overly accelerated, and contemporary reviewers noted the play's structural unevenness and thematic inconsistency. Reckord agreed with Cynthia Wilmot who said 'When it was very good it was very, very good and when it was bad it was awful' (2003, n.p.). The reviewer for *Punch* wrote that 'Reckord seems uncertain whether his play is about the problem or the characters he has chosen to illustrate it – he prepares us for a revelation of cosmic truth and instead involves us in the highly personal dilemmas of individuals' (Anon., 1958).[5] According to Milton Shulman, the problem lies mainly in the construction of Della's character: 'At no time does Della convince that she is a woman capable of grappling with [the] sociological and philosophical issues' in the play. Instead, she 'emerges as...a good girl whose men have done her wrong' (1958). I would argue that Della possesses greater political understanding of her own and her nation's situation than Shulman, writing in a 1950s context, credits. When she bids goodbye to the Doctor, she draws attention to his liability for her economic as well as her emotional distress: 'When I walk the street just now after the murder you did my love, and saw my people, every one of them a nasty poorhouse with a sweat smell, a vision come to me' (Reckord, 2010a, p. 43). Della's vision involves a graphic representation of the slave trade and black people's non-human status within it, and reveals her ability to make connections between slavery, colonial history and the impoverished condition in which her people live. However, she is given no politically constructive means of acting on this understanding. Brewster makes a similar point, and one that opposes her reading of Jamaican society as matriarchal, when she recognises that Reckord offers Della few ways of responding to events outside of some overly dramatic speeches (2010, p. 15).

In contrast, Reckord endows Annie Palmer not only with political consciousness, but also with the means to strike at her male oppressors. Mervyn Morris' introduction to *White Witch* states that it is based on a Jamaican legend about Palmer, a plantation mistress, who was rumoured to have numerous lovers and to have murdered four husbands (2010, p. 156). Reckord draws on this legend to make a trenchant critique of patriarchal authority in the colonial system, demonstrating how colonialism relies upon denying both black and white women sexual agency. Annie is introduced to the audience as an object of exchange between her father, an English duke, and Simon Palmer, a wealthy plantation owner. The duke wishes to be rid of her because she refuses to play the role of 'woman' according to the demands of polite society, whereas Simon needs to acquire a white woman to produce a legal heir. In gender terms, Annie resides on the same level as her husband's numerous black mistresses. Morris says that on the plantation, all women exist as an underclass – to serve the pleasures of men and to bear them children (2010, p. 156), and this is further demonstrated through men's use of rape as a tool to control both white and black women. Susan Brownmiller discusses how rape functioned as an institutional crime in slave systems. Black women's bodies belonged to their white masters and they had no legal right of refusal to sex (1975, p. 153). The institution of marriage affords Annie no greater protection from her husband, with whom she has intercourse only because she knows that otherwise he would rape her.

A conversation between Simon and the Doctor about Annie's repeated miscarriages draws another link between sexuality and race through the motif of licentiousness. Annie is described as 'high', which refers to her class status and her presumed racial purity, both of which are called into question because she takes pleasure in the sexual act. Active sexuality is deemed either a form of mental illness or wickedness in a white woman, whereas it is viewed as natural in black women because they are viewed as 'animal' (Reckord, 2010b, p. 222). The representation of black people as animalistic was core to the 'scientific racism' that was used as an apology for nineteenth-century colonialism. Commenting on the belief that black people were a distinct species, Robert Young asserts that the generally accepted test to determine distinct species was fertility, or rather that sexual intercourse between them would be infertile (1995, p. 7). The flawed logic of 'scientific racism' posited that even though sexual unions between black and white people produced offspring, their fertility, and its quality, would decline and ultimately cease through the generations (Young, 1995, p. 8). Annie's display of active desire, and the men's fear that she cannot carry Palmer's child full term, connects her to ideas of hybridity and to the assumed dangers of miscegenation, which in fact resulted more often from sexual relations (consensual and non-consensual) between white men and black women in a colonial context. Her association with black sexuality poses a threat to Palmer's plans to 'breed' heirs for his colonial dynasty, which can only be based on a racially unadulterated primogeniture. Moreover, on a macro-level,

Annie represents the colonial woman whose job is to ensure the continuation of the British race and its colonial dynasty, rooted in its ostensible white racial purity.

Even though Annie submits to her husband's sexual demands, she fights to keep some control over her body by refusing to produce a child through self-induced abortions, which Reckord styles 'carnal insurrection' (2010b, p. 220). Reckord uses witchcraft as a trope for black and white women's sexual autonomy by virtue of their ability to use it, or more precisely folk medicine, to determine if and when they bear children, and it is through 'carnal insurrection' that political revolt is generated in the play. From her arrival on the island, Annie seeks sexual liaisons with black men. She becomes pregnant by Cupid, the son of Palmer and his slave mistress. In defending her relationship with Cupid, Annie assesses critically both patriarchal gender relations and racial hierarchies:

> He doesn't care if I'm white, he doesn't think I'm a whore, he knows the politics are deranged, he isn't a blind creature of his time, passing down tried and tested lies. (Reckord, 2010b, p. 239)

What Cupid is able to see and that to which Palmer remains blind is the fact that, as Monique Wittig comments, 'the concept of difference has nothing ontological about it. It is only the way that the masters interpret a historical situation of domination' (1992, p. 29).

Simon's colonial framework of interpretation means that he cannot come to terms with Annie's infidelities or the growing disobedience of his slaves. His increasing isolation and frustration lead to a bout of what was popularly termed 'Jungle Madness' among colonialists, and during the slave's rebellion, Simon ultimately turns his aggression upon himself by committing suicide. His death frees Annie from the strictures of her marriage, but Reckord leaves it uncertain whether she and Cupid will defeat the advancing army on its way to quell the revolt. However, what is clear at the end of *White Witch* is how the repressiveness of social structures governing gender, race and sexuality in the colonial situation mirrors and reveals the oppressiveness of imperialist political structures, and thus, Reckord suggests, when racial, gender or sexual oppression is challenged, it generates potential for other forms of political resistance to spread, including armed rebellion.

Skyvers

The issues explored in *White Witch* and *Flesh to a Tiger* contributed over time to Reckord's reputation as a serious playwright. *The Guardian's* obituary for Reckord points out how these two plays in particular demonstrate the playwright's uncompromising 'espousal of unfashionable ideas' – about religion and politics, especially sexual politics – but, this 'did not necessarily make for good drama' (Busby, 2012, n.p.). For this reason, they received less critical attention than *Skyvers*, Reckord's most critically and commercially successful play. Its success is due not only to its aesthetic qualities, but also to the fact that its theme of educational reform was one of the most topical and contentious issues in post-war British society. Pam Brighton, who directed the 1971 Royal Court production, notes the important connection the play makes between educational attainment and social mobility:

> The gap, cultural, social and economic between the working class, or do we now call them the underclass, and the middle/upper class is a chasm. It is the running sore through our society and it amazes me how little it is written about. *Skyvers* was one of the first plays I ever read that really laid it out. (2010, p. 72)

Skyvers tells the story of a group of impoverished 15-year-old boys about to leave formal education. The relationship between the schoolboys and teachers is the main source of the action, with the clash between the reactionary standards of the middle-class headmaster and the disaffected values of the working-class pupils giving rise to dramatic tension. Reviews of the play emphasised its 'documentary honesty' (Anon., *Sunday Telegraph*, 1963a)[6] and 'unmistakable ring of truth' (Hope-Wallace, *The Guardian*, 1963).

The circumstances of the play's original production, however, resulted in a radical change to Reckord's script, and one that raises questions about how it should be read within the genre of realism. Deirdre Osborne records the Royal Court's claim that *Skyvers* had to be staged with white actors because no black actors could be found (2006a, p. 73). The presence of white actors enabled the play to be subsumed within a spectrum of realist plays about the British working-class that followed the 1956 production of Osborne's ground-breaking *Look Back in Anger*; this move may have led to more critical regard for *Skyvers*, but it further reduces the perception of British drama as anything but white authored.

The connection made between *Skyvers* and Arnold Wesker's *Chips with Everything* (1962) offers a case in point. Both plays offer a critique of social engineering and conformity. Wesker's play explores class conflicts among a group of military conscripts as they progress through basic training. In contrast *to Skyvers*, however, *Chips* ends with the rebellious young men passively accepting military authority. This prompted a reviewer writing for *The Observer* to suggest that *Skyvers* could serve as an apt prologue to Wesker's play because *Chips* 'shows us the military uses' to which the headmaster's lessons in conformity can be put (Anon., 1963b).[7] The parallels drawn between Skyvers and Edward Bond's controversial *Saved* (1965) is another example. Set in South London, Bond's play features a cast of young white men who act out their frustration over their bleak existence by engaging in sexist banter and random acts of violence. One critic noted that *Skyvers* seemed to involve the same characters, or types of characters, as *Saved*, but with the difference that Reckord treats them more sympathetically (Anon., 1971).[8]

Although a number of similarities in the adolescent experiences of poor black and white youths may well have existed, if Reckord intended staging a set of interior dialogues that represented black male experience, what critics and audiences witnessed was a very different interpretation of its subject. Certainly, the 'invisibility' of whiteness meant that race and identity did not emerge as a strand of critical debate about *Skyvers*, even though the play contains expressions of casual racism. However, one of the play's more interesting and unusual reviews highlights race: *The Times'* critic provocatively describes Cragge, on whom the narrative centres, as 'the first white Negro to appear on the British stage' (Anon., 'An Outsider in Search of Identity,' 1963c).[9] While remaining aware of the problematic nature of the term 'white Negro', this tag opens up another possible reading of the play, described by *The Times'* commentator as an allegory of an immigrant adrift in British society. Certainly, Cragge feels a deep sense of alienation, similar to that described by Reckord. Excluded from mainstream society represented by the teachers, as well as outside the youth culture symbolised by the gang leader Brook, Cragge's adolescent exploration of self and search for identity is doubly fraught.

Reading *Skyvers* as a narrative of young white boys' experience, Jack Lewis in the *Sunday Citizen* praised Reckord for capturing the boys' 'crushed morale' and anti-social attitudes, which is expressed primarily through their use of language (1963). Reckord employs a cockney idiom to forward his realist aim; he recounts, 'if the play sounds real it is because I've gotten down what these boys do in fact think and feel, although they are often too inarticulate to say it' (2010d, p. 77). Reckord's use of cockney may be linked to his position in the colonial race system. Cockney is a quintessential English dialect rooted in East London, working-class culture; hence, *Skyvers* presents a case in which a language identified as belonging to British white people of a lower economic class is being inscribed by a person who occupies a superior class position, but a lower status in terms of racial identity. His choice of cockney calls to mind M. M. Bakhtin's idea of hybridisation as 'a mixture of two social languages within the limits of a single utterance, an encounter within the arena of an utterance, between two different linguistic consciousnesses, separated from one another by an epoch, by social differentiation or by some other factor' (1981, p. 358), and the effect of hybridisation is to undermine the concept of linguistic unity and authority.

The extent to which critics were aware of Reckord's original cast intentions is unclear, but certainly no one identified the presence of a hybrid voice. To the contrary, the 'truth' of the boys' thoughts and feelings resonated with the all-white-male critical coterie and the predominantly white audiences at the Royal Court. The original production of *Skyvers* especially struck a chord among educationalists and young people, as did later revivals. A favourable review in *The London Teacher* encouraged people to take advantage of specially reduced ticket prices (Deslandes, 1963, p. 155), and, Robin Thornber's review notes that when the play toured Newcastle-upon-Tyne, the decision by the headmaster of Gateshead Comprehensive to withdraw an invitation to perform the play at the school sparked a walk-out by the fifth-formers (1963). The walk-out illustrates how the play generated fear among some in the educational establishment that exposure to *Skyvers* might make '*Students...think of smashing up schools*'; according to Thornber, as a result, fewer schools than usual opted to take the play with some education authorities refusing to provide the customary subsidy (1963).

Although the play does not advocate direct action on the part of students, it does call for a revolution in education, something that could only be achieved in tandem with overturning Britain's other established social hierarchies in order to create a genuine meritocracy. The play's setting in a Comprehensive school is significant, for this type of school embodies *Skyvers'* political or moral values. The glossary included in the programme for the 1963 production defines a Comprehensive as a school that provides 'a secondary education for every child according to his [sic] need and ability without introducing rigid intellectual and therefore, social, distinctions' (n.p.). Even though Comprehensives were set up with the aim of reducing, if not eliminating, class hierarchies, *Skyvers* makes the argument that they often hypocritically perpetuated them. *Skyvers'* analysis of British class politics unambiguously links the existing educational system with oppression. Ronald Bryden reflects that the play dramatically presents the same ruthlessly logical question as Michael Young's influential 1958 treatise *Rise of the Meritocracy*: 'if the top layer of our school system is an education for success, what can the rest be but an education for failure' (1963).

At a recent celebration of Reckord's theatrical legacy at the Bush Theatre, London, Warrington characterised Reckord as a playwright with a 'vision of how we all should live, and that's what he wrote about' ('Reckord Celebrations', 2012). Reckord viewed Comprehensives as sites where young people from lower socio-economic backgrounds become institutionalised into the reigning social order in the same way that prisoners become immured to having their lives controlled by their jailers:

> Schools are for teachers, not students. For teachers to impose a particular view of life that is medieval. To ensure that they're all disciplined – that they don't beat up teachers and they're not rocking the boat. (Qtd. in Thornber, 1963).

Ironically, Cragge, because he endeavours to play by the rules of the system, is more likely to spend his life labouring at an uninspiring and dead-end job than is Brook, who, rather than working for a 'few lousy nicker a week', plans to capitalise on what he sees as the easy option for escaping his poor environment – criminality – 'pinchin' cars and floggin' 'em' (Reckord, 2010c, p. 88). Brook's 'choice' for his future means that he and his gang are likely to end up in prison, something that was foreshadowed in *Skyver's* set design. Jocelyn Herbert's 1963 design, for instance, featured a 'tall grey set, with steel framed windows stretching up at the back of the stage', whereas Thornber's review notes that Trevor Coe (1963, Tyneside Theatre) used a set of school railings to emphasise a caged effect.

Cragge's outsider status is established in the opening scene when Helen comments that he is 'bottom on my list for going out and top a no one's' (Reckord, 2010c, p. 82). Whereas the other boys stand out in themselves, Cragge needs 'football and rock and roll to shine' (Reckord, 2010c, p. 81). Hence, he fantasises about transcending his lowly place by becoming a professional football player. He is not alone in his dreams of fame and wealth though. Nicholas de Jongh characterises the boys as a 'mass of dangerous discontent' in their longing to escape their indigent lives through money and sex (1971, n.p.). Each boy is aware that without exceptional luck he will play a pre-ordained role in society, one that is determined by his birth at the bottom of the social order rather than any individual talents he may possess.

The paucity of the boys' future expectations underscores that 'society, while hypnotically proclaiming the virtues of education, has a vested interest in producing what the school's headmaster considers "ignorant scum" to do its chores for it' (Anon., 1971).[10] For this reason, the education system is constructed not only to ensure Cragge's failure, but also to make certain that he accepts his inequality as part of the ordinary, tolerable way of things, and therefore, he will not seek to alter it. The way in which his school experiences ultimately impact on Cragge is left to the audience's imagination, however. Reckord offers a surprising twist in the plot when Cragge decides that he would like to continue his studies, having accepted that his aspiration to athletic stardom is illusory. He tells Jordan:

> I'm stayin' on 'ere. I can do better with my brains that with me feet, I know that. I can always see things that need arguin' and find the argument: that's brain. And it comes to me like birds come to Brook. (Reckord, 2010c, p. 143)

However, his new-found ambition to write for the school paper is thwarted by the nameless headmaster's view of him as unfit for further education. The headmaster, who homogenises his charges, assumes that Cragge is as guilty as Brook's gang of disrupting a prize-giving ceremony, and he tells Cragge that he will not be allowed to 'go on corrupting the school':

> The public don't read our magazines; they see your conduct. The Governors won't blame me if you never get G.C.E. God is responsible for your brains but I give you your character. (Reckord, 2010c, p. 151)

The sincerity of Cragge's desire to improve his life chances is evidenced when he accepts the headmaster's unfair and humiliating punishment, which is to be caned in front of the school assembly. Reckord closes the play with the image of Cragge bending over as the headmaster raises his cane to strike, and as the stage goes dark, the audience is left to ponder the sound of his strokes. In his review for the *Daily Telegraph* (1963), Darlington thought that *Skyvers* would have been a stronger indictment of the educational system had Reckord shown what happens to Cragge after he is beaten: will he be able to continue his schooling, or will he be propelled into delinquency? For *Daily Express* reviewer Herbert Kretzmer, though, to know whether Cragge's public humiliation represents a short-lived catastrophe or the beginning of a lasting personal tragedy is not necessary to communicate Reckord's social critique (1963). Given his aim of challenging what he believed to be the implicit agenda of comprehensive education in 1950s and 1960s Britain, the play's open-endedness leads the audience away from viewing it as a young boy's personal story rather than a political critique of the status quo, which they might conceivably act to change.

Conclusion

Skyvers, like *Flesh to a Tiger* and *White Witch*, represents an attempt to demystify what Antonio Gramsci terms the cultural 'common sense', those conceptions of the world – social hierarchies, whether they are grounded on racial, gender, class or sexual differences – that are imposed and absorbed passively and uncritically from outside (1988, p. 421). According to Warrington, who appeared in Reckord's television play *Club Havana* (BBC 1975), what made Reckord stand out as a playwright was his irreverence: 'Nothing was beyond question, everything, whatever it was, for its own sake, and ours, needed to be tested from time to time' (2010, p. 248). The acclaimed British director, Max Stafford-Clark, who directed Reckord's play *X* in 1974 at the Royal Court, also singles out the transgressive nature of Reckord's work, both in its form and content, and it is this quality, he suggests, that makes him a great playwright ('Reckord Celebrations', 2012). The recent celebration of Reckord's work at the Bush Theatre in London offers hope that soon we will have greater access to his theatrically accomplished irreverence,[11] but without doubt, his extant plays leave us an arresting and credible black cultural perspective on what it meant to be black and white British in the post-war era.

Notes

1. Brewster's 'Introduction' to *For the Reckord* states that the play would have been included in the volume could a complete copy have been found (2010, p. 12); however, the typescript to which I refer, a prompt book used by the English Stage Company, appears to be complete. It is held at the V & A Theatre and Performance Collection: PLAYS REC PROMPT 380441011511730. Three video clips are available of the Granada TV production; see www.screenonline. org.uk/tv/id/537722/index.html.
2. A small archive including files on some of the leading black theatre groups is maintained by the Victoria and Albert Museum (London). However, The Black Plays Archive, established at the National Theatre and funded by Arts Council England, serves as the main public project to redress this imbalance.
3. For more detail, see Shellard (1999).
4. The 1958 programme for the play defines Obeah as 'magic rites for bringing or getting rid of trouble'. Available at 'V & A Department of Theatre & Performance Core Collection': Production File: Reckord: *Flesh to a Tiger*.

5. Unsigned review from a clipping in the Victoria and Albert Museum, Department of Theatre and Performance Core Collection: Production File: Reckord: *Flesh to a Tiger*.
6. Unsigned review from a clipping in the Victoria and Albert Museum, Department of Theatre and Performance Core Collection: Production File: Royal Court, *Skyvers*.
7. Unsigned review taken from a clipping in the Victoria and Albert Museum, Department of Theatre and Performance Core Collection: Production File: Royal Court, *Skyvers*.
8. Unsigned review taken from a clipping in the Victoria and Albert Museum, Department of Theatre and Performance Core Collection: Production File: Royal Court, *Skyvers*.
9. Unsigned review in the Victoria and Albert Museum, Department of Theatre and Performance Core Collection: Production File: Royal Court, *Skyvers*.
10. Unsigned review in the Victoria and Albert Museum, Department of Theatre and Performance Core Collection: Production File: Royal Court, *Skyvers*.
11. 'Reckord Celebrations', a tribute to the late writer, Barry Reckord, was presented by Talawa Theatre Company and the London Hub on 23 September 2012. It featured video extracts of Reckord speaking about his plays, commentary on his work by the director Max Stafford-Clark and critic Michael Billington as well as performed extracts from his plays.

4
Home/lessness, Exile and Triangular Identities in the Drama of Caryl Phillips

Suzanne Scafe

Although better known as a novelist and essayist, Caryl Phillips began his writing career as a dramatist: his first play was produced at the Sheffield Crucible in 1980, and a year later at *The Lyric*, Hammersmith, where his subsequent work was also performed. His first novel, *The Final Passage*, was published in 1983. *The Shelter* and his first radio drama, *The Wasted Years*, were produced in 1984. In a recently published essay, he speaks of an enduring 'love' for the theatre that was frustrated by an 'accident of birth [that] meant I was unlucky enough to be coming to the starting line of my writing life at precisely the time that the sun was setting on a golden era of new writing in the British theatre' (Davis and Fuchs, 2006, p. 45). Like many other successful writers, including his contemporary Kwame Kwei-Armah, his 'love' of the theatre has found expression in the production of several radio plays that have been successfully performed for BBC Radio. This work, like much of Phillips' fiction and essays, is concerned with displacement, migration and the loss and pain that result from these forced or difficult journeys. Water is a dominant motif in the texts I have selected, evoking the distances travelled, the danger and the irrecoverable depth of buried cultures and histories, as well as through its use to suggest overlapping identities, the potential for transformation. As James Baldwin in his own voice says of the Atlantic in Phillips' radio drama *A Kind of Home* (2004), and expressing sentiments that Phillips himself has articulated: 'I have crossed that ocean often enough ... to see to what extent it connects and not to be afraid of the connection'.[1] In this chapter, I focus on Phillips' stage plays *Strange Fruit* (1981), *Where There Is* Darkness (1982), *The Shelter* (1984) and his most recent play, *Rough Crossings* (2005). Although Phillips' radio drama is as yet unpublished,[2] I also make reference to two early radio plays and I discuss these as radio drama, rather than as play scripts. The themes, formal structures and the preoccupation of his stage plays and radio drama overlap in what I suggest are significant ways: each genre enriches the other.

His first two stage plays, and the radio drama *The Wasted Years*, are concerned with, in his words, 'articulating the rage of the second generation of West Indian youth' (Phillips, 2006, p. 40): in these plays 'the youth' are in open and sometimes violent conflict with their immigrant parents, whose identities are grounded in an experience and memory of a Caribbean home. These conflicts perform several functions: they oppose fixed concepts of Britishness, as well as mythic concepts of home and are used to re-examine the relationship between blackness, slavery and Empire. They also dramatise the continued significance, in relation to the characters' identities, of triangular Atlantic crossings and their echoes in history (Rahbek, 2001, p. 116). The plays use repeated metaphors, themes and sets of relationships: agonistic identities produced within competing, and culturally defined discourses of masculinity; the conciliatory figure of the Caribbean mother, in *Strange Fruit* and *The Wasted Years* left on her own to bring up two sons; a dysfunctional or absent father figure whose absence or problematic presence is the root of the families' fragmentation, and an often fragile, abused white female character whose treatment in the first two plays replicates the misogynist attitudes that are in Phillips' early drama racially inflected. Whereas, as Deirdre Osborne has observed, 'contestation between masculinities' figured around the father–son conflict and misogyny, often in the form of female degradation, persists in the recent, popular work of playwrights Kwei-Armah and Roy Williams (2006a, pp. 90–2), both of whose work Phillips admires,[3] in Phillips's later drama these contestations are resolved through his work's focus on a presentation of more inclusive and interconnected – though still conflicted – identities. In his early drama, the white female characters provide the means by which his black male characters – Errol in *Strange Fruit* and Albert in *Where There Is Darkness*-vent their anger against a Britain whose racism they are otherwise seemingly powerless to confront. Despite this problematic representation, there is even in his first play, *Strange Fruit,* a sign of what Raimund Schäffner identifies as 'cosmopolitan multiculturalism' evident, not only as Schäffner argues, in the play's disavowal of Errol's black nationalism and its exclusionary rhetoric but also in the relationship that the play only tentatively establishes between Errol's mother and Shelley, her son's young, white girlfriend (1999). As her son Errol embarks on a fool-hardy mission of violent resistance, followed by the abused and accepting Shelley, the mother gives her the key to their house in a gesture of identification that transforms the house of her disintegrating family into a home for future generations of her children's children who are both black and British. Despite her tragic end and despite the play's critique of her political quietism, the mother, like the mother in *The Wasted Years*, emerges as the play's most sympathetic character, confirmed by Phillips' early comment that his intention was to write a play 'about a black mother, a single parent' (1984c, n.p.).

In the context of the familial conflict of his early plays, neither generation is fully 'at home'. Identities in *Strange Fruit* are produced in a kind of stasis. Its dramatic action is subordinate to long, self-presenting monologues, and the action itself is confined to one space – a 'cramped' but 'tidy' front room, where characters narrate their conflicted feelings, articulating the play's own concerns with nation, culture and identity. The descriptions of the room's décor and furnishings noted in the script have a specific, metonymic function. Its tidiness contributes to the mother's characterisation; she too is 'immaculately turned out', though like the mother in *The Wasted Years,* exhausted from over-work. The wallpaper, the 'heavy sideboard on top of which sits a brightly crocheted coverlet...and a yellow glass vase containing plastic flowers' (Phillips, 1981, p. 8) signify the Caribbean migrant mother's attempts to demonstrate her success but also her need to reproduce 'home'. The room's furnishings perform a similar function in *Where There Is Darkness*, where Sonje, the son's young black girlfriend notes the absence of plastic flowers in Albert's home: 'Most black people are brought up with plastic flowers all around them' (Phillips, 1982, p. 42). In the later play, this absence is a sign of Albert's success and acculturation as are his 'socks and sandals', and the: 'wooden leaves of peanuts, crisps, potato chips – largely undisturbed' (Phillips, 1982, p. 7). Through the use of realistic staging, the playwright locates his drama in a specific time and place, using the set not only to contribute to characterisation but also to convey the play's themes. The impersonal nature of the food, reminiscent of an office party is 'largely undisturbed', suggesting the fragility of Albert's success; hardly anyone has attended the party.

In the early years of his writing career, when Phillips was still defining himself as a 'dramatist', he acknowledged his connection to and dialogue with both an older generation of Caribbean-born playwrights such as Mustapha Matura and Michael Abbensetts and the then younger generation of black artists, Michael Macmillan, Linton Kwesi Johnson and

Hanif Kureshi. He also reflected on the influence of Ibsen and Chekov on his writing,[4] adding that traditions of naturalism and realism in Western European theatre were the only ones available to him. This is in fact what connects these early plays, stylistically if not thematically, to those of Matura and others (Phillips, 1984c, n.p.). Ibsen's influence is most evident in the second play, *Where There Is Darkness*, for which he received perhaps his best reviews. In this play, the characters' subjectivity is realistically imagined: their interiority is expressed through shifts in linguistic registers and through external signifiers such as the differences in dress, furnishings and so on. Time is fragmented; the past erupts in the present, and this temporal disruption is also used to reflect the father Albert's loss of control. He is haunted by the sound of the sea 'whispering' its guilt at having transported him across the Atlantic on the basis of a false promise (Phillips, 1982, pp. 15–16) The hurt and shame of his past is gradually revealed in the drama's present: Albert says of the young white woman he abandoned once she was pregnant, 'I did wrong by she. I did wrong by a lot of people' (Phillips, 1982, p. 34). The 'wrong' to his young Caribbean wife results in her leaving with a note telling him that their son has been left in a children's home. Albert's dis/ease is a symptom of what Phillips has described as the 'psychic wound' that originates with the rupture of forced migration and which, 'for countless millions of African people, continues to fester' (Tunstall, 2004, p. 220). Shame and guilt render him articulate. Albert heaps abuse on his son, on Sonje the son's girlfriend, and on his white wife Ruth, whose silent suffering prompted critic Rosalind Carne to remark that Phillips 'clearly has a problem creating women characters' (1982, p. 70). In this play, however, women characters are subject to Albert's misogyny, not Phillips': both women leave the raging, impotent Albert who, as Sonje observes, is homeless and can neither stay in England nor return 'home' to the Caribbean (Phillips, 1982, p. 47).

Critics whose work focuses on Black British drama, and playwrights themselves, have reflected on the continued use and appeal of realism as a mode of representation. The reasons for this, as Gabrielle Griffin has argued in relation to black and Asian women playwrights, are political, sociological and cultural and reflect most significantly the playwrights' use of realism in a bid for 'recognition' within traditions of British drama that privilege conventions of realism rather than 'traditions of a (post)colonial other' (2006a, p. 19).[5] While noting the tendency in black British women's drama to 'develop realist plots within clearly defined structures of conflict and resolution', Meenakshi Ponnuswami argues that this does not always preclude attention to 'fractured' subjectivities and a 'deconstruction of the processes of displacement, settlement and cultural mutation' (2000, p. 224). As these critics imply, however, to privilege and generalise the texts' socio-historic context would be to overdetermine 'concerns with possible *functions* of black texts in "non-literary" arenas rather than with their internal structures as acts of language or their formal status as works of art' thus limiting or inhibiting opportunities for formal experiment (Gates, 1984, p. 5). The playwright Roy Williams has commented on the demands, made by predominantly black audiences, for 'truth telling',[6] and in her introduction to a recent interview with Kwei-Armah, Osborne observes a potential contradiction between the 'impetus for black dramatists to create a black British aesthetic' and the 'binds of social realism', a genre that 'accommodated black drama's staging in the first place' (Osborne, 2007a, p. 255).

A desire for formal experimentation in the creation of a 'black British aesthetic' is evident in Phillips' third play, which did not receive the same 'recognition' as his first two more conventionally structured works. In a response characteristic of most other reviewers, John Barber, who applauded *Where There Is Darkness*, says of *The Shelter's* two characters: 'Invented to make a case, they [the characters] never achieve the odd, quirky flavour of real human beings'.[7] The cover of the play text of *The Shelter* reproduces a photograph of a man's black hands resting on the face of a white woman. It is a strange, grainy, disorienting portrait that has no context and that starkly contrasts his black hands with the woman's slightly harried white face. In the lengthy introduction to the play, Phillips suggests that the woman's expression reveals a highly charged emotional state. The man's hands exhibit both power and strength, 'but at this moment they were infinitely gentle, describing with eight fingers that moment when a grip of iron weakens to a caress of love' (Phillips, 1984d, p. 9). For the playwright, this work marks a significant change of direction, a refusal to present yet 'another... domestic tragedy which would have meant, as James Baldwin so eloquently put it, "Making peace with my own mediocrity" and stepping into an area whose parameters are defined not by what one can do but by what one perhaps ought to do' (Phillips, 1984d, p. 12). His lengthy 'Introduction', its use of ekphrasis to bring the photograph into the meaning of the drama, and the play's focus on language rather than dramatic action are signs that this play would mark a shift from the stage to the page in Phillips' work, a shift predicted by Ferdi Dennis (1983), one of its reviewers.

The first act is set in 'the eighteenth century' described by Phillips in the stage directions as 'the age of the Augustans, of all that is rational and exact' (1984a, p. 15): strains of Handel, a significant motif in the later *Rough Crossings,* introduce this play's first movement. Despite the use of realistic staging, the two characters in the first act are identified in the script only by their gender difference, through the use of object pronouns, 'Him' and 'Her'. Though neither name is used in the dialogue, 'Him', transformed to Louis in act 2, says to 'Her', now Irene:

> LOUIS: 'I'm a British subject'
> IRENE: Object, isn't it?
> LOUIS: I'm a British object.' (Phillips, 1984a, p. 43)

His namelessness in the first act is used to question the availability to contemporary representation of African subjectivities produced in the historical period determined by a 'semi-triangular structure which saw commodities and peoples shipped to and fro across the ocean' (Gilroy, 1993, p. 88). The 'gentle' quality of the man's hands is presented in the opening scene of the play where, in a second act of kindness, he ('Him') places his shirt 'over the woman to shield her from the sun' (Phillips, 1984a, p. 15). His first is to have rescued 'Her' from the shipwreck. Responding initially in fear, the woman quickly identifies the man according to prevailing stereotypes. At the same time, his calm, courteous manner, his use of an overly formal literary register and his English identity – he says, 'Like you I was of England whose chalk-cliffed fringes we may never again set our eyes upon' (Phillips, 1984a, p. 16) – spurs her contempt. Offended by his presumption that they share an identity, she quickly slips into the language of unreason and irrationality. He is an 'ape', a 'devil' 'a theatrical thing' (Phillips, 1984a, pp. 19, 20). In response to her continued refusal to see him as human and individual, he speaks to her 'whiteness', and of her implication in Europe's centuries long abuse of the African.

Although the man says that English is 'my only language' (Phillips, 1984a, p. 16), his stilted diction emphasises its borrowed form, an early example of Phillips' experimentation with voice. He ('Him') speaks from within a history of experiences that have been silenced and that are untranslatable in the present. He is, he says, 200 years old, representing himself not, as critics have commented, as a 'noble savage' but as an African whose selfhood and voice paradoxically emerge from the very discourses of Enlightenment, of reason, logic and argumentation, that justified his enslavement.[8] Like Olaudah Equiano and Frederick Douglass, his self-realisation is intimately bound up with a fluency in and a deep commitment to English literary language and rhetoric.[9] His language reflects what Stuart Hall has subsequently theorised as: '[T]his inner expropriation of cultural identity [that] cripples and deforms'. It produces 'silences' and creates individuals that are unmoored from their past and out of place in their present (Hall, 2003b, pp. 236–7). It is this silence and dislocation that Phillips attempts to address in the borrowed language of 'Him'.

Although the second act opens in a recognisably contemporary setting, and in the script the characters are named, there is very little dramatic movement: thus the second act reflects the first act's preoccupation with the inadequacy of language as a form of self-representation. The pauses in the dialogue are longer, and the miscommunication more intimately expressed. Whereas the now named Irene speaks in realistically imagined dialogue, Louis is a wordsmith, transforming grim reality through vivid metaphor: 'Out into the cold and foggy London streets where the light spills carelessly from lamp to tramp ... And from around the lazy corner the sharp leathery clicking of the dull man's shoes echoes in the chilly fifties air' (Phillips, 1984a, p. 36). Freighted with the blood of slavery and empire, the language in which Him/Louis is so proficient impedes rather than facilitates communication. Whereas in the first act these silences are filled with the sound of the sea, used to emphasise not only their entrapment, but also their overlapping and interconnected identities, in act 2 they are replaced with the sound of 1950s music-white versions of rock and roll, sentimental pop ballads that mock their own doomed love, ska and calypso, including Louis' own calypso inflected poem that speaks of the water crossings connecting both acts: 'Out yonder floats a spot, like a thin black slither,/This cruel boat taking people, my people, to where they will shiver; wither and die' (Phillips, 1984a, p. 45).[10]

This early experimentation is reflective of what critic Timothy Bewes reads as the absence of 'voice' in Phillips' novelised accounts of slavery: it is 'voice ... as ventriloquy' (2006, p. 47), that is, Phillips' refusal to present an 'authentic' or realistically imagined speaking voice for his characters. It is both 'eloquence and inarticulacy' (Bewes, 2006, p. 48). In addition, the gaps, silences and omissions that characterise his fiction function, for Bewes as 'the systematic evacuation of every discursive position that might claim freedom from implication in colonialism' (2006, p. 46). The texts' language and structure thus presents a discourse of impossibility in which the 'possibility of speaking is produced only by faithfulness to its impossibility' (Bewes, 2006, p. 51). In the context of slavery in Phillips' work, this impossibility is the experience of 'characters so destroyed by their suffering, or by the shame that results from it, that even if they live through it they are unable to speak of it' (Bewes, 2006, p. 42). The result is 'silence and shame' (Bewes, 2006, p. 43), characterised by the text's inadequacy, its failure to communicate, its incommensurability (Bewes, 2006, pp. 39–40).

This failure and the drama's incommensurability is signalled by repeated misunderstandings and by Louis' 'ventriloquy', evident in an early sequence where he recites what he calls his 'shunting' poem, using a metaphor from his workplace, the railways, to describe his own experience of migration. Through the implied root of 'shunting' – shun – he expresses the racism he experiences and that he locates in part in the hypocrisy of 'his woman's' smile. In response to Irene's description of her abusive marriage, Louis sings his calypso verse:

> My woman's smile is like a jagged knife
> ...It cuts deep, bleeds ugly, drains life
> From a man like me, born to be free
> And live in the shadow of a hot deep sea. (Phillips, 1984a)

In contrast to the first act, the sea signifies for this character longing, 'home' and an imagined Caribbean identity. For Louis, like Alfred in *Where There Is D*arkness, living in England has resulted in an erasure of personality. He came to England, a god-like creature, falling in love with what had seemed to have been a technicolour dream: 'The lights of the Empire Cinema in Leicester Square... And the traffic lights, roundabouts, lamp-posts, chimney pots like skyscrapers to me, and people pouring down the streets at the end of the day like it's World War Two about to break out again' (Phillips, 1984a, p. 51). But now he says: 'I look like nothing' (Phillips, 1984a, p. 49). As the play closes, the characters' dialogue becomes more and more fragmented, and less and less like conversation. The repetition of 'I want to go home... Back home' (Phillips, 1984a, p. 53) allows him to perform an act of return which, like all returns in Phillips' drama, involves abandonment: in this play it is of Irene, pregnant with their child, who will tie him either literally or metaphorically to England. These ties have already transformed the identities of Louis and Irene, his conception of 'home' and England's conception of itself.

Formal experimentation, particularly in relation to voice, is returned to in *Crossing the River* and *The Prince of Africa*, produced for radio in 1985 and 1987. Both are complex plays that extend earlier representations of intersubjective identities, focusing on their characters' emergence from historical interconnections and continuities and from the contemporary economic and political imperatives that produce scattered, fragmented but intersected selves. These identities are articulated at their most abstract in *Crossing the River*, in which a threnody of and for millions of lost African souls is presented by three voices in different temporalities and at different points of the triangular journey. As in the earlier plays, the disrupted family is central to the drama's meaning. Paternal abandonment is relocated to Africa, and Africa, masculinised through the figure of the father, is at the centre and origin of the drama's first moment of disruption.

The drama begins with the voice of Sarah: she is alone, outside the discourses of male power and authority. She is abused by the planters and left with children whom she longs to nurture in order to replace the familial bonds that were broken in the Middle Passage. Sarah repeats. 'Two men in my life, both then and now: a daughter is nothing to a father. I just watched my father' (1985). Although at different points in their lamentation each character cries out for their father, the father's 'shame' literally silences him and he cannot respond. The drama constructs a dreamscape of topographies and histories that are at once discontinuous and overlapping. Its language and structure reflect the 'complex poetry and dramaturgy of multi-layering between narratives' that as Stanton has noted, is suited to the medium of radio drama (2004, p. 104).[11] As with *The Shelter*, the characters are named only in the cast list: their use of language suggests distinct historical and geographical identities. There is the minimum use of sound but the characters' constant, rhythmic repetition of lines and phrases produce the complex threads that bind the characters together and serve to connect their experiences to what the listeners already know about the contexts from which they speak. Sarah's voice describes the experience of crossing the river to the slave ship that 'stank of the vomit of a million sick'. The sea – like the sea in the earlier plays – gives false reassurances: 'the ship made a loving movement, like a woman rocking a child, and the sea spoke to us, telling us to have no fear'. Her voice, flat and seemingly emptied of sorrow and longing, describes the plantation, her own rape and the removal and abuse of her child. It is this experience – the repeated loss of family – that closes the play. Her voice closes the drama: 'I listened to my two men. Brothers. My breasts hurt. I heard grey Mary [her dying baby] cry. Father, father! ... And we all cross the river' (Phillips, 1985).

The two men are located in Africa, in early-twentieth-century America and in contemporary England. A sense of a present time constituted by different pasts in locations marked by different crossings is reinforced by vocal repetitions. Through its circular structure, the lack of dramatic tension and of a 'realistic' sense of place and contextualising narration, the play refuses closure or the reassuring linearity of cause and effect. The drama achieves an effect of temporal simultaneity: it exploits the 'invitational structure' of radio drama, using the apparent incompleteness of the form to emphasise its 'expressive potential' (Cazeaux, 2005, p. 167). Words, phrases and occasional sounds structure the play's historical correspondences 'beckoning' or inviting the listener to create meaning through its gaps and patterns of repetition (Cazeaux, 2005, p. 165).

More is made of radio drama's acoustic elements in *The Prince of Africa* (1987), where much of the action takes place aboard a slave ship sailing for the Royal African Company. We hear the terrible groans of the Africans dying on board or being thrown overboard to 'collect on the insurance'; the clunking of chains; the sounds of the crew vinegaring, then 'scrubbing up the skin and blood from off the deck' to prevent the infection of the small pox virus. There are sounds of burning, lynching and the 'inner city riots' of England 1981. In the background is the constant sound of the sea 'beckoning' listeners beyond the gap created by the absence of visual elements, and inviting them to hear the thematic correspondences marked by the sea. In this play, the above elements connect the past and the present, Africa, Europe and the Americas and the living and the dead; those who jump overboard with those who survive the crossing to be sold, like the eponymous 'Prince', on an auction block. The use of sound creates a realistic topography, and each shift in setting – from Africa to the Americas and contemporary England – though not chronologically ordered, and conveyed through the voice of the narrator rather than through dramatic action, is clearly marked by shifts of sound. The opening lines are repeated throughout the drama, lending weight and significance to the first word: 'Marooned in the West; washed up on the shores of England, by the ever insistent tide of colonialism...Proud of my history because I understand it' (Phillips, 1987). 'Marooned' is used to evoke the resistance of the Jamaican Maroon slave rebels, and finds its echo in the late-twentieth-century black British youth rebellion that the drama re-enacts. The African father, like the father in the earliest 'domestic' dramas, is absent. His two sons, rendered homeless by the violence of slavery and colonialism, are reduced – like Louis in *The Shelter*, to nothing:

> Well, my two sons, without land, you are little more than chaff that the wind tosses and spins without respect...You are lost, blind, stumbling and ailing...you are nothing and you will have to begin again, a centuries long struggle to reassert yourselves. (Phillips, 1987)

The repetition of these lines diminishes the function of Africa as a site of recovery: in this drama, it does not deliver lost origins except as a 'deception' for the 'Pan-Africanists'. At the same time, its loss in the contemporary imaginary presents an obstacle to self-realisation: 'Always Africa. A sense of home. Africa, like a boll weevil eating away at the back of our brain' (Phillips, 1987).The impossibility of a return 'home' is figured through the use of an image which speaks of continued suffering and loss, and in the repeated sounds and references to water. The hollowed out but resonant voice of the 'African' narrator, played memorably by Trevor Laird (who also plays Will in *Crossing the River*) says to the other Africans on board the slave ship: 'Water has no paths and we may never find our way back home' (1987).

Several critics have commented on Africa's problematic absence in Phillips' fiction. Yogita Goyal for example, has argued that his fiction offers an 'ahistorical view of Africa' that 'creates a space of stasis for Africa, freezing it within the realm of myth rather than that of history' (2003, pp. 5–6) and in a more sympathetic reading Leela Kamali has suggested that for Phillips, the 'memory of Africa...awaits a form of narration able to dramatize the multiple temporalities of a diasporan experience' (2009, p. 215). In these radio plays, certainly Africa occupies a space of myth rather than history. Phillips' use of language self-consciously sustains the notion that a historical *experience* of Africa, for those stolen from it centuries ago, cannot be re-imagined. Phillips does not attempt to inflect the African voices with remnants of Africa, even as contemporary voices speak the 'new language' of coded gestures that 'like carefully blown wine glasses...contain more that you might initially imagine'. His narrator cautions: 'language can only accommodate so much subversion' (Phillips, 1987). Africa is in this work a loss, an absence from which the unnamed Africans voice their disembodiment. In contrast, representations of the English captain and crew are material and specific: they speak in conventionally structured dialogue, and provide the drama with a more conventional, linear narrative.

Although Phillips' most recent stage play, *Rough Crossings* (2007), seems to have marked a return to play writing after an absence of over 20 years, his prolific production of radio drama suggests that he had been honing his dramatic craft during this period and developing the themes and the attention to form and language that continue to characterise his work. He has said of the genesis of this stage adaptation of Simon Schama's historical text *Rough Crossings* (2005) that by coincidence he had made two visits to Sierra Leone in order to research a work of his own that was to have described the migration of African ex-slaves from Nova Scotia to Sierra Leone (Phillips, 2011, pp. 334–7). Phillips' adaptation echoes the concerns of his earlier drama: contested notions of 'home', of Britishness and British national identity, exile and home-lessness. Thomas Peters, one of the plays' two black protagonists, speaks lines that find echoes – in both content and register – in much of his earlier drama:

> British or American, it matters not what you call us, for the very trade which reduced us to homelessness, and this supplication, deemed that from this time on we would no longer be men who can be securely tied to your nations. We are men shackled to our race. Call us what you will...henceforth we shall always be black.' (Phillips, 2007, p. 81)

The play's multiple crossings are both a sign and effect of dislocation and displacement, resulting in the creation of plural identities. It opens on the Atlantic, with a vividly realised scene on board a slave ship. As with his earlier drama, Phillips' use of the material form of the ship serves as a reminder that the circulation of identities and of ideas and cultures during this period emerged from the horrors of the Middle Passage (Vivan, 2008, pp. 225–6). Here the dramatisation of the brutalities of the slave trade creates a context that heightens the exceptional achievements of Phillips' two African protagonists, whose first appearance is as the ship's 'cargo'. His adaptation revises and subverts the balance of lives presented in the original work in order to magnify the emancipatory significance of its two black protagonists, David George and Thomas Peters, thereby creating characters who live beyond a specific moment in history. These characters reflect his continued interest in fictionalised biographies of figures whose identities, like those of George and Peters, were shaped by their Atlantic crossings. Although the scenes that centre on these two characters are used to dramatise their ideological differences, the drama closes with two notes of reconciliation: between George and Peters but also, more tentatively between black and white settlers and colonists. The play ends with a dialogue between the white abolitionist Thomas Clarkson and David George, a figure who is more conciliatory than Thomas Peters. In response to Clarkson's assertion that 'some intemperate part of you is Thomas Peters', George replies: 'Some part of us all is Thomas Peters', thus closing the gap of difference between the two men and emphasising the characters' awareness of the importance of unity in the pursuit of freedom (Phillips, 2007, pp. 125–6). As Thomas Clarkson prepares to leave Sierra Leone, David George says: 'Over there, over the horizon, a new day shall soon rise up out of the ocean. To whom does this new day belong? To you?' Clarkson responds: 'To us?' (Phillips, 2007,

p. 126). In John McLeod's detailed and persuasive reading of the play, he suggests that Phillips' reconstruction of Peters and George provides him with the opportunity to revisit the 'missed opportunities for synthesizing and diverging forms of dissidence' represented by the opposing rhetoric of Martin Luther King and Malcolm X. Focusing on the lines cited earlier, he notes that not only is there a suggestion of reconciliation between the two characters after Peter's death, but also that the English Clarkson's 'To Us?' is 'perhaps Phillips's way of maintaining faith in a "post-racial" vision of brotherhood where "you" and "I" might no longer be separated' (McLeod, 2009, p. 203).

Phillips also uses the play's women characters to elaborate on themes of reconciliation. He creates a central role for Eliza Sharp, the harpsichordist and diarist, who is mentioned only briefly in Schama's text: her probing, assertive comments reveal both the effectiveness and the limitations of a joint articulation of race and gender oppression. In response to Thomas Clarkson's jibe that she might take a 'negro for a husband', she quickly retorts: 'And by doing so, bind inferior bondsman to inferior bondswoman' (Phillips, 2007, p. 38). Later she says of Clarkson: 'I am neither shackled to him nor to any other man' (Phillips, 2007, p. 71). With these words, the drama emphasises her difference from the enslaved African. Though unequal as a woman, she achieves voice and independence: she was never the ship's cargo and at no point in the play is her humanity in doubt. As McLeod notes, the closing scene includes Phillips' reimagining of another articulate and independent white woman, Anna Maria Falconbridge, who marries a black settler, Isaac, thus suggesting a potential for cross racial intimacy that had seemed impossible in his earlier stage drama.

Given these fictive reprisals, and their gesture towards a future not defined by racial separatism, it is surprising but perhaps predictable that several reviewers should have encoded Phillips' characters so strictly along racial lines. In a view that is shared by other critics, Charles Spencer laments: 'Worse still, many of the white characters, including the admirable English abolitionists, are caricatured, while all the leading black characters are models of resilience and nobility' (2007b, p. 1107).[12] Whereas these responses are more reflective of the limits of liberal guilt than of the themes presented by the drama itself, they are also a credit to Patrick Robinson's strong performance in his role as Thomas Peters. Delivering his uncompromising character with authority, eloquence and integrity, he creates a figure that demands an equally strong reaction from his audience. Rupert Goold's production achieved 'recognition', in part because of its reliance on realist dramatic structures and because of the play's focus on *individual* historically specific characters such as Peters. Unlike *The Shelter* and the radio drama discussed in this chapter, this play's focus is on the efficacy of language to communicate ideas within the drama and, as McLeod's reading suggests, to produce contemporary resonances. Although the characters' commitment to European structures of knowledge predicts the problematic differences that emerged in Sierra Leone between the Creole colonists and indigenous Africans, the play's reliance on realism, on coherent characters and on physically "real" settings, also offers what seems to have been a missed opportunity to subvert Western conceptions of Africa and to suggest alternative cultural paradigms within which African identities might emerge, without sacrificing the plays' historicity. As historian B. W. Rommel-Ruiz has noted, to eighteenth-century 'creole' colonists Africa 'was not a distant memory, but rather an opportunity to establish a New Africa, a black city upon a hill, a beacon of hope to blacks and their white supporters throughout the Atlantic world' (2006, p. 361).

The drama does achieve contemporary significance, however, and without and in contrast to the laborious explication of his first play. The presence of its eighteenth-century unhoused Africans is used to challenge contemporary as well as eighteenth-century discourses of race and nation, to reference political issues such as reparation, and to expose the limits of the abolitionists' commitment to freedom and justice. The structure of its very short split scenes, as well as the production's often effective synergy of African and European music, the use of film, photography and a tilting stage to emphasise simultaneous crossings, all successfully create a sense of backwardly looking forward, an avowal of the place of history in the present. Water, which in the early plays represents separation and dissolution, in this work is used to forge connections, present possibility and to facilitate dialogue across history's widest breaches.

In her essay on her work with Phillips' archive, Bénédicte Ledent argues that his published and unpublished drama provide a 'fascinating introduction to his later fiction and non-fiction' (2006, p. 190), revealing the 'intimate links' between the genres. McLeod (2009) too reads *Rough Crossings* through the lens of Phillips' better-known fiction, demonstrating the convergences in representation and using the fiction to elucidate the play. Without denying the importance of this approach, one endorsed by Phillips himself who has said in a recent interview that he has used his radio drama '(often subconsciously) to work out ideas that might well crop up later in fiction or stage drama' (Scafe, Unpublished Interview, 2011), I have attempted in this chapter to demonstrate that the drama itself offers a rich seam of meaning. A focus on the experimental nature of *The Shelter* and his 1980s radio drama, and close attention to the text's acts of language, suggests that Phillips sought a new direction in black British drama during the 1980s, one that did not merely offer new conceptions of Britishness but also attempted to break free from the issue based realism that had defined much dramatic production during this period.

Notes

1. Phillips, C. (2004) *A Kind of Home: James Baldwin in Paris*, (unpublished) BBC Radio 4, 9/01/2004
2. In her unpublished paper, 'Caryl Phillips's Drama: Fiction Under Construction' EACLALS, Istanbul (2011) Bénédicte Ledent notes that her 'next project will consist in preparing an edited collection of these unpublished plays and scripts', currently held at the at the Beinecke Library of Yale University.
3. See Phillips, 2006: 'I Could Have Been a Playwright' and 2005: 'Lost Generation'.
4. He has also spoken about the influence of these dramatists in a published interview with C. R. Bell (1991).
5. Griffin makes a similar point in her essay 'The Remains of the British Empire', where she cites black director Paulette Randall, who argues that 'it is still a political act to put a black person on stage' (2006b, p. 201)
6. In response to a scene of familial violence in his first play at London's Stratford East, a member of the audience argued that 'No black guy would treat his mother like that' (Sierz, 2006a, p. 116).
7. In addition Barber, who missed the connection between the play's two acts, described it as 'two plays for two people' (1983, p. 699), as did Robert Cushman in the *Observer* (1983, p. 700). Christopher Hudson in the *Standard* complains that 'nothing happens' in the first Act (1983, p. 699).
8. This identification was used by Ferdi Dennis in his review for *City Limits* and John Barber in the *Daily Telegraph* (1983).
9. Several critics have commented on Phillips' use of the 'voice' of Africans such as Equiano in his construction of his eighteenth-century fictional characters. An example of this line of criticism is Lars Eckstein's chapter on *Cambridge* (2006, pp. 63–98).
10. References to sound in the sound recording of the first performance of *The Shelter* (1983) at the Lyric Hammersmith, directed by Jules Wright.
11. See also Martin Esslin's influential essay 'The Mind as Stage' (1971).
12. See also Philip Fisher's review of *Rough Crossings* (2007). Not all reviewers were unsympathetic: Siobhan Murphy in *The Metro* (2007) described Robinson's performance as 'outstanding'.

Part II
Second Generation

5
The Social and Political Context of Black British Theatre: 1980s–90s

Meenakshi Ponnuswami

Concepts of Britishness were vigorously contested during the 1980s and 1990s, a period bracketed between 1979, when Margaret Thatcher was elected after a campaign that invoked British fears of being 'swamped by people with a different culture' (Burns, 1978) and 2002, when Home Secretary David Blunkett warned that immigrant children would soon be 'swamping' local schools (Qtd. in Travis, 2002). These two decades witnessed the institutionalisation of anti-racist and multiculturalist state policies as well as backlash from nativists and white supremacists. At the same time, complex post-modern formulations of race, ethnicity and national identity emerged on several fronts, in academic studies as much as in the cultural avant-garde and on the streets, prompting wide-ranging investigations of British history and politics and of national, ethnic and cultural identity. It was against this contentious backdrop that black British theatre had its first major groundswell.

Roy Williams and the two other playwrights discussed in this section, Kwame Kwei-Armah and Winsome Pinnock, were among those black artists whose careers were established and flourished in these decades. Each writer was born to immigrant parents in the 1960s: Pinnock to Jamaican parents in 1961; Kwei-Armah to parents from Grenada of Ghanian origin in 1967; and Williams, also to Jamaican parents, in 1968. All three were raised in London and navigated the turbulent years from Brixton through Cool Britannia: a period when, as Onyekachi Wambu succinctly puts it, 'We moved from post-colonialism to multicultural Britain' (Qtd. in Arana, 2005, p. 236). This essay will map this history in two stages, outlining first the emergence of a new wave of playwrights and companies in the 1980s following the riots in Brixton, and then tracing the proliferation of black British identities and 'new ethnicities' (to use Stuart Hall's phrase) in the late 1980s and 1990s.

Brixton 1981: anger and after

Kwesi Owusu calls the 1980s a 'transformatory decade', which saw 'the emergence of a broad radical movement of scholars, cultural practitioners, media personalities and politicians as the new intellectual voice of Black Britain' (2000, p. 6). To understand this movement in context, it is necessary to start with the urban uprisings of the period. Spurred by the anti-immigrant violence and police harassment endemic in the years leading up to and during the Thatcher administration, the riots of the 1980s played a critical role in demonstrating that the black community in Britain saw itself as fully British, ready to respond as a citizenry. The Race Relations Act of 1976 had outlawed discrimination in key sectors such as education, housing and employment, and established the Commission for Racial Equality as a watchdog group. But 'in the recession-hit Britain of the seventies and eighties', relates Kenan Malik, 'hostility to blacks and Asians was an everyday fact of life. Racism then was vicious, visceral, and often fatal. Stabbings were common, firebombings almost weekly events' (2010, pp. 38–9). Malik reports that 'no fewer than thirty-seven Blacks and Asians were killed in police custody' between 1969 and 1989, 'almost one every six months' (2010, p. 41). The consequent protests, marches and riots that shook Britain through the late 1970s and early-to-mid-1980s were wide-spread and varied in cause, provoked by confrontations with the far right and the police. In Deptford, riots followed police attempts to break up a peaceful march to protest the cursory investigation of a fire at a New Cross Road birthday party in which 13 black youth died. According to Paul Gilroy, 'the Deptford inferno' would 'hang over the race politics of Britain for the next few months like a pall of thick acrid smoke'. The Brixton riots followed the launching of the aggressive 'Operation Swamp', when 943 people were stopped and searched by the police in just four days (Gilroy, 1987, p. 104). The riots spread to several areas around London and far beyond, lasting several months and presenting the Thatcher government with its first significant domestic challenge. [1]

The 1981 riots had a direct and dramatic impact upon the development of black British arts and culture. The Scarman inquiry commissioned by the Thatcher government blamed the riots upon the 'endemic, ineradicable disease' of 'racial disadvantage' and 'racial discrimination', and recommended immediate remediation in the form of measures that would encourage the full participation of blacks in British life and politics. For the Conservative government, this was understood to mean the creation of a black bourgeoisie – a commitment to 'back the good guys, the sensible, moderate, responsible leaders of ethnic groups', in the unfiltered words of Sir George Young, Thatcher's first minister in charge of race relations (Qtd. in Malik, 2010, p. 57). The playwright Caryl Phillips, who graduated from Oxford just as Notting Hill exploded, translates dryly that the British public was 'clamouring for an articulate second generation that was not throwing bricks' (Qtd. in Jaggi, 2001, p. 4).

The new funding created as a result of the Scarman report provided significant opportunities for a variety of black and Asian artists. As Helen Thomas's essay in this volume has shown, black British cultural organisations had been proliferating during the 1970s, bringing together people of African, Caribbean and Asian descent to foster community relationships and tackle the problems of racism and policing.[2] In the 1980s, these merged into a Gramscian vanguard of intellectuals and artists.[3] The pace accelerated after the post-Scarman funding began pouring in, and a number of state-orchestrated initiatives were also launched. Channel Four was established in 1982 with the explicit charge of providing programming relevant to minority communities, and the next decade witnessed a bourgeoning of arts funding and programming along ethnically specific lines. In 1983, the Ethnic Arts sub-committee of the Greater London Council (GLC) initiated its Black Theatre Season, which during its six seasons provided significant opportunities for black artists to showcase their talents. Its productions included Trevor Rhone's *Two Can Play* and Michael Abbensett's *Outlaw* (both 1983); Earl Lovelace's *The Hardware Store* (1985); *The Pirate Princess* by Barbara Gloudon (1986); and Derek Walcott's *Beef, No Chicken* (1989).

The Black Theatre Season was organised by the Black Theatre Forum, which offered workshops and training even after 1990, when funds for the Black Theatre Season were terminated. In 1985, the Black Arts Alliance was established with SuAndi as its freelance Director, and alongside Common Word and Contact Theatre served as a vital cultural enclave for black artists at this time. Michael McMillan (2006), Lynette Goddard (2007) and Colin Chambers (2011), among others, have charted the significant range of playwrights and companies which launched in the 1980s under these circumstances. Paulette Randall, Bernadine Evaristo and Patricia St Hilaire founded Theatre of Black Women in 1982 (the same year that, coincidentally, Brewster became the first black woman drama officer at the Arts Council). A year later in 1983, Jacqueline Rudet started Imani-Faith, also dedicated as a theatre for black women, while Gloria

Hamilton started Umoja. The Black Mime Theatre and the Double Edge Theatre Company were established in 1984; Brewster, Mona Hammond, Carmen Monroe and Inigo Espejel started Talawa in 1985.

It was also in 1984–5 that two umbrella organisations merged, the Black Theatre Forum and the Black Arts Alliance. Temba, which had been founded in 1972, took a new direction in 1986 under the artistic direction of Alby James, seeking new audiences by producing the work of new writers such as Irish Cooke, Felix Cross and Benjamin Zephaniah. A number of theatre companies run by white artists also began turning their attention to work by black playwrights: Foco Novo, the English Stage Company at Royal Court, Oval House and Tricycle Theatre took on plays by Mustapha Matura, Ikoli, Alfred Fagon, Winsome Pinnock, Fred D'Aguiar, Maria Oshodi and Michael J. Ellis. The Women's Theatre Group introduced a multi-racial policy in 1985.

Although playwrights and practitioners who had been active since the 1960s and 1970s remained on the arts scene in the 1980s, including Matura, Brewster and Abbensetts, an impressive roster of new playwrights saw their careers begin to flourish in this period. By 1987, Brewster would edit 'the first anthology of plays written by and about black people written in Britain' (p. 7), *Black Plays: One*. Interestingly, in her introductory note, Brewster describes a 'vibrant' black British theatre scene but cautions:

> The work of those who live in this country must become more accessible; if not, then the work of playwrights living in the Caribbean and Africa will continue to dominate the scene as their plays are more readily available in the Educational editions meant for the schools of the Third World. These 'source' plays establish vital links with essential cultural roots, but the indigenous voice is just as important. (1987, p. 7)

Plays by Derek Walcott and Wole Soyinka were indeed popular in the 1980s. By 1987, however, several 'indigenous' playwrights (Brewster's use of the term includes both British-born and immigrant) had seen their work performed, including Pinnock, Randall, Ikoli and Don Kinch.

In spite of the difficulty of generalising from such a diverse body of material, it is possible to identify some key trends and preoccupations in the playwriting of the 1980s. 'For our generation', Linton Kwesi Johnson has commented, 'the question of identity was paramount' (Qtd. in Jaggi, 2001, p. 4). Inevitably, most playwrights examine the complex interplay of cultural identities not only between blacks and whites but also among disparate groups of blacks: the relationships between middle and working classes; immigrants and British-born; West Indian and African. Authenticity is a key concern in the drama of the period, apparent in the quest for languages and rhythms appropriate to class, ethnicity and generation. The young Rastafarians depicted in Matura's celebrated *Welcome Home Jacko*, the inaugural production of the Black Theatre Cooperative (1979), were not authentically 'other': rather, they 'helped turn Matura's language into authentic street expression, representing a texture, vocabulary, and rhythm belonging to those who were born or raised in Britain rather than the older diasporic emigrants' (Chambers, 2011, p. 176). Both Phillips (2006, p. 43) and Yvonne Brewster recall the particular success of Fagon's *Lonely Cowboy* (1985) in capturing the 'rhythms and the speech eccentricities of a generation raised by immigrants' (Brewster, 1987, p. 8).

This concern for authenticity is apparent also in the recurrence of themes of fidelity and 'selling out', as can be seen in plays by immigrant as well as British-born playwrights. Matura's *One Rule* (1981) focuses on younger black Britons in a reggae band, whereas Abbensetts's *In the Mood* (also 1981) highlights class differences between a group of well-heeled and assimilated Guyanese immigrants. Similarly, *Lonely Cowboy* depicts the conflicts which arise when a member of the community joins the much-hated police force. When Jack is accused of having sold his 'birthright to the Englishman' by becoming a policeman, he retorts, 'I am an Englishman' (Brewster, 1987, p. 43). This affirmation seems to signal the arrival of a distinctly 'multicultural', post-immigrant voice, one which would strengthen through the 1990s and eventually find fuller articulation by the end of the millennium. However, it is difficult to demarcate the post-colonial from the multicultural too strictly, as playwrights of the 1980s and 1990s depict a vastly polymorphous black Britain in which both immigrant and British-born characters can be variously 'assimilationist', or not; nostalgic or contemptuous of the past; politicised and agitational or unwilling to rock the boat.

Cultural conflicts between immigrants and second-generation Britons are sometimes handled as comedy, as in Ellis's 1985 *Chameleon*, which depicts the conflict between an assimilationist immigrant 'Black Achiever' and his politicised second-generation co-worker. Such conflicts are also handled lightly in Pinnock's *Leave Taking*: Viv, the younger of two British-born daughters of a Jamaican mother, mocks her mother's loyalty to England by bursting into a parodic patriotic recitation of Rupert Brooke's 'The Soldier', whereas Viv's elder sister Del establishes a brusquely comic camaraderie with Mai, an elderly obeah woman whose profession Del derides as 'mumbo-jumbo' even as she apprentices herself. However, the generational conflict between Enid and Del is far from comic, and Pinnock suggests that the gulf of incomprehension that separates mother and daughter is premised upon irreconcilable disagreements over the lived experience of Englishness: Enid clings, albeit with increasing desperation, to a Thatcherite vision of benevolent England as a promised land, whereas Del is trapped in a harsh Thatcherite reality in which 'Every day we go out and they can do what the hell they like with us' (1989, p. 157).

The social upheaval of life under Thatcherism is, inevitably, a dominant theme in the plays of the 1980s. Some playwrights directly addressed the uprisings and their aftermath; Michael McMillan's *Day of Action* (1981) was based on events surrounding the New Cross Fire, and Edgar Nkosi White's *Man and Soul* (also 1981) features the aftermath of a riot in Notting Hill. A number of plays explore the dire economic circumstances confronting black Britons in Thatcher's England, such as Oshodi's 1986 *From Choices to Chocolate* and Amani Naphtali's 1989 *Ragamuffin*, which are both focused on urban youth, and Jacqueline Rudet's *Money to Live* (1984), in which an underemployed young woman finds success and independence when she consents to work as a stripper. McMillan's *On Duty* (1983) examines black workers' lives in the Thatcher era: the National Health Service nurse in McMillan's play is radicalised by her more political co-worker and joins a strike.

Plays of the Thatcher era also often depict a more generalised disillusionment and malaise, an exhaustion of spirit brought on by the immigrant generation's unfulfilled hopes and desires. Nigel Moffatt's 1985 *Mama Decemba* depicts an elderly Jamaican woman who finds herself facing old age in England unemployed and friendless, whereas Pinnock's *Leave Taking* compares the disenchantment and survival strategies of two women of the Windrush generation. In White's quasi-expressionist play *The Boot Dance* (1984), a young South African immigrant is driven mad by his desire to gain white acceptance and approval. *The Boot Dance* was performed in 1984 just as the anti-apartheid movement was beginning to regain momentum, following protests against the South African constitution of the preceding year. The play is one of many that situates black British concerns in relation to contemporary international, diasporic ones, such as Pinnock's *Talking in Tongues* (1991) and *A Hero's Welcome* (1988); and Cooke's *Running Dream* (1993). These and other plays explore diasporic histories, including histories of slavery, imperialism and independence movements: Yemi Ajibade's *Waiting for Hannibal* (1986) is set in Carthage in the third century BCE; Dennis Scott's *An Echo in the Bone*, is a murder mystery set in Jamaica in 1937; Pinnock's *A Rock in Water* (1989) is a biography of Claudia Jones and *A*

Hero's Welcome (also 1989) is set in the Caribbean in 1947 and captures the critical moment between the end of the war and the departure of the Windrush.

Quests for roots in the ancestral past occasionally take emigrants as well as their British-born children back home, where they are seen to encounter rejection as often as roots. White's *The Nine Night* (1983) takes a family through a ritual for the dead because the father believes the journey back to Jamaica will help reunify the family, whereas Evaristo's *Silhouette* of the same year depicts an encounter between a contemporary woman and the spirit of an enslaved woman who died in the Caribbean two centuries ago. Retrospection also often prompts a reckoning with the present and the (often wasted) years spent in Britain, as happens in Phillips' *Where There Is Darkness* (1982), in which returning to the Caribbean compels its protagonist to take stock of his quarter century in Britain: a common narrative in many plays of the look-back-in-anger genre.

Black British feminism was a vital force in the 1980s as well. Women had been in the frontlines of black workers' struggle against racism in the 1970s, and black feminist scholars and activists built upon this heritage in the 1980s. Two path-breaking works, Hazel Carby's 1982 essay 'White Woman Listen' and a special issue of *Feminist Review*, 'Many Voices, One Chant' (Amos et al., 1984), offered a critique of mainstream, white, Anglo-American feminisms while mapping the discursive boundaries of black feminism. At the same time, the influential volumes *The Heart of the Race: Black Women's Lives in Britain* (Bryan, Dadzie and Scafe, 1985) and *Let It Be Told: Black Women Writers in Britain* (Ngcobo, 1988) documented the histories and experiences of black British women.[4]

Significant women playwrights who emerged during this period include Pinnock, whose *Picture Palace* explores violence against women, especially in the media, an issue touched upon also in Rudet's *Money to Live* (1984). Zindika's *Paper and Stone* (1990) is a coming-of-age story focused on a girl's breaking away from her domineering mother. Women are situated historically in several plays, where the search for a matrilineal past can evoke a sense of transhistorical gender solidarity based on the oppression of women through all time. Jackie Kay's 1986 *Chiaroscuro*, which adapts the choreopoem form of ntozake shange's *for colored girls* to examine the lives of four black British women, is a good example of this genre, although its radical feminist evocation of women's history as a unifying gesture is complicated as the play progresses by issues of difference, specifically of homophobia and cultural chauvinism. Rudet's *Basin* (1985) and Kay's *Chiaroscuro* examine lesbianism and homophobia as part of their depiction of women's lives, but Kay's 1988 youth play

Twice Over centres the black lesbian experience and, moreover, reverses the typical coming-out narrative by featuring a young girl who discovers that her recently deceased grandmother was a lesbian.[5]

Family dynamics are a key recurring concern in plays of the 1980s. Ikoli's celebrated *Scrape Off the Black* (1981, set in the 1970s) explores the raw racial and class dynamics of a mixed-race family where the younger son Trevor naively tries to celebrate his elder brother's release from prison by organising a family reunion with their uncaring white mother and absent African father. The tensions between immigrant parents and their British-born children are often as fraught, as in White's 1984 *Redemption Song* (where a Jamaican Briton returns to Jamaica to confront his father, his squandered inheritance and his lost identity); Abbensett's *El Dorado* (also 1984, where a grandson returns to his ancestral home in the West Indies); Pinnock's 1987 *Leave Taking* (which depicts a pitched domestic conflict between an immigrant mother and her pregnant teen daughter). This dynamic plays out especially in dramas that explore the contours of the often fraught relationship between emigrants and those who stayed 'back home'. Several first-generation characters struggle with the disapproval of parents back home who condemned their decision to leave for England: Lazarus in *The Boot Dance* recalls parental disapproval with guilt and bitterness, as does Enid in Pinnock's *Leave Taking*. Pinnock suggests here and in *Talking in Tongues* (1991) that sentimental longing for 'home' is emotionally dangerous because it is so often based on falsified memory and desire.

Although so many plays depict Windrushers as weary and broken, relatively few address disability. Two notable exceptions are Ruth Harris's *The Cripple*, which was produced by Theatre of Black Women in 1986 and depicts the true story of a Jamaican-born woman who suffered cerebral palsy; and Oshodi's 1988 *Blood, Sweat and Fears*, which examines the problems that confront a black employee at a fast food restaurant who has Sickle Cell Anemia.

New ethnicities in the 1990s: 'From post-colonialism to multicultural Britain'

According to a 1992 British Social Attitudes report, 'for the first time, people in Britain were more optimistic than pessimistic about race' (Storry and Childs, 1997, p. 17): a remarkable turn-around when one considers the magnitude of the troubles just a decade earlier. The 1990s were also, of course, a period of continuing tensions between black communities and the mainly white Metropolitan Police Service, most significantly in relation to the murder of Stephen Lawrence in 1993 and the 1995 riots following the death of Wayne Douglas in police custody.[6] In his 1997 essay 'A Reporter at Large: Black London', Henry Louis Gates observed that despite the progress made in the 1980s and 1990s, 'the growing prominence of black culture there doesn't mean that racism itself has much abated'.[7]

However, although the Scarman report attributed the problems of Brixton to deprivation and poverty, finding no systemic or intentional racism in the police force, the McPherson report into the murder of Stephen Lawrence categorically stated that the police force was 'institutionally racist': a shift that would have far-reaching consequences. By mid-decade, the sun finally set upon the British Empire: in 1997, when Hong Kong was returned to China and when the process of devolution began with the United Kingdom; and then again in 1998, with a different and perhaps more positive emphasis, in the festive commemorations of the 50th anniversary of the arrival of the *Empire Windrush*. In 1998, Hall wrote: 'Black British culture is today confident beyond its own measure in its own identity – secure in a difference which it does not expect, or want, to go away, still rigorously and frequently excluded by the host society, but nevertheless not excluding itself in its own mind. Blackness in this context may be a site of positive affirmation but is not necessarily any longer a counter identity, a source of resistance' (p. 127).

Not all black Britons embraced the specific forms of the emerging multiculturalism of the late 1980s and early 1990s. The anti-racist alliances of the 1970s had emphasised a unified political action based in a commonality of interests across divergent lines of identity. But state subsidy in the post-Scarman era initiated the gradual ascendancy of anti-racism in state policy on terms which, many argued, diminished the impact of coalition politics. For critics, the emerging politics of difference signalled the end of collective resistance. As Amina Mama put it, 'a growing focus on identity and a new competitive cultural politics replaced the 1970s/early 1980s notions of black unity and wider anti-imperialist and black liberation struggles' (1992, p. 97). Pratibha Parmar specifically lamented that the solidarity of black feminist groups at the beginning of the 1980s was replaced by a 'ghettoised lifestyle "politics"...unable to move beyond personal and individual experience' (1997, p. 68). An influential critic of difference politics, A. Sivanandan remained defiant in the face of the increasing splintering of the Afro-Caribbean and Asian alliances: 'Cultural segmentation...is deeper and more complex today. But that is the more reason to fight it, before it becomes inward-looking and reactionary' (Qtd. in Owusu, 2000, p. 12).

Malik places the blame for this 'segmentation' on the Left, arguing that whereas the Tories envisioned unity, the Leftists celebrated difference:

conservatives under Thatcher imagined that state funding for ethnic projects would produce an acquiescent and assimilated black middle class, but the Labour-backed local authorities, dominated by New Leftists set adrift after the Tory victories, redefined racism to mean 'not the denial of equal rights but the denial of the right to be different' (2010, p. 94). 'By the end of 1980s', argues Malik, 'concepts of a common humanity and universal rights' had begun to be repudiated by a new emphasis on difference: 'The celebration of difference, respect for pluralism, avowal of identity politics – these have come to be regarded as the hallmarks of a progressive, anti-racist outlook and the foundation stones of modern liberal democracies' (2010, p. xix). Sharply critical of the multicultur-alist and anti-racist policies that emerged from the Scarman report, Malik claims that 'cynicism about the idea of "Britishness"', coupled with a discovery of 'surrogate proletariats in the so-called New Social Movements', swayed the New Left to privilege culture over class:

> Black people, so the argument went, should not be forced to accept British values or to adopt a British identity. Rather, different peoples should have the right to express their own identities, explore their own histories, formulate their own values, pursue their own lifestyles. In this process, the very meaning of equality was transformed: from possessing the same rights as everyone else, to possessing different rights appropriate to different communities. (2010, p. 59)

In short, as James Clifford put it, '"Identity politics" [was] under attack from all sides': 'The political right sees only a divisive assault on civili-zational (read national) traditions, while a chorus on the left laments the twilight of common dreams, the fragmentation of any cumulative politics of resistance' (2000, p. 94).

Whereas some on the Left lamented 'the twilight of common dreams', many others were pulling what Clifford called 'the anti-essentialism trigger' (2000, p. 94) by arguing that new social formations were begin-ning to take root. At a pivotal transitional moment when immigrant, post-colonial concerns were beginning to encounter second-generation perspectives, 'anti-essentialism' was in full deployment by post-structur-alists of the late 1980s, such as Hall, whose influential theorisation of 'new ethnicities' I discuss below. Post-structuralist and anti-essentialist articulations of the new black Britishness were indeed significantly Leftist in origin. For Owusu, for example, Gramscian praxis was at the heart of Hall's intellectual and political project in the 1970s and 1980s: 'forging a link between academic scholarship and public debate, intellectual property and its wider circulation, [Hall] provided his collaborators with a new vocabulary of political engagement and a corresponding disposition to creative experimentation' (2000, p. 5). Further, as Mercer argues, at a moment when the institutions of the Left 'were crumbling under three terms of Thatcherism', 'black interventions' (such as the critiques by Hall, Gilroy and others of the New Left's ethnocentric and nationalistic conception of 'culture') revived an emaciated Left and created 'a more inclusive conception of cultural democracy' (1994, pp. 20–1).

The political groups and artists of the late 1980s and 1990s thus shared many of the priorities of the earlier coalitions but also moved forward to provide the foundational articulations of a new black Britishness. Several commentators have noted that the urban uprisings of the 1980s played a formative role in fashioning the new black British identity in the 1990s. Playwright Kwei-Armah recalls watching the Deptford marchers on television as a teenager, and for the first time, experiencing 'us, as a black community, standing up as a community in that way. This was black Britain – the ones who only knew this country as home' (Qtd. in Akwagyiram, 2011). In Wambu's useful description, 'the British-born generation...began, uniquely, to map out the contours of their own identity as Black British people, not as rejected outsiders, but as critical insiders' (Qtd. in Arana, 2005, p. 236); while Owusu describes 'a new revisionism that foregrounded the experiences of Black people in Britain as a distinctly "British" or "English" experience' (2000, p. 5). In a similar vein, R. Victoria Arana suggests that the literature of the 1980s and beyond 'takes possession of the definition of Englishness' by insisting upon 'diversity *within* Englishness' (2005, p. 232).

Arana also insists that black British writers of the period repudiate 'globalisation' and 'internationalisation' (2005, p. 232). In some ways, this bracketing off of identity echoes the kind of cultural specificity attributed to the emerging black Britishness by Mercer when, for example, he examines the 'postcolonial hybridity' of Hanif Kureishi's *The Buddha of Suburbia* and Bally Sagoo's remix of a Nusrat Fateh Ali Khan composition:

> [this] is the music that most evokes for me [the England I know]...the 'ordinariness' of its multiculturalism which finds no counterpart in the different hybridity in the States, despite the shared centrality of 'race' in both countries. (1994, p. 29)

However, elsewhere in *Welcome to the Jungle*, discussing the 'exhilarating prospect of radical democracy', Mercer appears to celebrate the possibility of 'living with difference without need of nation as the basis of community or solidarity' (1994, p. 29). His discussion of the 1980s and 1990s in Britain as a 'highly creative and productive moment' focuses upon the ways in which emergent black British cultures 'widened aesthetic diversity within the expressive codes of diaspora culture': 'a time when your local movie cinema might be showing *A Passage to India*, *My Beautiful Laundrette* or *Handsworth Songs* in the same week' (Mercer, 1994, pp. 18–19).

For Mercer, the creative ferment of the period thus involved a 'dual movement of demarginalization and decentering', a phrase he uses to describe the transformation of cultural structures of power and authority as they 'become increasingly de-centered and destabilized, called into question from within' (1994, pp. 18–19). This key point is one of many that Mercer associates with Hall's discussions of the new cultural formations that emerged in the late 1980s. (Indeed, my own bifurcation of the 1980s and 1990s in this article takes its cue from Hall's foundational 1988 essay 'New Ethnicities', which describes a 'significant shift' in 'black cultural politics' of the late 1980s.) Hall describes not the emergence of a new movement but 'two phases of the same movement, framed by the same historical conjuncture and...rooted in the politics of antiracism and the postwar black experience in Britain' (1988, p. 163). What Hall sees as the first phase (implicitly that of the 1970s and early-to-mid-1980s) is a moment in which the signifier 'black' had a unifying power by 'referencing the common experience of racism and marginalization' and producing an oppositional 'cultural politics designed to challenge, resist, and, where possible, transform the dominant regimes of representation' (1988, p. 163).

Emerging from this moment in the late 1980s, Hall argues, is a 'shift' (but not a rejection or repudiation) towards an understanding that discursive practices – 'how things are represented and the "machineries" and regimes of representation' – occupy 'a formative, not merely an expressive, place in the constitution of social and political life' (1988, p. 165):

> What is at issue here is the recognition of the extraordinary diversity of subjective positions, social experiences, and cultural identities which compose the category 'black'; that is, the recognition that 'black' is essentially a politically and culturally *constructed* category, which cannot be grounded in a set of fixed transcultural or transcendental racial categories and which therefore has no guarantees in Nature. What this brings into play is the recognition of the immense diversity and differentiation of the historical and cultural experience of black subjects. (1988, p. 166)

Cautiously acknowledging that this shift is 'the effect of a theoretical encounter between black cultural politics and the discourses of a Eurocentric, largely white, critical cultural theory,[8] Hall proposes that 'it marks...the end of the innocent notion of the essential black subject' (1988, p. 166).

As Owusu illustrates, Hall's analysis of the British state and civil society was widely influential in the 'cultural renaissance' of the 1980s and 1990s, apparent in an impressive range of works, including films, photography and the visual arts. However, while crediting Hall's influence upon the arts, Owusu observes that 'the reverse was also true': that Hall's 'involvement with the young artistic avant-garde' shaped his theorisation of race (2000, p. 5). Gates likewise notes that the 'cultural ferment associated with black London happens much closer to street level', citing the example of black newspapers such as the *Voice*, the *New Nation*, and 'even...the crudely satiric *Skank*', designed for younger readers (1997, p. 172).

But the dynamism of the period was not simply a grassroots bourgeoning brought on spontaneously by the avant-garde, the intellectuals and the street. Goddard makes the important point that while '[a]rts funding cuts led to the closure of a number of black theatre companies during the 1990s, appearing to sound the death knell of a dedicated black British theatre sector', such 'closures coincided with the Arts Council of England's development of cultural diversity initiatives that aimed to foster greater inclusion of black practitioners in mainstream theatre venues'. The Arts Council was thus instrumental in opening out opportunities for black artists. Goddard, writing on the renaissance in black British drama in the 1990s in an article for the National Theatre Black Plays Archive, specifies that the Arts Council's 1989 'Towards Cultural Diversity' report demonstrated a 'commitment to recognising the fundamental role that black arts could play in diversifying British culture' (n.d.)

Black British theatre thus thrived in spite of the cutbacks and participated fully in the cultural effervescence of the period. Colin Chambers comments regretfully that 'the sheer number of groups and initiatives that have been launched since the end of the 1980s makes it impossible to offer a meaningful survey' (2011, p. 194). He discusses Mahogany Carnival Arts (1989); Femi Elufowoju's 1997 theatre Tiata Fahodzi; and efforts to 'secure a national centre' for black performance (such as Oscar Watson's 1996 plan for a National Black and Asian Theatre Development Centre and the 1998 Birmingham centre, The Drum) (2011, p. 194). To these I would add Oshodi's Extant (1997), 'Britain's only professional performing arts company of visually impaired people'[9] and Half Moon Young People's Theatre (1990).

Several British-born writers built active careers in the 1990s, including Cooke, Zephaniah, Valerie Mason-John, Paul Boakye, Jenny McLeod, Elufowoju, Dona Daley, Steven Luckie, Zindika, Sol B. River and others. First-generation playwrights such as African-born Biyi Bandele and Caribbean-born Tyrone Huggins and Felix Cross were also prolific in the 1990s. Naturalism maintained, as Chambers puts it, its 'historic function of being a remedial and provocative force, offering counter images to those that confirmed marginalization and discrimination' (2011, p. 196). However, despite the preponderance of naturalist and realist plays, this was also a period of significant experimentation. A range of performance practices offered a 'challenge to conventional theatre' and 'allowed greater expression of the diversity behind being British': the dance companies Posse and Bibi Crew developed musicals, revues and satirical sketches; and several artists produced 'live/performance art and performance poetry', such as Patience Agbabi, SuAndi, McMillan, Dorothea Smartt and Zephaniah (Chambers, 2011, p. 194). This work has been documented in Catherine Ugwu's 1995 collection *Let's Get It On*, and discussed at length in Goddard's *Staging Black Feminisms*, which also features a chapter on the work of Black Mime Troupe and its 1990 offshoot, Women's Troupe (2007, pp. 133–78). Benji Reid's late-90s hip-hop theatre Breaking Cycles should also be mentioned in this context; his hip-hop musical *Avalanche* played in Nottingham Playhouse in 1998. Many of the performance poets discussed by Chambers and Goddard also worked in the 'conventional' theatre in the 1990s.

Chambers notes that the 'commercial black theatre' has been more successful in finding a black audience. In spite of featuring divisive 'sexually and politically conservative stereotypes', Oliver Samuel's 'Bawdy Jamaican comedy' and shows by the popular 1989 group Blue Mountain Theatre 'make a point of being populist in all aspects of the theatre-going experience' and providing a '"good night out" environment'. As a result, comments Chambers, 'the active audience rapport at such shows is the envy of the theatre world' (2011, pp. 194–5).

The 1990s gave rise to a strong sense of optimism about black arts in Britain as the millennium approached. In 2000, Yasmin Alibhai-Brown would celebrate the vibrancy of a London in which 'evidence of real and irreversible integration is everywhere': 'Multicultural London is coming of age, and it is this that is igniting such energy, buzz and creativity.' As John McLeod has argued, London's 'imagined geography is positively reconceptualised and remade' by the 'millennial optimism' of Alibhai-Brown's article, and by works such as Zadie Smith's 2000 novel *White*

Teeth, which portrays a buoyant, richly plural London (2004, pp. 160–1). Hall had indeed spotted this trend a decade earlier:

> I've been puzzled by the fact that young black people in London today are marginalized, fragmented, unenfranchised, disadvantaged and dispersed. And yet, they look as if they own the territory. Somehow, they too, in spite of everything, are centred, in place: without much material support, it's true, but nevertheless they occupy a new kind of space at the centre. (1987, p. 44)

Ten years later, Hall would explain to Gates that young black Britons had 'turned marginality into a very creative art form…They've *styled* their way into British culture' (Gates, 1997, p. 171). Comparing his visits to London in the early 1970s and late 1990s, Gates remarks upon the sea change apparent in black life: whereas the earlier generation had seemed disempowered, 'joyless', and ghettoised (Gates, 1997 p. 170), London in 1997 presented utopian possibilities: 'if the barriers of class seem higher in England, those of race seem far more permeable', he observes. 'I'm always struck by the social ease between most blacks and whites on London streets.' 'In no small measure', he comments, 'black culture simply *is* youth culture in London today' (Gates, 1997, pp. 174–6).

This essay is dedicated to the memory of my mother, who during our last summer together in 2013 created an extraordinarily beautiful and peaceful study space for me in Coimbatore, where I completed my research for this essay.

Notes

1. See Gilroy, 1987, pp. 98–103 and Malik, 2010, pp. 39–40.
2. The Caribbean Artists' Movement (CAM) and the black nationalist Radical Alliance of Poets and Players were active during the 1960s and 1970s. Owusu lists also the Organization of Women of African and Asian Descent (OWAAD), the Brixton Defence Committee, Southall Black Sisters and others (2000, p. 6). Notable also were Camden Black Sisters and the socialist–feminist Brixton Black Women's Group of 1973–85 (Donnell, 2002, pp. 62, 58).
3. Several influential organisations and movements were founded at this time by black British and diasporan literati and activists, including the International Book Fair of Radical Black and Third World Books and the Afro-Caribbean Education Resource Project (ACER). New presses – Akira, Tamarind, Dangaroo, Karnak House, Karia – were established, and the journals *Race and Class* and *Race Today* were published by the Institute of Race Relations.

4. For an overview of black British feminist history and theory, see Mirza, 1997.
5. For a more comprehensive discussion of black lesbian theatre, see Goddard, 2007.
6. In 1993, black British teenager Stephen Lawrence was murdered by a gang of white men who beat and stabbed the young man as he waited for a bus, leaving him to bleed to death on the pavement.
7. Focusing on Afro-Caribbeans alone, Gates cites 'dire' numbers: 25% unemployment (nearly 50% 'in some parts of London'); 'only 2 per cent' representation 'in the professional class'. He cites a study which estimated that there would be 'as many as sixty-one thousand racially motivated assaults against Afro-Caribbeans over the course of a year', even though they constituted only 1.2% of Britain's population (Gates, 1997, pp. 174–5).
8. Mercer similarly comments that 'one of the strangest things about...the eighties was the experience of finding a voice in the language of "theory"' (1994, p. 20).
9. From the company's website, www.extant.org.uk.

6
Looking Back: Winsome Pinnock's Politics of Representation

Nicola Abram

'[O]ne of the current stars in the women's writing firmament': this celestial praise was written of Winsome Pinnock just three years after her first theatre production (Crabbe, 1989, p. 207). Pinnock was born in 1961 in Islington, London, to Jamaican parents. Her aptitude for drama has found a range of outlets: her work has been produced on the radio, including an adaptation of Jean Rhys' short story 'Let Them Call It Jazz' for BBC Radio 4 in 1998, and she has written screenplays and television episodes. But, whereas many of her contemporaries have now turned their creativity wholly towards television, film or prose, the fact that Pinnock continues to write for theatre demonstrates her commitment to its embodied, communal experience (Phillips, 2006, p. 38). Such longevity characterises her work, too: several plays have enjoyed revivals, evincing their critical acclaim in an institutional context that often privileges new writing. Indeed, the 1995 remounting of *Leave Taking* – nine years after its début – made Pinnock the first black British woman to have a play staged at the National Theatre (Chambers, 2002, p. 596).

This chapter profiles two of Pinnock's plays: *A Hero's Welcome* (1989) and *Talking in Tongues* (1991). It begins by considering the works' thematic innovations, as Pinnock brings new locations and lives to the nation's stages, before turning to her formal innovations, mapping how certain subversive aesthetics imagine social co-existence beyond race and gender hierarchies.

The relations of representation

A Hero's Welcome was given a rehearsed reading at the Royal Court in 1986, before its full production by the Women's Playhouse Trust, at the

Court's Theatre Upstairs, in 1989. It is set on an unspecified Caribbean island, after the Second World War. The eponymous Len has returned from Britain with only a limp to show for it. His injury was incurred during thankless work in a munitions factory – this was the ostensible hero's closest encounter with life at the front line. Reinstated in his grandmother's home, Len is openly disillusioned with England and disappointed by the racial hostility he encountered. Nonetheless, the imaginations of his neighbours persist; they wilfully believe that England boasts 'cars as long as rivers, houses that touch the sky' (Pinnock, 1993, p. 45). As posters appear recruiting migrant labour, some of the characters find the appeal of the 'motherland' irresistible. Responding to this setting, Gabriele Griffin groups *A Hero's Welcome* among a cluster of plays that address the historical and contemporary issue of migration (2003, p. 17). This follows on from scholarship by Meenakshi Ponnuswami, who highlights the significance of migration stories persisting into the work of second-generation playwrights. For Ponnuswami, *A Hero's Welcome* is one of many dramatic 'acts of retrieval and [...] nostalgia' (2000, p. 225).

Contrary to the play's title, however, the plot centres on three female friends – Minda, Ishbel and Sis – in their shared quest to escape from poverty and inopportunity. They have a single strategy in their pursuit of freedom: to marry. However, despite the girls' desperate appeals to Obeah rituals and sexual promiscuity to encourage this dream along, *A Hero's Welcome* provides no such comedic resolution.[1] By the final scene, Ishbel is pregnant by Stanley, an opportunistic idler with a pocketful of dubiously acquired cash. Stanley, meanwhile, has set sail for England with Minda; she had married Len, only to find his conservative demands less than satisfying. Len, abandoned by his new wife, continually fails to notice the affections of Sis. Eventually, with one friend seaboard and the other due to be dispatched to her Aunt's care, Sis decides to leave the district in search of an education.

Critics perceived *A Hero's Welcome* as offering relief from the overtly didactic plays dominating contemporaneous black British theatre. Their reviews describe it as 'gentle' (Edwardes, 1989, p. 207; Crabbe, 1989, p. 207) and 'mellow' (Hiley, 1989, p. 209), and they embraced Pinnock herself as 'one of a welcome crop of black writers who have seen that polemical, anti-racist plays [...] have had their day' (Arnott, 1989, p. 207). Yet the play is no less political for its entertaining plot. Although Pinnock does not repeat the tired statements critics anticipated, she certainly upholds an anti-racist agenda. Indeed, her approach in *A Hero's Welcome* typifies a wider black cultural politics that has been identified by theorist Stuart Hall.

In his essay 'New Ethnicities' (1988), Hall observes that black cultural representation in Britain operates in two modes. The first is a reaction against white hegemony. It demands entry into the regimes of representation, and inverts the Manichean binary to provide positive images of blackness. As necessary as it is, this strategy has its limitations. It locks black artists and activists in a defensive position, which cultural critic Kobena Mercer has dubbed the 'burden of representation' (1994). Refusing to yield to this pressure to produce only positive representations, we see Pinnock boldly drawing complex characters.

Pinnock presents the male characters in *A Hero's Welcome* with a particularly incisive critique. Landowner Mr Walker falls foul of his own misplaced passions, dying *in flagrante* in a barn. Stanley exemplifies the stereotype of sexual voracity without responsibility. The young Charlie, deluded that his observations of the small district are of significance to British Intelligence, is taunted and ignored. Len is at least thoughtful, though his naïveté loses him a wife, Minda, and a friend, Sis.

Pinnock's refusal to idealise her characters corresponds with her treatment of the cultural context. She refrains from defending the island society against accusations of primitivism. This is notable in the gendering of the relationships she constructs. Pinnock lays bare the three friends' reliance on male wealth and mobility, admitting the uneven positions of men and women in the small community. She emphasises this marginalisation by naming the women as their familial relationships to men (Sis, Nana, Mrs Walker), or with diminutions (Minda, Ishbel) that are further reduced to monosyllables (Pinnock, 1993, p. 24).

Pinnock does not offer these observations without contestation, however. I identify two linguistic motifs through which she critiques the gender and class divisions of the post-war island culture. Both images play on the primacy of the body in structuring such social arrangements: the hand functions as a metonymic signification of household tasks, and the foot as a cipher for freedom. Each will be evaluated here in turn.

Scenes illustrating the negotiation of domestic labour open both plays. Their differences emphasise that such arrangements range across historical and geographical settings, refusing to support a singular story of black domestic life. In *Talking in Tongues*, the brief prologue nostalgically portrays three women communing while washing clothes at the gully – an event that men were unable to witness. This gendered event contrasts with the opening of *A Hero's Welcome*: Len busies himself with the mundane tasks of household laundry and planning the next meal, while his grandmother looks on.

Charlie, the youngest character in *A Hero's Welcome*, charges himself as spokesperson on gender roles in response to this scene. He unequivocally articulates the normative position on the division of labour: 'Man not supposed to wash clothes…it's woman's work' (Pinnock, 1993, p. 23). His words preserve a polar distinction between male and female, refusing to admit any continuity across gender categories or heterogeneous variance within them. Further reifying the dyadic gender difference, Charlie's patois transforms a statement inflected towards the local – a comment on the arrangements between a particular grandson and grandmother – into a universal law, reliant on the singular and essential archetypes 'man' and 'woman'. This appeal to gender as a timeless fact obscures its socially contingent construction. By destabilising the division of male and female roles, Len's behaviour threatens the social order Charlie espouses.

Pinnock has a number of onlookers comment on this same scene. Sis muses admiringly that Len's willingness to undertake such tasks distinguishes him from other men, while Minda frets that it is a sign of immaturity: 'How many men of that age do you know who still live with their grandmother? He even wash clothes and cook dinner' (Pinnock, 1993, p. 25). While both Sis and Minda measure Len against a perceived norm, he remains within a scale of possible masculinities; this contrasts with Charlie's less nuanced perspective. Pinnock does not provide a unifying, conclusive statement. Instead, the fact that she convenes a chorus of opinions on Len's actions provokes her audience to reflect on the scene, too. This willingness to engage discussion displays her security and ambition. Such qualities supersede the reactive stance characterising the first phase Hall observes in black cultural politics.

After this opening scene, the plot proceeds conservatively: Charlie's favoured organisation of housework prevails, as Minda is charged with all of the domestic tasks when she and Len marry. It is within this arrangement that Minda becomes a protagonist in Pinnock's analysis of gender. She performs her duties poorly, and thereby echoes Len's earlier disruption of the naturalised gender binary. Further, she explicitly articulates her displeasure. Here, we see Pinnock deploying linguistic imagery to mount her cultural critique: she uses hands to metonymically indicate availability for certain roles. Minda discredits the corporeal organisation of domestic tasks by invoking it *ad absurdum*, repeating and redeploying the image of the hand:

> See those hands? Nice and small, eh? Do these look like the kind of hands cut out for doing an old woman's dirty laundry? More like hands that a prince would kiss. (Pinnock, 1993, p. 43)

Minda plays with biological determinism by re-reading her body as destined for another kind of life. Her laudable conclusion exposes the class privileges inherent in the negotiation of domiciliary duties; hands in line to be kissed by a prince are unlikely to be engaged in any household activity, regardless of their size.

Minda is not alone in her sardonic critique of this social structure. Anticipating Minda's lexicon, Nana speaks of her own familiarity with the island: 'I know this place like the back a me hand' (Pinnock, 1993, p. 21). Nana's use of this worn simile to describe her local knowledge is not simply lazy expression. Like Minda, she uses the term to confront the biological determinism embedded in language. Nana's appeal to a corporeal knowledge of the place, 'like the back a me hand', asserts that her body refuses the restrictions ascribed in its name – Len's demands that she refrain from leaving the house due to being both old and female. Rather than her body legitimising or necessitating her captivity, Nana celebrates it as symbolically mapping her journey to the bush. For both Minda and Nana, the imagery of the hand provides a locus to examine the assignation of gendered domestic duties.

Pinnock repeatedly engages her plays in political debates through the visual texture of her characters' dialogue, prioritising aesthetic integrity above polemical statement. Elsewhere in *A Hero's Welcome* – and indeed, persisting into *Talking in Tongues* – another corporeal image appears: the foot. This facilitates a discussion of freedom.

Many of the characters in *A Hero's Welcome* are troubled by the limitations of life on the island. The 1989 production underscored this claustrophobia by restricting the performance area to a traverse stage, enclosed by two parallel tiers of seating (de Jongh, 1989, p. 209). Len incarnates this sense of limited movement in his limp. He and Charlie repeatedly recall Len's fabricated explanation for this injury: a valiant military confrontation that sees him shot in the big toe (p. 24). This invented encounter attributes his wound to a conflict determined by nationality, British versus German. Yet, as its true occasion was his industrial work, its actual cause was the nation's *refusal* to accommodate him as its representative on the front line. A similar symbol appears in *Talking in Tongues*. Here, black female partygoer Claudette finds her toe crushed in a 'stampede' when a white woman enters the room (Pinnock, 1995, p. 175). For both Claudette and Len, a pedalian injury somatises the debilitating racism encountered in Britain. Pinnock extends this metaphor of movement further in *A Hero's Welcome*. Mrs Walker describes marriage as curtailing her flight from numerous suitors:

> When I was your age *(smiles)* I had to run away from them all. *(Slight pause, smiles)*. And then Gregory came along. And I didn't run any more. You understand? (Pinnock, 1993, p. 30).

The change of gait she articulates is confirmed in her marital name; wife to Gregory Walker, she found her running slowed to a respectable pace. Her staccato sentences aurally enact the restrictions implied in this marriage.

Continuing the imagery, Minda's success is measured by the state of her footwear. She boasts of her new shoes, acquired through her affair with Mr Walker, as evidence that she 'knows how to survive' (Pinnock, 1993, p. 28). Thus, when she and Mrs Walker quarrel, the older woman's confrontation draws upon a cruelly corresponding lexicon to quash her upward mobility: 'You not even fit to lick my Gregory shoes' (Pinnock, 1993, p. 40). Enraged on discovering the affair, Mrs Walker demands her stolen stockings back, leaving Minda barefoot. The young woman is stripped of her spoils and returned unadorned to her former social class. Mrs Walker's final threat to Minda perpetuates the imagery. Here, the foot is a synecdochical representation of unauthorised presence: 'if I catch you even setting foot here again I swear I'll kill you' (Pinnock, 1993, p. 40). Mrs Walker and Minda both perpetuate the foot and its paraphernalia as indicative of potential freedoms; in Mrs Walker's vocabulary the image refers to the self-determination of her past singleness, whereas Minda's longed-for liberty is from her restrictive socio-economic status.

Within this catalogue of corporeal imagery, Len features to facilitate a critique of race relations, while Minda, Nana and Mrs Walker expand the discussion to incorporate gender and class. These are multidimensional, intersectional characters. *A Hero's Welcome* thus refuses to collude with the idea of a monolithic blackness, corroding the organising principle of racism: absolute otherness. As such Pinnock moves beyond the impasse of positive representation into the second phase Hall identifies in the trajectory of black creative practice. In place of a singular blackness, she profiles 'the extraordinary diversity of subjective positions, social experiences and cultural identities which compose the category' (Hall, 1996b, p. 443). Examining subjectivities as contingent and constructed heralds 'the end of innocence' for black cultural politics (Hall, 1996b, p. 443).

Talking in Tongues continues where *A Hero's Welcome* concludes, examining the British-born generation that resulted from the trans-Atlantic journey of that early play's closing scene. This second generation continues to refer to an ancestral place of origin; Griffin observes that for the children of migrants, 'the question of where you belong is not easily resolvable, either in terms of a spatialization of belonging that points to a geographical place [...] or within the imaginary' (2003, p. 77). Such complexity informs the content of *Talking in Tongues*; the play parallels a group of young professionals in contemporary London with the men and women populating Jamaica's tourism industry.[2] This bipartite structure is integral to the play's semantic strategy, as experiences and events from one cultural context comment on those from the other.

In the prologue, a Jamaican woman muses on female friendship and spiritual fulfilment. Although her name, Sugar, is invested with the cash crop history of the plantation colony, this appellation is not made apparent to the theatre audience until she returns in Act Two. By leaving her anonymous, the prologue conceals Jamaica's colonial past and its history of intercultural relations. Instead, Sugar's speech directs attention towards the intracultural conflicts of the country's inhabitants, as organised through gender. She recalls a childhood experience of witnessing three women enjoying spiritual and social communion at the gully. Though the men of the village were apparently intrigued, their attempts to follow were thwarted by bizarre events. Here Sugar suggests that female sociability, founded on co-operative labour, precludes the presence of men.

Sugar's prologue is populated by Jo-Jo, Dum-Dum and Mary; this triad anticipates Claudette, Curly and Leela, guests at the New Year's Eve party of the following scene – it also recalls the three female protagonists in *A Hero's Welcome*. Act One of *Talking in Tongues* opens with the three girls hiding from the other partygoers, disillusioned by their disadvantaged social status. Claudette complains about black men pursuing white women and crushing black women in the process. Her anger, catalysed by a literal injury, signals a more endemic experience of imparity. This scene repeats the prologue's exploration of gender differences, and adds to it ethnic division in the context of sexual rivalries.

The juxtaposition of Claudette's complaint with Sugar's account presents the invisibility of black women to black men as common across the two cultures. Yet the characters' differing responses continues

Pinnock's project of disavowing monolithic representation. In the black West Indian culture of the prologue, the women's invisibility is given as liberating. White émigré Kate, recently settled in the contemporary Jamaica of the second act, also finds that passing unnoticed is desirable: 'the best times are when I feel myself stateless, colourless as a jellyfish' (Pinnock, 1995, p. 209). In London, black intersex partygoer Irma confirms the social mobility available to women due to going unseen. Considering 'corrective' surgery for her newborn child, Irma's mother understood that presenting as female might prove advantageous: 'she felt that black men were too often in the limelight, and that a woman might quietly get things done while those who undermined her were looking the other way' (Pinnock, 1995, p. 193). Yet, Irma's mother did not ultimately authorise the operation; the adult Irma is insistently visible, wearing a colourful outfit, shaven head and ostentatious jewellery.

Leela's experience contrasts with both the enjoyed invisibility of Kate and the trio in the prologue, and the hypervisibility propounded by Irma. She is disempowered by her unchosen invisibility, and unable to challenge her assigned social position. Her boyfriend Bentley confirms his failure to see her:

> Sometimes you – I can't bring myself to look at her, say I've got a lot of work to do. So it gets worse. You can't rest. (Pinnock, 1995, p. 189).

As Bentley's account oscillates between the first person pronoun – the I/eye that originates the gaze – and the second person, it grammatically enacts his inability to look directly at Leela. Later, the women's invisibility affords them an unexpected sight. Hiding beneath a pile of coats – a literal illustration of being socially overlooked – they inadvertently witness Bentley's affair with the white host of the party, Fran. The group's fraught relationships finally collapse.

Act Two sees Leela and Claudette travel to Jamaica to seek solace. There, Leela gets to know the island almost as intimately as Claudette connects with the local men. Ponnuswami has commented that although Leela's experiences are comparatively 'more self-effacing', the women's encounters with Jamaica share a consumerist orientation (2007, p. 217). Both exploit their positions as paying guests to reproduce the imparity they experienced in London. For instance, Claudette develops an insatiable quest for sexual agency, acting without concern for the lives she disrupts. This answers to her experience of being ignored by Bentley and other black men in the first act. As the disempowerment experienced in the pair's London lives is displaced onto these new surroundings, it culminates in a violent act of jealous revenge directed towards Kate.

Whereas *A Hero's Welcome* explores the limitations imposed by socio-economic status alongside restrictive gender roles, the protagonists of *Talking in Tongues* attribute their alienation to the intersection of gender disadvantage with racism. Pinnock continues the earlier play's metaphor of mobility to scaffold this theme. She first deploys the metaphor in the prologue, as Sugar tells of the women's transformation by observing changes in their gait: 'them women leave dragging themselves like them have rock tie to them foot, then come back skipping like children' (Pinnock, 1995, p. 173). This story prefigures a broader trajectory towards positive embodiment. The metonym persists from Claudette's crushed toe in Act One, hurt in a 'stampede' (Pinnock, 1995, p. 175) towards a white woman at the party, to Leela's compulsion to take long barefoot tours of Jamaica, at the close of Act Two. Pinnock's stage directions foreground the physicality of the transformation. Claudette is instructed to 'practice [...] putting weight on the injured foot' (Pinnock, 1995, p. 176), a tentative step that anticipates Leela's growing confidence when walking the island's treacherous paths. *Talking in Tongues*, like *A Hero's Welcome*, imaginatively enquires into the social conditions shaping women's lives by examining their experiences of corporeal movement.

The protagonists' individual progression within this metaphoric frame of mobility differs somewhat, though. Leela began by refusing to dance at the party, claiming:

> I'm not very good. I bump into people. It takes all my effort to keep myself upright...I never forget my body. That's the trouble. (Pinnock, 1995, pp. 182–3)

She later comes to inhabit her body as a familiar home in a new land, learning that 'you've got to be in touch with your body. It soon gets used to sudden challenges' (Pinnock, 1995, p. 225). To be in touch with one's own body is a self-referential corporeality, becoming both subject and object of a reciprocal exchange. Conversely, Claudette remains focused on her body as an object of others' sexual – imaged as alimentary – appetites. She feels empowered by the desiring gaze of those, like the old American, who watch her 'like a man ain't eaten for months' (Pinnock, 1995, p. 206). Although Leela progresses further than Claudette in learning to value her own body, she is not yet willing to share her walk with Kate. Interpersonal healing, which might more fully address the legacy of colonial power relations, remains to take place.

Pinnock's strategy of juxtaposition contrasts individual characters as well as structuring scenes and settings. This web of comparisons continues her commitment to staging blackness as multiple. So, whereas Claudette is angry and alienated, both Curly and Irma are content with their lives. This contrast disavows the reasoning that social dislocation is an inevitable consequence of a diasporic heritage. Further de-essentialising black identity – an agenda that Hall identifies in the second phase of black cultural politics – Pinnock also depicts affinity between those named by distinct identity categories. For instance, she has white British characters express sentiments of alienation and discord. Jeff recounts that at the end of a day's work: 'I'm so stressed I can't move...I can barely get up to go to bed' (Pinnock, 1995, p. 180). Here, Pinnock incorporates Jeff into the framing metaphor of mobility, aligning his condition with the inhibited movement experienced by Claudette and Leela – and, indeed, by Len, Minda and Mrs Walker in *A Hero's Welcome*. Pinnock here refuses to invest in ethnicity as fully explaining lived experiences.

Jeff attributes his dissatisfaction to the trials of life in the capital: 'Of course it's home, I was born here, but it doesn't feel like a home, more like a place you rest at overnight on your way to somewhere else' (Pinnock, 1995, p. 180). His lament about London could conceivably have been spoken about Britain by Leela. That Pinnock has Jeff, Kate and Leela each independently articulate their dislocation figures it as a contemporary metropolitan condition rather than a uniquely diasporic one, affirming the spirit of Hall's observation on 'the Antillean as the prototype of the modern or postmodern New World nomad' (Hall, 2003b, p. 243).

Significantly, Pinnock has the contemporary cultural crisis articulated by Jeff precede its more specific incarnation as Leela's diasporic unbelonging. White spectators (the predominant population of the Royal Court) are thus invited into a primary identification with Jeff; this affinity is then transferred to Leela, as the resemblance of the characters' experiences is revealed. Pinnock's commitment to producing intercultural affinity, already at work among the characters onstage, is thereby extended to her audiences. She creates channels of cross-ethnic and cross-gender identification that explode any attempt to demarcate uniquely black, white, male or female experiences.

Further denaturalising ethnic affiliation, Pinnock writes a variety of temporary alliances based on gender and culture. She has Leela and Kate agree in opposition to the Jamaican Mikie. Kate responds disapprovingly to his callous description of slaughtering the pig for that night's barbecue: 'that's the difference between men and women. A woman could never see it as just a pig' (Pinnock, 1995, p. 212). Although Kate attributes this alliance to a shared female sensibility, it points more convincingly to shared cultural assumptions. It is not that Mikie really slaughters each meal by hand; rather, the women's horror exposes the colonial bias latent in their shared British heritage, as their failure to question the veracity of his story implies their subscription to the stereotype of the primitive islander. Mikie exploits this supposed superiority in his tall tales, performed in a tourist industry that trades on the production of authenticity. Later, Kate comes to understand the function of the pig story in this global marketplace (Pinnock, 1995, p. 213). Leela is thus the most culturally naïve of the two women; Pinnock gives no credence to an intrinsic solidarity between her and Mikie based on phenotype.

Pinnock does not suggest that intraracial affinity is entirely impossible, of course. Rather than offering a community grounded in natural or automatic biological kinship, she postulates the performance of a linguistic identity. Language is of central concern to *Talking in Tongues*; Pinnock describes the play as 'about a black woman finding her voice' (Pinnock, 1991, n.p.). More accurately, Leela's discovery is of a culturally located language. She experiences a lack of identity due to her linguistic orphanhood (p. 195); this anguish finally finds expression and healing in the spiritual and corporeal utterance that titles the play.

Claudette does not experience the same ecstatic release as Leela. Yet to read the two women as opposites – as Griffin has, in understanding Leela as 'being reunited with the abjected body through a spiritual experience' and Claudette as simply 'using the body for sexual purposes' – is perhaps to elide Claudette's more subtle personal journey (2006b, p. 204). Through language Claudette begins to adapt to this new environment; a poetic familiarity with the place manifests in her metaphor. In the first act, her lexicon is markedly English in its cultural referents. She uses the simile 'hunting dogs on the scent of a fox' to describe the relation between black men and white women, for example (Pinnock, 1995, p. 175). Yet in Jamaica, her vocabulary is notably different: 'the sky seemed so low you could pluck the moon out and eat it like a ripe mango' (Pinnock, 1995, p. 204). Thus, when Mikie answers Kate with a corrective metaphor, his imagery tacitly affirms Claudette's successful participation in the local speech community:

KATE: Plenty more fish washed up gasping on the shore, eh?
MIKIE: Plenty more ripe mango fallen off the trees, yes. (Pinnock, 1995, p. 214).

Indeed, Claudette metonymically expresses her affinity with Mikie as linguistic: 'Me and Mikie speak the same language. When he's kissing me under the stars and telling me he loves me, I know exactly what he means' (Pinnock, 1995, p. 212). Although not exactly like Leela's glossolalia, Claudette also experiences a kind of tongued communion.

Racism is enabled by, and perpetuates, impassable boundaries between black and white. As we have seen, Pinnock begins to undo the notion of natural identities by foregrounding intraracial difference, as well as by staging interracial and interethnic continuities. Yet, another impasse is at play in the theatre form; structuring dramatic realism is a constitutive chasm between actor and audience. This opposition echoes the binary terms, black and white, that Pinnock so diligently unpicks. The following analysis will therefore examine how, and to what effect, these two productions also begin to denaturalise the actor/audience divide.

'New ways of being': new ethnicities and new aesthetics

The relation of absolutist racial categories to the separation of performer from spectator is not simply symbolic. Recent efforts to orchestrate outreach programmes remind us that venues like the Royal Court and the National Theatre command a majority white audience. Yet Pinnock works towards reconfiguring this historical demographic: 'when a play by a writer like myself is presented on a mainstream stage, the profile of the visiting audience is radically changed' (Pinnock, 1999, p. 32). Specifically, Pinnock's plays engage older black women (Griffin, 2006b, p. 200). This development of new audiences means that oppositional racial categories no longer map as easily onto the stage and the auditorium. Pinnock thereby labours towards a more nuanced regime of representation.

As well as engaging new audiences, culturally diverse productions challenge the expectations of regular (white) attendees. As new kinds of characters demand recognition, they initiate the 'integrat[ion] or normaliz[ation of] diversity as part of the everyday of contemporary culture' (Griffin, 2006a, pp. 12, 25). For instance, the subject matter of Pinnock's *Leave Taking* demanded that National Theatre audiences identify with characters unfamiliar to such prestigious stages, such as the older Jamaican immigrant, Enid. This transposition of experiences across cultures was apparently successful; Pinnock recalls respondents saying '"Yes, that's me" or, "that's my mum", irrespective of their class or race' (Pinnock, 1997, p. 49). Such avenues of emotional affinity dissolve the borders demarcating identity categories.

However, such an affinity remains unidirectional: it proceeds from the audience to the dramatic characters, and so retains the dynamics of an unevenly powered relationship. While such ontological boundaries persist between actors and audience, true parity will remain elusive. An anti-racist art form must therefore exceed content-orientated interventions, to engage in formal innovations that disrupt the actor/audience division. Pinnock's subtle efforts towards achieving these changes long went unacknowledged. Her theatrical form was dismissed as naturalistic until Ponnuswami carefully charted her inheritance of Bertolt Brecht's epic theatre and Samuel Beckett's absurdist aesthetic (2007). Ponnuswami comments that Pinnock relates formal choices, like Brecht's alienation effect, to the real, historical experiences of migration that inform her plays' narratives: 'the formal techniques that connect Pinnock's work to the wider contours of British theatre ... are also reconfigured aesthetically in relation to the issues of diaspora and identity' (2007, p. 210).

Reviewers reported that *Talking in Tongues* was traditional in form, saying it declined to participate in the subversive aesthetic projects of Pinnock's contemporaries: 'In the current rush to challenge theatrical form, Winsome Pinnock's new play *Talking in Tongues*, which deals in naturalism, might be dismissed as terribly old-fashioned' (Scott, 1991, p. 32). Critics failed to recognise how the traditional content of naturalistic drama was being reconfigured. Lynette Goddard corrects this oversight, arguing that Pinnock's Jamaican setting, non-linear structure and inclusion of a hermaphrodite character are revolutionary acts (2007, p. 52). I would add that the critical insistence on Pinnock's supposed naturalism overlooks the mechanics of specific productions. At the Royal Court, home of 'kitchen-sink' drama, *Talking in Tongues* disrupted expectations of a naturalistic viewing experience. Most of the cast played two roles across the two acts; only two characters, Leela and Claudette, make the journey from London to Jamaica within the story. This cast doubling was dismissed by many critics, with one attributing it to 'the bad influence of Caryl Churchill' (Coveney, 1991b, p. 1045). Again, Goddard has acknowledged the effect of this deliberate aesthetic choice, detailing the semantics of the specific character pairings (2007, pp. 77–8). However, this unconventional casting carries further meaning that is yet to be fully articulated.

In the first instance, the cast doubling was motivated by an accident of theatre policy. Pinnock recalls:

> When I was writing it, Max [Stafford Clark, then artistic director of the Royal Court] asked me how many characters it had, and when I told him [12] he said, 'But you're only allowed seven!' (Bayley, 1991, p. 29)

Pinnock was committed to presenting a full complement of characters and a complex plot: 'the more characters you have the more interesting the story you can tell' (Bayley, 1991, p. 29). Cast doubling enabled her to realise this ambition. That actors recur as different characters calls attention to the material reality of the bodies onstage, and so renders *Talking in Tongues* a comment on its own circumstances of production. Thus, cast doubling points towards the limited resources available to new black playwrights.

Further, cast doubling can highlight the limited availability of black actors. This, in turn, comments on the accessibility of hospitable training programmes, the availability of varied roles to develop actors' skills, and enough professional opportunities to make performance a viable career. Sadly, this equitable environment has not always been a reality. Two years after *Talking in Tongues*, Britain's foremost black theatre company struggled to find a suitable performer for its production of Michael Abbensetts' *The Lion* (Brown, 1993, n.p.). Talawa's then Artistic Director, Yvonne Brewster, wrote to the actors' union, Equity:

> In spite of exhaustive efforts on our part we have been unable to iden-
> tify a black female Equity member who is resident in this country, is
> at least 5'10" tall and in the 50-year-old grouping, let alone one who
> we consider appropriate and is available.

Tellingly, the union was unable to make any suggestions; Madge Sinclair, a Jamaican, was eventually employed. Aware of this straitened industry context, Pinnock has diligently provided central roles for older black actors – particularly women. In *Leave Taking*, for example, she created Enid Matthews, a woman in her early 50s, Mai, a woman in her late 60s, and Broderick, a man in his late 60s.

A Hero's Welcome also makes radical interventions into expected dramatic form, albeit more subtly than *Talking in Tongues* does through cast doubling. Pinnock responds to the 'kitchen-sink' realism champi-oned by her producing venue, and thus anticipated by her audience, by eschewing the cramped interior settings characteristic of John Osborne et al. Instead, the action takes place entirely outdoors; stage directions indicate that to go 'inside the house' is to exit the playing area (Pinnock, 1993, p. 25). Pinnock thereby brings the setting and archetypal char-acters of a traditional Caribbean format, the yard play, into dialogue with an esteemed English theatre tradition rooted in nuclear domestic arrangements (Goddard, 2007, pp. 48, 80). This continues a foray begun by Errol John, whose *Moon on a Rainbow Shawl* (1958), hailed by some as the prototypical yard play, also premiered at the Court (Chambers, 2002, p. 135). Accompanying this syncretism of setting in *A Hero's Welcome* is an important linguistic innovation. Pinnock disavows standard English, the language of the 'patriarchal, (neo)colonial regime', and instead has her characters speak with a local language (Goddard, 2007, p. 66).

The Royal Court's 1989 production of *A Hero's Welcome* further subverted its heritage in realism by disavowing the traditional proscenium arch: director Jules Wright staged the play in traverse. Critics interpreted this with varying degrees of generosity. For one, the arrangement attempted 'to capture the atmosphere of a backwater' (Edwardes, 1989, p. 207). It emphasised the island setting, creating a claustrophobia befitting the 'small district' announced in the stage directions (Pinnock, 1993, p. 21). For another it was 'oddly discomfiting' (Armitstead, 1989, p. 208), as naturalistic dialogue was compromised by the difficulty of seeing two characters at once. This interrupted spectatorship visually enacts 'the distances between people' (ibid.), allowing the play's thematic concerns to shape its formal arrangements.

Further, the traverse stage blurs the boundaries 'between the onstage and the auditorium realities' (Goddard, 2007, p. 77). It undermines the unidirectional gaze that attends naturalism, as the parallel seating arrangement forces the audience to see each other across and beyond the play's action. Seeing their own spectatorship returned, audience members are continually reminded of the play's fictional nature, and of themselves as being reciprocally seen. This self-reflexive gaze announces spectators' complicity in the representational production of meaning and ideology, as its consumers.

A Hero's Welcome builds on this metatheatricality with moments of direct audience address. This reflexive mode surfaces in the first and pre-penultimate scenes, bookending the realism that serves the central action. As Nana grumbles that Len restricts her freedom, she hints that she is alert to the presence of the audience: 'Lord, the day does run slow if you got people watching you every minute' (Pinnock, 1993, p. 22). Len responds: 'You free to come an' go as you please. As long as you don't go further than that line I mark out over there' (Pinnock, 1993, p. 22). Confirming this exchange as metatheatrical, the boundary of the performance area was marked by a washing line (Armitstead, 1989, p. 208). Nana and Len's bickering highlights that the divide between spectators and the play's action is as provisional as a casually slung coil of rope. When Len prohibits his grandmother's movement, then, he not only exercises patriarchal control within the world of the play, but operates to preserve realism in a production that threatens – like Nana – to exceed its boundaries.

The closing scene finalises this shift towards a reflexive theatre praxis. Ishbel and Sis, the friends left behind, sit atop a grassy bank overlooking the harbour as the optimistic migrants begin their voyage to England. Ishbel implores: 'Oh. Take me with you. Please' (Pinnock, 1993, p. 48). The statement is framed within the narrative as an appeal towards the departing boat, yet the stage directions mandate that her words are orientated 'Into audience' (Pinnock, 1993, p. 48). As in the interaction between Nana and Len, this momentarily releases the dialogue from its narrative context and makes it address the present reality of the theatre. Ishbel's gaze transforms her character's desire for a new life in post-war England into a startlingly real demand for inclusion in the world the spectators are shortly to return to, as they step out of the venue onto the privileged streets of London's Sloane Square. Sis and Ishbel stare into the audience in silence, before the lights fall to curtail the scene. This powerful vignette finally turns the act of spectatorship back towards the audience: the actors become the originators of the gaze, and the audience its object.

This chapter began with Hall's assessment of the twin strategies characterising black cultural participation in Britain. Eschewing the reactive stance that marks the first phase Hall documents, Pinnock mounts a series of imaginative challenges to the concept of a single, knowable blackness. The above analysis suggests that Pinnock's creative politics exceed the deconstructive work of Hall's second phase, too. Ultimately, her dramatic representation is not simply mimetic – a retrospective reflection of multifarious black British experiences – but productive: it looks forward to new possibilities for equal co-existence. Pinnock herself articulates this belief in the value of imaginative labour: 'We have the opportunity to create new ways of being, theatrically' (1997, p. 53).

I have argued that Pinnock undertakes this visionary task by negotiating the dramatic gaze. She not only rewrites who is seen onstage but reconfigures who *sees*, and the conditions of that ocular encounter. As such, her plays undermine the separation of producer and consumer that structures theatrical realism. In *A Hero's Welcome*, the gaze becomes reciprocal: the performers look back, and the audience is seen. In *Talking in Tongues*, cast doubling looks behind the dramatic fiction to alert the audience to the material realities of the cultural industries.

These unsettling metatheatrical moments return spectators to their own realities, and invite recognition that their position as audience members, like that of the actors, is temporary and voluntary. Understanding these roles as conditional then translates into a progressive conception of identity, where 'race' and gender classifications lose their dividing hold. In *A Hero's Welcome* and *Talking in Tongues*, the dyadic categories that ossify difference – black and white, male and female, performer and spectator – are meaningful only as constructed and contingent states. Through her playful exploration of what it is to participate in the theatre, then, Pinnock imaginatively posits alternative ways of being in the world.

Notes

1. Obeah refers to the folk medicine or witchcraft practiced in some areas of the Caribbean, and derived from West African traditions. For a scholarly discussion of the practice, see Diana Paton and Maarit Forde's edited volume, *Obeah and Other Powers: The Politics of Caribbean Religion and Healing*. For further analysis of Obeah in Winsome Pinnock's plays, see Goddard's *Staging Black Feminisms*, pp. 69–73.
2. In its exposure of sex tourism, and comparison of black women on either side of the industry, *Talking in Tongues* anticipates debbie tucker green's *trade*.

7
(Black) Masculinity, Race and Nation in Roy Williams' Sports Plays

Lynette Goddard

Roy Williams is one of Britain's leading black playwrights of the early twenty-first century, sustaining a high-profile career since the mid-1990s and widely acknowledged for 'provid[ing] the multicultural perspective absent from mainstream British theatre' (Barry and Boles, 2006, p. 298). His urgent and edgy 'state-of-the-nation' plays foreground social commentary and debate about race, national identity and belonging, exploring how multiracial demographics affect black *and* white Britons' sense of self and place in contemporary urban communities. Several analysts have mentioned the prominence of sports in Williams' plays, which this chapter seeks to develop with an examination of the social impact of these plays as a genre.[1] Williams admits to being 'hopeless' at sports as a child, stating 'to be a footballer then was the only thing black kids had going for them, and all my other black mates were really good at sports' (Hattenstone, 2010, p. 19). His plays examine how racially coded expectations surround black men's ability as players of sports and illustrate how understanding sporting support as an index of national identity and belonging is made more complex by the presence of black players and fans.

This chapter examines Williams' portrayals of (black) masculinity, race and nation in two plays depicting players and fans of sport in Britain that premiered in London's most prominent mainstream theatres. *Sing Yer Heart Out for the Lads* (National Theatre, 2002 and 2004) debates how new millennial racial anxieties manifest in the racist and xenophobic behaviour of a group of England football fans. *Sucker Punch* (Royal Court, 2010) examines how the racist exploitation of the black macho that underpins black male boxing careers is further exacerbated by the Thatcherite context of 1980s Britain.[2] By foregrounding football and boxing, Williams highlights issues in two of the key sporting arenas in which ideas about (black) masculinity, race and nation are created and sustained.

Scholarship on 'black masculinity and sport' has mainly been conducted within cultural and sociological analyses that map how expectations surrounding black male achievement in sport are linked to the perpetuation of neo-colonial discourses of black male sexuality, often in opposition to white men.[3] Williams' realistic plays interrogate how black men's experiences within British sporting discourses reflect socio-cultural assumptions and anxieties about race and nation; thus, these debates provide useful reference points for assessing the social imperative of his explorations of connections between race and sport in Britain. When asked about what influences his playwriting, Williams states, 'I get inspiration from what happens around me, what I see on the news or read in the paper' (Kennedy, 2004, n.p.). His characters and narratives closely resemble some key incidences of racism in British sport, and thus an understanding of these events and the sports personalities that inspire his writing can be used to ground analysis of his plays in the specific social and political contexts from which they arose. Williams uses sport as a dramatic metaphor to illuminate his political concerns, which raises questions about the social impact of black playwriting that interrogates contemporary issues. I am particularly interested in how black British playwrights' representations resonate with the real, adding black-informed perspectives to prominent contemporary debates. However, as I discuss later, Suzanne Scafe (2007) warns against prioritising the polemical value of black British plays and demands mindfulness of the limits that a sociological approach might impose, especially the risk of eliding the distinction between theatre and real life and overlooking the aesthetic aspects of these plays. With these reservations in mind, I examine Williams' plays with close reference to how the issues portrayed are discussed within cultural theory and sports sociology, coupled with analysis of the dramatic and theatrical devices used in the writing and productions, as a way of assessing the parameters for how we can understand the social, political *and* aesthetic resonances of contemporary black British playwriting.

Race and sports sociologists have drawn attention to how race relations and attitudes about national identity in England manifest within sporting fan cultures, particularly football. Adrian Smith and Dilwyn Porter argue, for example, that 'the possibilities for defining or redefining what it means to be "English" are inextricably linked to what happens on the field of play' (2004, p. 2). A quick trawl through English football's recent history uncovers racism as a deep-seated issue, with some stadiums (notably Millwall) notoriously used as recruiting grounds for the British National Party (BNP), and non-white players remaining prone to being racially abused on the pitch. When John Barnes first played for Liverpool, opposing fans chanted 'Everton are white', 'N*****pool' and 'Better dead than a N***** in red'. Kevin Hylton reports that 'in the 1980s, monkey chants in UK stadia along with banana-throwing were commonplace [...and] one of the iconic images of football in this period was John Barnes back-heeling a banana skin off the pitch whilst playing for Liverpool' (2010, p. 239). White fans questioned the loyalty of England's black players, and poor results were linked to a sense of antipathy and decline in national pride within an increasingly multiracial society. The 'Let's Kick Racism Out of Football' campaign was started in 1993, and in April 2004, it was reported in the news that ITV sports commentator Ron Atkinson had resigned following the accidental airing of his racist remark that black Chelsea captain Marcel Desailly is 'what is known in some schools as a f[***]ing lazy thick n[*****]' (Qtd in Prior, *The Guardian*, 22 April 2004).[4] Debates about racism in football hit the news headlines again in late 2011, when England captain and Chelsea player John Terry was charged with the racial abuse of Queen's Park Rangers' Anton Ferdinand and stripped of his captaincy, and Liverpool's Uruguayan player Luis Suarez was given an eight-match suspension for racially abusing Manchester United's Patrice Evra.[5] In early 2012, Manchester City player Mario Balotelli was subjected to monkey chants, another high-profile instance of racism in football that prompted Prime Minister David Cameron to hold a summit in collaboration with the 'Kick It Out' Campaign (now also addressing homophobia) in February 2012. In the summer, Euro 2012 launched amidst fears about racial violence and abuse towards black players and fans in Poland and Ukraine.[6]

Williams explores questions of race, nation and racism in football fan cultures in *Sing Yer Heart Out for the Lads*, which was first produced in 2002 as part of the National Theatre's experimental 'Transformation season' in the newly created Loft Theatre in the Lyttleton's Theatre bar, directed by Simon Usher; it was later revived for a larger-scale production in the Cottesloe in 2004, directed by Paul Miller. The play is set in the King George Public House in South London, which is heavily decorated with St George flags on the afternoon of 7 October 2000 as a group of (mostly white) working-class men gather to watch England's defeat to Germany in a World Cup qualifying match. The match was significant for being the last game played at the original Wembley Stadium before it was demolished and rebuilt, thus ending historic associations with notions of empire.[7] The play's realism is emphasised by being constructed in 'real' time as the 90-minute match is screened on a large plasma television above the bar; the dialogue is carefully crafted to move continuously between conversations in different areas of the pub and incorporate the men's reactions to key moments in the match, such as Dietmar Hamman's early goal, David Beckham's free kicks and England manager Kevin Keegan's sudden resignation in the televised post-match interview immediately after the game. Multiple levels of signification are created as the theatre audience is positioned to respond as spectators of the match as replayed live on screen (which may also link to their memories of the actual past event) while also watching the characters' immediate responses. Seating some of the audience members at tables and bar stools in the 2004 production further implicated them at the centre of the racial conflict that arises from the men's reactions to England's poor performance on the pitch.

Williams is an avid football fan and wrote the play after being in a pub watching England's clash with Germany in the first round of the Euro 2000 Championship and witnessing the behaviour of a group of drunken fans: 'I was enjoying myself and then all these drunk guys came barging in, chanting En-ger-land and shouting racist obscenities. And the most appalling things about [David] Beckham's wife. It was uncomfortable but, at the same time, I realised it was a great stage set' (Sierz, 2006b, p. 184). The incident coincided with his ambition to develop his playwriting to interrogate ideas about nation: 'I very much wanted to write a bigger play, not just simply about race, but about British Nationalism: what does it mean to be British in the twenty-first century, who's more British now, the blacks or the whites?' (Williams, 2004, p. x). Conservative politician Enoch Powell's notorious 'Rivers of Blood' speech (Conservative Association Meeting, Birmingham, 20 April 1968) marks one of the most controversial moments in the history of race relations in Britain, promoting an anti-immigration stance that galvanised bigoted racist separatism and violence. Powell's rhetoric on racial integration and multiculturalism is a backdrop for Williams' assessment of contemporary race relations in Britain, which invites audiences to consider the extent to which attitudes about the place and belonging of black people have shifted in the intervening three decades. Williams explores links between tribal nationalistic mentalities and football hooliganism within English working-class football fan cultures, looking at how heightened patriotic emotions can be evoked by international sports matches and drawing particular attention to how the presence of black fans can complicate ideas about national allegiance, inclusion and belonging.

England's longstanding rivalry with Germany goes back to the glory of England's 1966 World Cup victory in the team's halcyon days and reflects Paul Gilroy's assertion that football and war rhetoric are inextricably linked in the English public imagination. Gilroy observes that the England fans' chant of 'two world wars and one world cup' offers 'valuable insights into the morbid culture of a once-imperial nation that has not been able to accept its inevitable loss of prestige in a determinedly post-colonial world' (Gilroy, 2001, p. xi). Winning (the game and/or the war) is associated with masculine pride, virility and strength, and poor fortunes for the team are thus deemed to be a source of shame that is linked to a decline in national pride and the gradual loss of status as an imperial world power. Using war rhetoric in football chants reflects desires to hold on to nostalgic ideas of an England in which common values are shared among (white) men, but Williams explores how the growth of multiracial communities has ruptured such ideas of an unquestionably 'united kingdom'.

Debates about playing for the pride of one's nation or uniting in support of national teams are complicated by the presence of black and Asian players and fans who may share allegiance with teams from their countries of heritage (the West Indies, Africa, India or Pakistan). In the early 1990s, Conservative MP Norman Tebbit's controversial 'Cricket Test' (also known as the 'Tebbit Test') claimed that second-generation black and Asian fans who supported the teams of their parental heritage countries in international cricket matches against England have not fully integrated into the British society into which they were born.[8] However, Carrington highlights a different perspective on integration when he argues that 'the fact that the majority of the black population living in England had either a large degree of ambivalence towards England or openly supported "anyone but England" underscores the points being made that the form of national identity produced failed to be inclusive and actually alienated large sections of the nation' (1998, p. 118). The 2002 World Cup saw a move away from use of the Union flag to the flag of St George as a distinct symbol of support for England, and Martin Polley suggests that the 'many England fans of Afro-Caribbean and Asian backgrounds sharing in the celebrations [...was evidence of] the newly-visible diversity of England football followers' (2004, p. 11). However, despite an increase in the number of black fans openly supporting England in international football fixtures, sensitivities around black sporting allegiance remain evident, as shown in one (presumably black) fan's discomfort with seeing footballer Ian Wright draped in the St George's flag at an England match:

I looked at him [Wright] on the screen and I thought 'What the fuck is he doing – has he lost his mind completely!' I mean the St George Cross! That's the worst thing for a black person because according to them people you can't be black and English. Maybe Britishness would be something else because you can be 'black British' but English? Never. (Qtd. in Back et al., 1998, p. 99)

At the same time, Carrington observes that 'the very presence of Black athletes wrapped in the Union Jack still provides a distressing sight for the far right in visibly and publicly challenging the claim that "there ain't no black in the Union Jack"' (2000, p. 134). A reputation for yobbish racism at football grounds also seems to preclude the comfortable integration of black fans, whose 'inclusion within such arenas can be dependent upon their conformity with the "white" working class masculine normative structures associated with certain aspects of football culture' (Back et al., 1998, p. 235).

Williams' play emerges from within these contradictory debates, highlighting how 'us' and 'them' mentalities resonate with ideas about integration and separatism for black British-born people living in England. A familiar picture of a group of testosterone-fuelled, sexist and homophobic, white working-class football fans is established at the start of the play, but this image is soon ruptured by the arrival of black character Mark and his younger brother Barry who represent contrasting opinions in the debate about integration or separatism for black British-born people in contemporary England. Barry allies himself with white working-class culture, symbolising his ardent support for England by painting the St George flag across his face and proudly showing the British bulldog tattooed onto his lower back. His claim that he is not comfortable around black people and his refusal to visit his ailing father imply that he has distanced himself from his black cultural heritage. Barry behaves like a stereotypically loutish football fan, bragging about involvement in the hooligan violence abroad for which England fans were becoming renowned, loudly 'singing for England, "EN-GER-LAND"' (Williams, 2002, p. 37), and joining in with the xenophobic chants towards the German players during the match: 'Stand up, if you won the war!' (Williams, 2002, p. 38). As the star player in the pub's football team, scoring the goals that saw them victorious against the Duke of York pub earlier in the day, the macho hero's welcome that Barry receives from his white team mates suggests that he is an integral member of the group. [9] However, his race complicates straightforward understandings of his place within the group, exemplified by audiences having to reconcile the incongruity of a black man whose body is visibly marked with symbols of Englishness with recognition that he is kept outside of the group, arriving last because he drew the short straw and was left to walk back from the earlier match alone while his white team mates returned together in shared cars.

The attitudes of the other black characters in the play also undermine Barry's support for England, epitomised in teenager Bad T's retort 'I ain't watching no rubbish English match. They lose at everything' (Williams, 2002, p. 14). Similarly, Barry's brother Mark previously had a relationship with the pub's white landlady Gina and joined the army, swearing an oath of allegiance to queen and country; but he left after becoming disillusioned by the racism of his superiors and has developed an acute sensitivity of racial dynamics that underline his separatist stance. Mark's initial refusal to stay and watch the match echoes the discomfort of the fan's comments cited earlier when he tells Barry to 'wipe that shit off your face' (Williams, 2002, p. 39), and warns his younger brother against naïvely believing that being born in England assures automatic inclusion as one of 'the lads'.

The tenuousness of Barry's place within the group is further under-lined by the variety of explicit and latent racist expressions throughout the play, for instance, the blatant old-fashioned racism of pub landlord Jimmy. His daughter Gina's tolerance of the multicultural milieu is tested by her concern that her teenage son Glen is getting into trouble because he is hanging around with the local black youth and bullying Asian children at school. Neo-Nazi racist thug Lawrie calls black people 'coons' and openly expresses his desire to beat up people of colour. His ambiva-lence towards a changing nation is captured through his association of England's glorious footballing past with a period of racial separatism and national pride at a time 'when Enoch [Powell] best prime minister we never had, spoke the truth' (Williams, 2002, p. 72). Lawrie criticises the current poor match-play as evidence of a lack of manly qualities caused by increased diversity and a decline in national pride, stating 'We better [win], restore some pride after that fuck-up in Belgium. I mean, how fucking bad was that? The nation that gave the world football. (*Roars.*) Come on, you England!' (Williams, 2002, p. 27).

Whereas Lawrie's demeanour can be dismissed as the poor behaviour of a typical football lout, the most controversially racist character in the play is far-right extremist Alan, who underpins his racist opinions with articulate explanations for racial separatism: 'If *they* want to prac-tice *their* black culture and heritage, then *they* should be allowed to do it in *their* own part of *their* world' (Williams, 2002, p. 60, emphasis added). Williams drew inspiration for Alan's character from British National Party

(BNP) literature, and states '[i]t was important to me not to make him a devil. I wanted him to be charming, cool, and able to completely justify what he says' (Williams, 2004, p. x). Alan's long speeches are deliberately uncomfortable to watch, containing extreme views that provocatively tap into rarely spoken about sensitivities of race and nation, such as his opinion that even third-generation black children have only 'squatters' rights' (Williams, 2002, p. 90) because they do not have a long enough cultural history in England to be counted as English.

The tension between conceiving of black people in England as either black British or black English is one whereby African Caribbean people in England might be holders of a UK passport, whereas the claim to Englishness remains the preserve of white people. Slippage between using the terminologies British or English often occurs in relation to white people in parts of the UK other than England, such as when Scottish people are mistakenly referred to as English rather than the political qualification of British.[10] The issue is further complicated by acknowledgement that Great Britain is constituted of three countries – Scotland, England and Wales, whereas the UK also includes Northern Ireland – and compounded even more by the idea that even when born in England, black people are generally thought to be British rather than English. Mark draws attention to these complexities when he contests Alan's notion that only white people have a genuine claim to be labelled 'English', and Alan's response to Mark's challenge demonstrates the confusion when he collapses country (England) with nation (Britain) and moves between the categorisations of 'English' and 'British' without acknowledging the difference between them.

> MARK: I'm English
> ALAN: No you're not.
> MARK: I served in Northern Ireland. I swore an oath of allegiance to the flag. [...] How English are you? Where do you draw the line as to who's English? I was born in this country. And my brother. You're white, your culture comes from northern Europe, Scandinavia, Denmark. [...] Where do you draw the line?
> [...]
> ALAN: The fact is, Mark, that the white British are a majority racial group in this country, therefore it belongs to the white British. (Williams, 2002, p. 90)

Alan's arguments for white supremacy stir cultural anxieties about how the changes wrought through waves of immigration disadvantages the white working classes who, in his view, are potentially sidelined in politically correct endeavours for multicultural equality, and he predicts an Enoch Powellian 'rivers of blood' fallout if the resentments caused by the quest for multicultural equality are not addressed. The topicality of such rhetoric is apparent from the increased profile of the BNP during the 2000s when they contested for seats in the 2002 elections and won a seat in Barking and Dagenham in the 2008/9 local elections, which they subsequently lost in the 2010 General Election.

However, Williams also examines how histories of immigration have changed the racial demographics of the country, particularly in urban communities, which challenges purist ideas about 'English' national identity. The very boundaries of 'Englishness' that Lawrie and Alan seek to protect are unsettled by the language and behaviour tropes of the younger black and white characters who talk and act similarly. Gina's teenage son Glen behaves in a manner typically associated with urban black youths, listening to loud rap music and speaking a contemporary generational 'urban patois' (Sawyer, 2008) that the younger characters in Williams' plays often speak. But Glen's identification with black culture is undermined when Bad T evokes stereotypical ideas of a contrast between virile, strong black boys and feeble white boys to bully him and take his jacket and mobile phone: 'White boy love to cry, ennit' (Williams, 2002, p. 17). As Scafe argues, Glen's 'posture of blackness [...is] based on his fear of the menace of his black school-mates, itself a defensive posture' (2007, p. 83). Like Barry, Glen has to negotiate a position in contemporary England where his allying with his black friends is challenged by the other white male characters' old-fashioned ideas about racial separatism.

At the start of the play Glen and Barry appear to be products of a well-integrated multiracial society, but the racist banter circulating around them throughout the course of the match finally forces them to choose sides as the tensions build into destructive violence. Significantly, it is the entry of a black woman into the pub space that breaks the tenuous homosocial bonds between the black and white men. Duane's mum Sharon condemns the men's mistreatment of her son, and the literal 'manhandling' of her as they throw her out of the pub incites an angry gathering of people protesting in the offstage space outside the pub door. The conflict between 'us' and 'them' is symbolised by a separation between the pub's interior as a space of inclusion for white English nationals, and its exterior, an exclusion zone for black people whose claim to 'Englishness' is contested by those within. The offstage space is symbolic of those excluded from full participation in old-fashioned constructs of an English nation, and who challenge the boundaries of

'Englishness' by hurling bricks through the window and trying to break down the door. The men's questioning of Barry for staying within the pub's 'nation' space interior as the commotion begins outside is a further reminder of his struggle for acceptance if race is taken as a key credential for being a fully fledged England supporter.

PHIL: [...] Barry shouldn't you be out there?
BARRY: ENGLAND!
PHIL: He's your brother, you should be backing him up.
BARRY: I'm watchin the game.
[...]
What you trying to say, Jase?
[...]
I'm not white enuff for England? (Williams, 2002, p. 66)

Spatially, it is also notable that important conversations about race between Mark and Barry occur in the toilet, a marginal space from the main pub, seen through a Perspex screen that obscured our vision of them in the 2004 production. Such racial-spatial divisions prevail when the play culminates with Glen stabbing Mark to death in the toilet and re-enters the main space of the pub shouting 'He's a black bastard, they all are' (Williams, 2002, p. 106), which highlights the ultimate effect of him imbibing the racist ideas that have been circulating throughout the match. Barry responding to his brother's murder by calling his teammates 'white cunts [sic]' (Williams, 2002, p. 107) and symbolically renouncing his allegiance to England by wiping the St George flag from his face leaves audiences with a sad final image of a racially divided nation that is struggling to reconcile ideas of old and new 'England'.

Reviewers found this ending pessimistic, as the younger generation's eventual resort to angry racism carries an air of hopelessness about peaceful coexistence between different races in a multicultural society. One of the main criticisms of the production was that Williams raised important debates but failed to provide answers on how to eradicate racism. David Benedict writes that 'while it's salutary to be presented with unpalatable facts about society [...] facts alone are not what drama is for. Isn't the point of art to leap beyond the constraints of reality and use the imagination to explore and express alternatives, even hope' (2002). Scafe also bemoans that '[t]he development of a twenty-nine page Education pack to accompany the touring production suggests that, like so much Black expressive art, it is more valued as polemic than as theatre' (2007,

p. 81). Yet, these issues are otherwise hardly tackled on the contemporary British stage, and Williams raises important concerns about race relations that are rarely discussed in mainstream theatrical contexts. He probes beneath the surface of the polite middle-class liberalism and political correctness of the presumed audience by highlighting uncomfortable ideas such as Alan's claim of latent racism towards black and Asian Britons: 'Show me one white person who has ever treated you as an equal, and I will show you a liar. [...] Because in order to do that they have to see you differently. It will never come as naturally as when they see another white person. All this multiculturalism. Eating a mango once a year at the Notting Hill Carnival is still a long way from letting your kids go to a school that is overrun with Pakis [sic] and blacks' (Williams, 2002, p. 89). Although Alan's views are uncomfortable to watch, they share Williams' sentiments that some of these sensitive issues need to be openly discussed to increase understanding between races. Although black British playwrights (trained in theatre practice rather than social work) should not be expected to offer solutions to these urgent societal concerns, airing these difficult issues within the context of mainstream British theatre contributes to debates that remind audiences about the latent and explicit anxieties and hostilities that inform race relations in the UK and of the dialogue that is needed to promote an understanding of the landscape in which we live.

Williams continues his explorations of racism in *Sucker Punch* (Royal Court Theatre, 2010), which uses boxing as a backdrop to explore ideas about black masculinity and belonging in 1980s Britain. Under Margaret Thatcher's Conservative Government, escalating unemployment and an economic recession impacted particularly on opportunities for black and working-class men, and tense race relations between black youth and the police were compounded by the controversial SUS laws that saw an increase in the number of black boys and men routinely stopped and searched on London's streets. Anger about inner-city deprivation, inequality and continued police brutality towards black people led to race riots in Brixton, Handsworth (Birmingham), Toxteth (Liverpool) and Chapeltown (Leeds) in 1981 and in Brixton and Tottenham in 1985.

A long association between boxing and tropes of black male violence is evident from reports of slaves being paid money for beating each other up, and many of the world's most eminent black sportsmen have been boxers. However, as social analysts have observed, boxing is a sport that reproduces neo-colonial ideas about black male bodies' 'natural' propensity for physical strength over intellect. Mike Marqusee highlights that boxing is a degrading sport, a capitalist commodity that reiterates the exploitation of black male boxers who must acquiesce to the demands of promoters, managers and television companies in order to develop and sustain their careers: 'Boxing today appears highly individualistic but the individuals involved, the boxers, have less power over their bodies and careers than almost any other sports people. Even successful boxers, with few exceptions, are bound like serfs to promoters, managers and satellite TV companies.' (1995, p. 3). Hylton also identifies that participation in sports is framed as a way of keeping young black (and working-class) men out of trouble, and a boxing career in particular is deemed as a way of legitimately channelling aggression while potentially securing a lucrative income.

In Williams' play, white gym owner Charlie takes childhood friends Leon and Troy under his wing after catching them breaking into his premises, thus seemingly fulfilling the stereotypical idea of a white male father figure using sport to 'save' young black boys from a life of crime and poverty.[11] Like many of the black fathers in Williams' plays, Leon's biological dad Squid is unreliable and feckless, scrounging money for womanising, drinking and gambling, while leaving his son to fend for himself. But Charlie's potential role as a surrogate father is undermined by his racism, exemplified when he agrees to help Leon build a professional boxing career only if the youngster breaks off his budding relationship with Charlie's daughter. Nonetheless, Charlie uses Leon's boxing success to keep the gym afloat in the midst of the 1980s recession, despite his personal feeling towards his young charge.

Boxing opponents often use insults towards each other as a way of getting the upper hand in the pre-fight build up, and Leon's blow-by-blow accounts of key encounters in his rising boxing career show how he channels pent-up anger and aggression about racial insults in the ring. However, racial 'trash talk' takes on yet another dimension when insults are traded between black men, such as when Muhammad Ali notoriously called Joe Frazier an Uncle Tom in the lead up to their much-anticipated 1971 encounter in Madison Square Gardens. Williams' characters fit Marqusee's contention that black boxers are historically contrasted as one of 'two equally tragic role models: the "bad N[*****]" and the "Uncle Tom"' (1995, p. 7), respectively aggressive hoodlums, or humble, subservient and compliant with white authority.[12] Such a noble/savage distinction is epitomised in the contrast between heavyweight fighters Frank Bruno (UK) and Mike Tyson (USA), the former deemed a 'coconut' (black on the outside, white on the inside), a patriotic royalist who sought assimilation, and the latter an uncontrollable aggressive 'monster'; Williams' characterisation of Leon and Troy closely resembles these real life boxers. Troy accuses Leon of being an Uncle Tom, who acquiesces to the demands of an exploitative white manager and seeks to integrate with white working-class culture in Britain. Charlie throwing in the towel to stop the bout between Leon and Troy near the end of the play reflects Frank Bruno's heavy defeat to Mike Tyson in 1997, and Leon's rebuke to being called an Uncle Tom echoes Bruno's emotional outburst in his post-fight interview after winning the WBC Heavyweight Championship in 1995:

> I'm not an Uncle Tom, I'm not an Uncle Tom, no way, I love my brother, I'm not an Uncle Tom [...] I love my people, I'm not an Uncle Tom, I'm not a sell-out. [...] I'm no Uncle Tom, I'm no Uncle Tom, believe that, please, please, just believe that I'm no Uncle Tom. (Qtd in Carrington, 2000, pp. 150–1).[13]

Such close parallels between the theatrical representation and real life add a further layer to understanding the resonance of Williams' play.

Troy fulfils the 'bad n*****' stereotype, getting involved in violent confrontations with the police on London's streets before moving to the USA in pursuit of a stronger sense of black identity based on the unity forged by separatist racial politics. However, Williams highlights the tenuousness of Troy's belief that black men fare better in the USA when his black manager Ray asserts control over his protégé, reminding him 'You fight who I tell you. You are mine' (2010, p. 83). Ray's sentiment of ownership is further revealed when he refers to Troy as 'bitch' in a similar derogatory way to Charlie calling Leon 'boy' earlier in the play, highlighting how both of the young black men lack the autonomy that a boxing career promises while being subject to the particular dangers associated with the brutality of this sport.

Some critics found the play to be 'overly schematic' (Brown, 2010, p. 699) with a simplistically predictable plot that drove towards a final showdown between Leon and Troy, but others praised the production's aesthetic qualities and it received a number of awards.[14] Miriam Buether's design spectacularly transformed the Royal Court auditorium into an authentic boxing arena into which audiences entered through a corridor where the walls were lined with sponsors' adverts and newspaper cuttings of past prize fights and were then seated ringside. Strobe lights, dry ice and mirrors enhanced the visceral nature of a performance environment in which 'you can almost smell the stale sweat and the disinfectant' (Brown, 2010, p. 699). The visceral nature of the production resonates with another level on which we might seek to understand how the play responds to predominant discourses of black masculinity through an exploration of ideas about the erotic and virile black male body on display. Former professional boxer Errol Christie was brought in to train the actors in boxing and skipping techniques, which were coupled with Leon Baugh's stylised choreography of the fights to make impressive visual displays in the show. Although no actual fights were shown on stage until the final showdown between Leon and Troy, the production highlights the physical display of a toned and muscular black male body as Leon impressively performs complex boxing training moves – skipping, dancing and shadow boxing – while delivering the monologues describing his fight encounters. Leon's unorthodox trademark dance, 'The Leon Shuffle', draws further attention to the actor's physicality and dancing skills, while evoking Muhammad Ali's memorable catchphrase 'float like a butterfly sting like a bee, the eyes can't hit what the eyes can't see.' These performances emphasise stereotypical views of the physicality of the black male body on display, while the beautifully choreographed dance-fighting sequences also somewhat undermine ideas about animalistic ferocity that are often associated with black male boxers, such as Mike Tyson.

Barry and Boles liken Williams' plays to politicised verbatim theatre that responds to current events, indicating that '[a]lthough Williams does not use material from real transcripts or interviews, this proximity between theatre and real life has meant that his theatre has had a particular social relevance' (Barry and Boles, 2006, p. 312). I have also positioned the two sports plays discussed in this chapter within specific realistic frameworks by highlighting how they are inspired by real life contexts, events and sports personalities. Williams' sports plays are social documentations of contemporary Britain, thus rendering the sociological debates contained within them pertinent to understanding their importance and impact. They contribute to important debates about how participation in and spectating of sports can play an important role in fostering a sense of belonging in Britain. London's winning bid to host the 2012 Olympics was largely strengthened by a commitment to building a lasting legacy of diversity in sporting activities within a multicultural milieu, and producing Williams' plays on London's main stages promotes white audiences' awareness of complex issues of race and nation. Williams recalls a heritage of black sporting activity that invites contemporary audiences to recognise issues that black players and fans of sport are forced to confront in the UK, such as the questions about national allegiance that underline Tebbit's 'cricket test' or the ways that black and white men respond to sexual and sporting stereotypes in constructing and understanding their identities as British males. Analysing Williams' sports plays as a genre highlights how he uses motifs of gladiatorial combat, and sporting oppositions such as home or away, us or them, or win or lose, as useful allegories for questioning the politics of inclusion and exclusion in contemporary Britain. The significance of these debates is further exemplified by how Williams' portrayal of issues of integration and separatism within his sports plays resonate with his own position as a black dramatist within the context of mainstream contemporary British theatre. His pioneering engagement with Britishness *vis à vis* black and white males' relationship to sport contributes to increasing the diversity of representation in key theatre venues that are starting to give black playwrights some recognition at the heart of British theatre discourse.

Notes

1. See Peacock (2006b), Derbyshire (2007), Scafe (2007), Osborne (2011b).
2. In addition to the plays discussed in this chapter, Williams uses sport as a context for *The No Boys Cricket Club* (Theatre Royal Stratford East, 1996), *Joe Guy* (Tiata Fahodzi/Soho Theatre, 2007) and *There's Only One Wayne Matthews* (Polka Theatre, 2007 and Crucible Sheffield, 2010).
3. See, for example, Carrington, (2000, 2002 and 2010) and Hylton (2010).
4. Atkinson thought that his comments were being made off-air and their broadcast led to his immediate resignation from his job at ITV and newspaper column work at the *Guardian*. See Eboda (2004) for an interview with Atkinson about the incident.
5. Further analysis of these issues can be found in Back, Crabbe and Solomos (1998). At a magistrate court hearing in July 2012, Terry was subsequently cleared of a racially aggravated public order offence, but an FA disciplinary hearing in September 2012 found him guilty of using abusive language and he was fined £220,000 and banned for four matches.
6. Evidence of violent racist attacks and anti-semitic chanting were shown in *Panorama, Euro 2012: Stadiums of Hate*, which was broadcast on BBC1 on 3 June 2012.
7. The original Wembley Stadium, formally known as the Empire Stadium, was opened in 1923 for the British Empire Exhibition.
8. See Polley (2004) for further discussion of the ramifications of the Tebbit Test.
9. Both pub names allude to the historic battles of the past.
10. These issues are likely to become further complicated if Scotland votes in favour of Scottish independence in the 2014 referendum.
11. See Carrington (2000) and Hylton for detailed analysis of this idea.
12. See Mercer (1994), Marqusee (1995) and Carrington (2002) for explorations of how these stereotypes relate to boxers such as Mike Tyson and Frank Bruno.
13. Gilroy (1993) and Mercer (1994) also present detailed accounts of the significance of this moment.

14. Awards for *Sucker Punch* include Roy Williams – Writers' Guild of Great Britain Awards, Best Theatre Play (2011), Daniel Kaluuya – *Evening Standard* Award and Critic's Circle Award, Outstanding Newcomer (2010), Miriam Buether – *Evening Standard* Award, Best Designer (2010), Leon Baugh – Olivier Award, Best Theatre Choreographer (2010) and Peter Mumford – 4th Knight of Illumination Award for Lighting Design (2010).

8

Kwame Kwei-Armah's African American Inspired Triptych

Michael Pearce

Introduction

Kwame Kwei-Armah, né Ian Roberts, was born in England in 1967 to Grenadian parents and grew up in Southall, London. He attended the Barbara Speake Stage School as a child and began his adult career as an actor. Kwei-Armah achieved a national profile playing the role of paramedic Finlay Newton in the BBC's television programme *Casualty* from 1999 to 2004. Kwei-Armah consolidated his presence in television through appearances in *Comic Relief Does Fame Academy* (BBC, 2003), as a regular on panellist shows such as *Newsnight Review* (BBC) and as a documentary presenter on the series *On Tour with the Queen* (Channel 4, 2009).

Kwei-Armah also diversified into writing and directing. He wrote his début play, *A Bitter Herb* (2001) in 1999, which was produced in 2001 at the Bristol Old Vic. Prior to that, his play *Big Nose* (2001), based on Rostand's *Cyrano de Bergerac* and co-written with Chris Monks, opened at the Belgrade Theatre in Coventry in 1999. That same year, his soul musical *Hold On* (2001), then entitled *Blues Brother, Soul Sister*, premiered at the Bristol Old Vic before touring nationally. In 2003, *Elmina's Kitchen* premiered at the National Theatre's Cottesloe theatre, before transferring to the Garrick Theatre in 2005, where it became the first drama by a black British-born writer to be staged in the commercial West End. *Elmina's Kitchen* (2009) was also performed in Baltimore and Chicago, making it one of a handful of plays written by British-born blacks to have crossed the Atlantic. Kwei-Armah followed *Elmina's Kitchen* with two new plays, both of which also premiered at the Cottesloe: *Fix Up* (2009) in 2004 and *Statement of Regret* (2009) in 2007. Together these three plays comprise what Kwei-Armah refers to as his 'triptych'.[1]

After *Statement of Regret* followed *Let There Be Love* (2009) in 2008 and *Seize the Day* (2009) in 2009, both of which premiered at London's Tricycle theatre and were directed by Kwei-Armah. In 2011, Kwei-Armah relocated to the USA where he became Artistic Director of Center Stage Theater in Baltimore. Despite this shift in his career, Kwei-Armah continues to write. His latest play, *Beneatha's Place* (unpublished), opened at Centre Stage in 2013, playing in rep with Bruce Norris' *Clybourne Park* (2010). Like Norris' play, *Beneatha's Place* is also inspired by Lorraine Hansberry's *A Raisin in the Sun* (1959); but, *Beneatha's Place* also responds to *Clybourne Park* in its structure and often shockingly open and humorous debate about race.

Prior to *Beneatha's Place*, Kwei-Armah's plays have largely been set in contemporary London, demonstrating his commitment to representing the contemporary metropolitan black British experience.[2] Nevertheless, Kwei-Armah's relocation to the USA follows a long infatuation with African American politics and culture. Indeed, two African American writers played a decisive role in Kwei-Armah's life: Alex Haley, whose books *Roots* (1976) and *The Autobiography of Malcolm X* (1965) re-configured Kwei-Armah's identity and honed his political consciousness, and August Wilson, whose work inspired Kwei-Armah to become a playwright and whose style has highly influenced his dramaturgy.

African America as cultural, political and symbolic resource

Whilst growing up, Kwei-Armah felt disconnected from his parents' Caribbean culture and struggled to find his place in Britain. Looking back at his youth, Kwei-Armah expresses a profound sense of dislocation:

> When I was young I never had a home. I used to call myself at sixteen famously a 'universal alien'. When I walked out on the streets in London, they'd say 'Go back home, you black bastard.' When I went to the West Indies they'd say, 'You're English.' When I go to Africa, they say 'Go home. Look at you, Bob Marley.' I'd never had a home until I discovered that I was an African and that actually I was a diasporic African. (Qtd. in Davis, 2006, p. 247)

For a number of black people growing up in Britain during the 1960s and 1970s, the paucity of black role models, lack of a mainstream black British cultural presence, no precedent of a critical mass of British-born blacks and a racist environment meant that youths had to look elsewhere for their cultural and political reference points. This, combined with widespread assumptions that blacks born in Britain were not really 'British', opened the door to African American identification, particularly among activists and artists, and coincided with the ascendancy of black American popular culture in the USA and its global dissemination.

The Black Power movement in the USA and its legacy had a fundamental impact on black British political organisation, cultural expression and identity (Gunning and Ward, 2009; Malchow, 2011; Wild, 2008). A key aspect of Black Power politics was an Afrocentric world-view. Afrocentrism has broad interpretations. Tunde Adeleke defines it as a racially essentialist ideology that uses Africa in order 'to advance a monolithic and homogeneous history, culture, and identity for all blacks, regardless of geographical location' (2009, pp. 10–11). Stephen Howe, on the other hand, highlights its less extreme interpretations that place 'an emphasis on shared African origins among all "black" people, taking a pride in those origins and an interest in African history and culture – or those aspects of New World cultures seen as representing African "survivals" – and a belief that Eurocentric bias has blocked or distorted knowledge of Africans and their cultures' (1998, p. 1). Nevertheless, fundamental to both interpretations is the notion of the African diaspora.

The view of African Americans and Afro-Caribbeans as an African diaspora who share a common origin and cultural similarity with continental Africa emerged as an important ideological accompaniment to black political and cultural discourses that sought to highlight essential differences between blacks and whites in reaction to white racism. In the USA, Black Power's rhetoric of self-determination and solidarity had an equally important cultural dimension, which drew on Africa for inspiration and was applied at the very root of some people's identity. For instance, during the 1960s and 1970s, some individual artists such as Amiri Baraka (formerly LeRoi Jones) and Ntozake Shange (formerly Paulette Williams) rejected their family 'slave names' and adopted names that proclaimed their African ancestry. It was also at this time that a group of radical black artists emerged, who, identifying themselves as members of the Black Arts Movement (BAM), gave artistic representation to Black Power ideology. The principal aim of the playwrights of the BAM was to harness African American urban cultures to their aesthetic and dramaturgy. This was accompanied by a desire to establish continuity with Africa by utilising indigenous cultural forms or 'survivals', which were seen to have their roots in African practices. By the 1970s, these ideas and approaches were brought to popular attention and into the mainstream with the publication of Haley's Pulitzer Prize-winning novel *Roots: The Saga of an American Family* (1976).

It was through *Roots* that Kwei-Armah literally 'discovered' Africa and decided to change his name. When the television series of *Roots* was broadcast in the UK, it had a profound impact on the young Kwei-Armah (then Ian Roberts): 'It was on when I was 11 and I changed my path. It inspired me to start connecting myself with Africa and to find my true identity' (Qtd. in West, 2008). In his 20s, the then Ian Roberts went to Ghana where he traced his family genealogy and, on his return, changed his name to Kwame Kwei-Armah. His identification with Afrocentric ideology was the direct result of his experiences of racism and marginalisation growing up in the UK in the 1970s and 1980s; but crucially, his understanding of it was accessed through African American popular culture.

Kwei-Armah does not explicitly identify with African America. He sees himself as a 'diasporic African' occupying an interstitial position between three cultures that define his identity: 'I call myself tri-cultural: I'm African, Caribbean and British. And each one of those has an equal part to play and I can be one or all at the same time depending on what it is' (Qtd. in Davis, 2006, p. 240). Kwei-Armah's plays certainly exhibit a deep awareness of Caribbean and British cultures. More interestingly, they stage the unique ways in which they have intersected and given rise to new cultural hybrids and histories. Arguably, however, Kwei-Armah's sense of self- and political consciousness as a 'diasporic African' is not refracted through the third space of Africa but rather through black America. For instance, his Pan-African, Afrocentric politics stems in the main from African American cultural nationalist thinkers. On the political influences that have shaped his work, he states:

> My work comes from a cultural perspective that is supported by my Pan-Africanist politics [...] My politics is a diasporic, black politics influenced by the philosophies of Marcus Garvey and Malcolm X and the writings of James Baldwin and Amiri Baraka. It is non-apologetic politics. (Qtd. in Osborne, 2007a, p. 253)

Apart from Garvey, the above mixture of activists and writers are all African American – and even Garvey spent a substantial time in the USA. Indeed, it is in black America that we see the dominant influences that have shaped Kwei-Armah's identity, politics and art.

Similarly, black America has had an important influence on his creative output. In a number of his plays, the African American experience provides the starting point for Kwei-Armah's engagement with the black situation in Britain: The title of his play *Let There Be Love* is taken from Nat King Cole's version of the song and uses its message of harmony and compassion in a plea against prejudice and intolerance of minorities in Britain; *Seize the Day* revolves around a candidate in the running to become London's first black mayor and was inspired by the election of Barack Obama in 2008 as the first African American President of the USA; *Fix Up* was inspired by a book of African American slave narratives that Kwei-Armah received as a gift from his agent on the opening night of *Elmina's Kitchen*; and in *Statement of Regret*, Kwei-Armah bases the play's central exploration of the continuing impact of slavery on the black psyche on African American social scientist Dr Joy DeGruy-Leary's theory of 'post traumatic slave syndrome'. In *Post Traumatic Slave Syndrome* (2005), DeGruy-Leary argues that the trauma of slavery continues to impact upon the psychological development of black Americans.

The Caribbean experience of racial segregation under colonialism and the hostile and racist treatment of black people in Britain in the post-war period have had, in Kwei-Armah's opinion, a similarly damaging effect on black people in Britain as the USA's history of slavery and segregation/Jim Crow laws: 'My parents' generation, who came here from the Caribbean in the 50s, had what was literally a legal colour bar in the Caribbean before they came here and brought that with them. Even though a lot of people say it's not the same in this country as in America, technically with colonialism, we are running in direct parallel' (2007).

August Wilson, in particular, has been an inspiration. In 1990, Kwei-Armah attended his first August Wilson play. It was *Joe Turner's Come and Gone* at London's Tricycle Theatre where Kwei-Armah admits he became a devotee of Wilson: 'I really got turned on to August in a big, bad way. I was smitten by its spirituality, by its haunting refrain to Africa, its exploration of the pain of the diaspora' (Qtd. in Edwardes, 2006). In Wilson, Kwei-Armah would find a powerful role model. In particular, Kwei-Armah's triptych reveals a debt to Wilson's plays in their style, thematic exploration and underlying political belief system. Indeed, it is through Wilson's influence that one can trace the fundamental impression black America has had on Kwei-Armah's dramaturgy.

The influence of August Wilson

Kwei-Armah's inspiration for his triptych of plays was a production of Wilson's *King Hedley II* (2005), which he saw while in Washington, D.C. in 2001.[3] In an interview about *Elmina's Kitchen*, Kwei-Armah recounts: 'I was so touched by the magnitude of this man [August Wilson] and his commitment to talk of and chronicle the African–American experience through the art form [...] I went back to my hotel room that night and said, "O.K., I now know what I want to do; I want to chronicle the black

British experience"' (Qtd. in Wolf, 2005). Kwei-Armah's triptych takes its lead from Wilson's Pittsburgh Cycle. For the Cycle, Wilson wrote ten plays, each set in Pittsburgh and each representative of a decade in the twentieth century. Similarly, Kwei-Armah sets all three of his plays in London, and, although the plays occur within the first decade of the 2000s, they are divided according to class: *Elmina's Kitchen* – the underclass, *Fix Up* – the working class, and *Statement of Regret* – the middle class.

In *Elmina's Kitchen*, the action takes place in a fast-food takeaway called Elmina's Kitchen in Hackney's notorious 'murder mile'.[4] The play examines the failed attempts of restaurant owner Deli to keep his son Ashley from entering into a life of gangs and crime. Brother Kiyi's black-consciousness bookshop provides the setting for *Fix Up*. In the play, Brother Kiyi's struggle to keep his shop afloat is undermined by his lodger Kwesi, who plans to take over the premises and turn it into a black hair products shop. The conflict yields a debate centred on whether black self-determination is best won through intellectual or economic means. When Brother Kiyi's mixed-race daughter arrives, looking for the father who gave her up for adoption and for an explanation as to the whereabouts of her mother, a concurrent theme emerges around identity and the importance of historical knowledge and truth if individual and collective freedom is to be achieved. *Statement of Regret* is set in a black political think-tank. The play explores the role of black politics in contemporary British society and the differing generational and ethnic approaches taken by the think-tank's black British, Caribbean and African employees. At the play's core lies an examination of the continued legacy of slavery and its impact upon the black psyche.

Themes of inter-generational conflict and the struggle against racial oppression and for racial identity are as central to Kwei-Armah's work as they are to Wilson's. This has led a number of reviewers to comment on echoes of Wilson's work in Kwei-Armah's plays. For instance, one reviewer wrote of *Statement of Regret*: 'For all that the suited black British characters exist an ocean apart – and an economic class or two above – the black milieu unforgettably chronicled in the US by the late August Wilson, *Statement of Regret* seems in *numerous* ways to want to answer many of Wilson's ongoing concerns, adapting them for a UK audience. The result makes for an intriguing theatrical case of call-and-response, whereby one feels very directly the cultural and thematic baton being passed from one important dramatist to another' (Wolf, n.d.).

A number of thematic and situational similarities exist between Kwei-Armah's triptych and Wilson's ten-play cycle. In *Elmina's Kitchen*, Deli, an ex-boxer and reformed criminal, is determined to reform his and his son's life. The relationship is reminiscent of Wilson's *Fences* (1986). In *Fences*, Troy, the play's protagonist, like Deli, is an ex-convict and ex-sportsman whose dreams never came true and who struggles in his job to provide enough money for his family. However, the relationship between father and son in *Fences* is reversed in *Elmina's*. In *Fences*, Troy's jealousy prevents his son going to college on a football scholarship. In *Elmina's*, Deli is desperate to remove his son from a world of gangs and violence and his motives are entirely altruistic. Nevertheless, the father–son relationship is destroyed in both plays. The similarity lies in both works' exploration of the themes of failed ambitions, the inability of the father to prevent history repeating itself and of death. When *Elmina's Kitchen* was produced by Center Stage in Baltimore, the reviewer for *The Washington Post* could not help draw a comparison between Kwei-Armah and Wilson: '"Elmina's Kitchen" clearly owes a debt to, among other dramatists, Wilson; the play's setting – a funky diner in a marginal black neighbourhood is practically interchangeable with that of Wilson's "Two Trains Running"' (Marks, 2005).

However, while the setting may be familiar, the themes of *Two Trains Running* (1992) more closely resemble the issues explored in *Fix Up*. The setting of *Two Trains Running* in the declining neighbourhood of the Hill District in the 1960s, which was once a politically and culturally vibrant black area, resembles Brother Kiyi's struggling black-consciousness bookshop. In both plays, the setting (the restaurant in *Two Trains Running* and Brother Kiyi's bookshop in *Fix Up*) provides the locus for the exploration of a generational and gendered debate on approaches to black political activism and the route to self-determination. *Fix Up*, like *Two Trains Running*, stages an ideological debate through the conflicting viewpoints of its central characters. In *Fix Up*, Brother Kiyi's political stance is based on the belief that historical knowledge should be sought to bring about emancipation from 'mental slavery', whereas Kwesi views economic power as the best means by which to achieve self-determination. Through the mixed-race character of Alice, Kwei-Armah brings a critical voice to the Black Nationalist debate. Alice's arguments, for example her summation of Claude McKay's poem, *If We Must Die*, as 'sexist' because in it 'he only talks about the race by imagining the aspirations of men' (2009a, p. 126), highlight the hypocrisy of black men who critique white oppression yet continue to oppress black women.

In *Two Trains Running*, it is the character of Risa who fulfils this similar function. However, Kwei-Armah complicates the debate my making Alice mixed-race. As a mixed-race, or, as she points out, woman of 'dual heritage' (Kwei-Armah, 2009b, p. 130), her presence in the play not only exposes the male-centricity of black intellectual and political leaders but also her exclusion from black discourses of belonging as a mixed-race woman. She is treated with contempt by Kwesi who accuses mixed-race people of choosing their allegiance to black people only when it suits them:

> Kwesi: I don't trust you type of people. I see you coming in here trying to be down, so when the white man thinks he's choosing one of us you're there shouting, 'Hey, I'm black.' But you ain't. (Kwei-Armah, 2009b, p. 134)

Alice's search to find her black father and learn the truth about her white birth mother's identity echoes broader political debates raised in the play around racial belonging and highlights how Britain's growing mixed-race population poses a challenge to assumptions of how blackness and whiteness are defined and experienced.[5]

In the same way that a triptych describes three individual yet correlated pieces of art intended to be appreciated together, *Elmina's Kitchen*, *Fix Up* and *Statement of Regret* are linked by a common thematic thread: despite differences in age, gender, birthplace, sexuality and ethnicity, Kwei-Armah asserts that black commonality may be found in a legacy of oppression which began with slavery and continues to manifest itself in the present. The most striking echo between Kwei-Armah's triptych and Wilson's Pittsburgh Cycle is the treatment of the impact of the past on the lives of the characters.[6] The interplay between past and present is a hallmark of Wilson's work and defining element of his dramaturgy. In plays such as *Joe Turner's Come and Gone* (1988), *The Piano Lesson* (1990) and *Gem of the Ocean* (2004), Wilson inserts moments which pull apart the unities of time and place and force the characters into a space in which they must confront not only their specific pasts but the collective past of African Americans. It is only by going through this terrifying process that past injustices can begin to heal.

Wilson encases his explorations of the relationship between the past and present within a dramaturgy that melds realism with ritual, and which allows for the collapsing of the time and space of the present with that of the past. This unique style is achieved through a combination of music, African American folk traditions and mythology and ritual re-enactment. In *The Past as Present in the Drama of August Wilson*, Harry Elam writes: 'Wilson (w)rights history by invoking rites that connect the spiritual, the cultural, the social, and the political, not simply to correct the past but to interpret it in ways that powerfully impact the present.

In a space and time outside of time, within the liminal dimensions of theater, Wilson (w)rights history' (2004, p. 4).

In the same way, Kwei-Armah's plays attempt to access a larger cosmos. Although the settings of a café (*Elmina's Kitchen*), a book shop (*Fix Up*) and a small, floundering think-tank (*Statement of Regret*) are parochial, Kwei-Armah inserts devices that link the ordinary people of his plays with the larger historical events of the trans-Atlantic slave trade and colonialism. The plays' themes in common (inter-generational conflict, the struggle against racial oppression and the search for identity) are placed within a broader continuum of black experience. In *Elmina's Kitchen*, contemporary Hackney is firmly planted on the foundation of slavery. Elmina's Kitchen, named after Deli's mother, is also a reference to Elmina Castle, built in Ghana by the Portuguese in 1482, which later became a key slave trading post in the early seventeenth century. The reference to the Atlantic slave trade suggests, as Wilson does, that the origins of intra-racial violence lie in the violent historical treatment of blacks by whites. Although the references to slavery point to an under-lying cause of the intra-racial violence in the play, Kwei-Armah is also at pains to highlight that it is through knowledge of the history of black suffering and a connection with one's cultural and spiritual roots in Africa that black people in the diaspora can find healing.

Kwei-Armah also adds a 'griot' figure into *Elmina's Kitchen* who appears as a man in the prologue to Act One, and as a woman at the start of Act Two. Such figures occupy the position of mystic and signify the perform-ance's ritual element and link to Africa. In *Elmina's Kitchen*, the griots' appearances symbolise the play's connection with an original homeland and anchor its aesthetic choices and performance modes in a notion of an 'authentic' Africa to which the diaspora are direct inheritors of its cultural and spiritual traditions. From the onset, the play's prologue situates the play in this historical and ritualised time/space:

> The stage is in darkness. A single spotlight slowly reveals a costumed man, standing absolutely still with a gurkel (a one-string African guitar famed for possessing the power to draw out spirits) in his hands [...] The music starts. It is a slow lament-sounding concoction of American blues and traditional African music. The man then covers the length and breadth of the stage flicking handfuls of powder on to the playing area. (Kwei-Armah, 2009a, p. 5)

Traditionally, the West African gurkel is an instrument associated with exorcising malevolent spirits and the sprinkling of powder implies that the space is being consecrated and that a healing is about to take place.

Although there is no interaction between the African figure and the characters in the play, his appearance signifies the presence of the ancestral past in the present and suggests that the play is a ritual re-enactment that will bring about a healing by providing a bridge to the liberating space of the collective memory.

In *Fix Up*, the melding of past and present is more fully realised and embodied. The set, comprising towering bookshelves, encases the performance space. The towers of books draw attention to the substantial contribution of black intellectuals and artists, reinforcing the idea that the play's setting within a black-consciousness bookshop is a space that harbours the thoughts, dreams and creativity of the past contained within the tomes. The most vivid depiction of the melding of past and present occurs when Alice, alone in the shop, begins to read from a volume of slave narratives that Brother Kiyi has recently purchased. These slave narratives provide the catalyst for Alice's self-discovery. Alone in the shop, Alice begins to read aloud about a mixed-race slave from Grenada named Mary Gould. Gould recounts the difficulties facing the mixed-race 'yella' (Kwei-Armah, 2009a, p. 133) children who occupied a social positioning between the black slaves and the plantation owner's white children. Betrayed by her colouring, a visual reminder of the plantation owner's infidelity, Mary Gould was routinely whipped and then sold on by the owner's wife. The extract plunges Alice into the painful truth of her mixed-race ancestors. As she reads, she takes on the voice and persona of Mary Gould. The transformation is accompanied by a shift in the lighting state to a spotlight upon Alice and a physical transformation as Alice's voice changes and takes on a Grenadian accent. Possessed by the 'spirit' of Mary Gould, Alice is forced to confront an aspect of her history that had otherwise been unavailable to her growing up with white foster parents in Somerset. The event further provides Alice with an understanding of her feeling of dislocation in the present. She is now able to begin the process of coming to terms with growing up without a father and her isolation from her black heritage.

Kwei-Armah's debt to Wilson also has a political dimension located in Kwei-Armah's cultivation of a 'Black' aesthetic. Accordingly, Kwei-Armah's plays draw on a plethora of black British cultural and linguistic forms so as to represent the complex cultural heritage of the black community in Britain. Kwei-Armah acknowledges Wilson as an inspiration for this approach:

> What he was doing with the African–American community, with his own community in Pittsburgh, inspired me to create what I perceive as the theatre of my front room. Validating your language, giving

equal cultural status to the syntax, to the rhythm in which your own people speak: this is cultural equality. (Qtd. in Edwards, 2006)

Kwei-Armah does this deftly through his use of Caribbean and Black London vernacular, calypso and his representation of multiple generations with different cultural backgrounds. Kwei-Armah's self-described 'theatre of my front room' reveals a front room as a transnational hub through which diverse cultures move, meet and form anew. Through his plays' depiction of multiple generations and ethnicities, we are presented with the genealogical diversity of the black community, which encompasses different histories, cultures and geographies. The very specific stage directions, indicating the characters' accents, reveal his acute awareness of language as a primary marker of such complex identities. In *Elmina's Kitchen*, 'Digger's accent swings from his native Grenadian to hard-core Jamaican to authentic black London' (Kwei-Armah, 2009a, p. 6), Anastasia, who is black British, is able to use 'authentic, full-attitude Jamaican at the drop of a hat' (Kwei-Armah, 2009a, p. 17) and Clifton, who is from Trinidad, 'uses his eastern Caribbean accent to full effect when storytelling' (Kwei-Armah, 2009a, p. 34). Identity is further complicated in *Fix Up* through the character of Alice, who is mixed-race but was brought up in an all white environment, and whose physical appearance is in conflict with social assumptions. At one point, she remarks: 'Cos I'm brown, everybody expects me to somehow know everything black. And I'm like, 'Hey, how am I suppose to know what ... raaasclaat means, I'm from Somerset' (Kwei-Armah, 2009b, p. 128). The inclusion of multiple generations fulfils Kwei-Armah's aim to chronicle the black British experience by grounding it within its historical context, which takes into account the remembered history of colonisation, the Caribbean migration of the Windrush generation and the contemporary phenomenon of large-scale African migration to the UK.

The influence of Black Power politics and the Black Arts Movement

Kwei-Armah's approach to aesthetics is one that combines an educational aspect, demonstrative of his commitment to using theatre as a means to raise the self-awareness of his audience. When asked by Osborne if he agreed with Linton Kwesi Johnson that 'no black writer working in England today can afford "art for art's sake"', Kwei-Armah responds: 'Correct, and I believe in that. Let's not mince words here, my work is political work' (Osborne, 2007a, p. 253). The impact of Wilson on Kwei-Armah's playwriting, alongside cited influences such as Baraka and James Baldwin, places Kwei-Armah as an inheritor of the USA's 1960s Black Arts Movement (BAM).

Black Power cultural politics distinctly informs the aesthetic in Kwei-Armah's triptych. His plays are written with a black audience foremost in mind. The absence of white characters in all three plays signals Kwei-Armah's reluctance to enter into a discussion of racism or protest art that centres white people as the principal subjects by attacking them:

> I'm not interested in talking about race. What I'm interested in is presenting stories from my cultural lens that are about my humanity [...] What I'm saying is, we must not define ourselves purely in relation to racism. (Qtd. in Kwei-Armah et al., 2003)

Following the precedent set by the African American BAM, Kwei-Armah's aesthetic aligns ideological didacticism with black cultural forms in order to provide a vehicle for black-consciousness and self-determination. Like Anastasia's collection of self-help books she passes on to Deli in *Elmina's Kitchen*, the principle of self-help informs the message of Kwei-Armah's plays, which explain their multiple references to black intellectual, political and cultural icons.

In *Fix Up*, the space of the bookshop offers such a resource for the play's characters. In the dramatis personae Kwei-Armah lists three 'non-present characters': Garvey, Baldwin and McKay. Their presence throughout the play is given voice. For instance, at the start of the play, Brother Kiyi is playing a tape of one of Garvey's speeches; Brother Kiyi cites Baldwin in his conversations and Carl reads McKay's poem, *If We Must Die*. Through references and quotations, the intellectual, political and cultural life of these seminal black icons imbues the piece with their legacy and provides intellectual and spiritual nourishment to the characters and audience. Norma comments that Brother Kiyi has taught her to love herself: 'you love Black. And all of my life I have been taught to fear it, hate it. That ain't right!' (Kwei-Armah, 2009b, p. 119).

Kwei-Armah's authorial voice is clearly of the opinion that black improvement lies in knowing one's racial history. For those that embrace it, such as Deli, there is hope; for those that do not, there is despair, plainly demonstrated with Ashley's death at the end of *Elmina's Kitchen*. The need to know yourself, your roots and your people rings throughout the three works. For Kwei-Armah, pride in one's history is as important as coming to terms with the painful experience of the collective past. His plays provide a wealth of examples of extraordinary black achievement.

As he states in an interview: 'Art is there *solely* to reflect ourselves. And it is only in that reflection that we are able to be self-critical and able to improve and remove some of the subconscious inferiority that has been placed in us since slavery' (Qtd. in Davis, 2006, p. 243). Running in parallel with Kwei-Armah's depiction of characters struggling in life is a strong seam of positivity to bolster and nourish the audience and characters if they choose to see it. For instance, in *Fix Up*, which takes place during Black History month, the discussions between characters are peppered with historical information about Caribbean culture and how it was shaped by slavery, from people's names to the food they eat.

The didactic elements in Kwei-Armah's work operate on the level of character as well as dialogue. Kwei-Armah creates characters grounded in African mythology as a means to root his plays in an African cosmology, and, presumably therefore, to access a collective culture and memory shared between continental Africans and the diaspora. For example, in *Elmina's Kitchen*, Anastasia arrives unexpectedly carrying a home-made macaroni pie and looking for a job. Her superior cooking secures her the job, and she quickly becomes a major force of change in the play. She convinces Deli to clean up the image his restaurant is projecting by getting rid of patrons like Digger, whose presence Anastasia describes as giving off 'the stench of death' (Kwei-Armah, 2009a, p. 45). She also helps Deli to give the restaurant a fresh image, a new name, and exposes him to self-help books. Her positivity strengthens Deli's resolve to extricate Ashley from mixing with gangs. As a character, she is almost too good to be true. There is something artificial about her, leaving the impression that she is more archetype than a three-dimensional representation.

It is the macaroni pie, a traditional southern American 'soul food', that further hints at her more supernatural purpose. The power of food is not underestimated, as Digger comments before Deli takes a bite: 'Mind she obea you, boy!' (Kwei-Armah, 2009a, p. 18). Yet from his first taste of the food, Deli's life begins to change for the better and Anastasia secures a place in his life. As Harrison writes, 'Black Theatre is not merely the social inscription of victimization arrested in the lens of social realism' (2002, p. 5). Its critical engagement, he argues, requires an understanding of African diasporic cultural traditions: 'It is not uncommon to discover in the ritual forms of Black Theatre characters that are more representative archetypes than individuated, full-dimensioned characters located in the conventions of realism. Characters configured as archetypes serve a universe that allows both the living and the dead to drive the actions of a dramatic event' (Harrison, 2002, p. 5).

The stage directions describe Anastasia in such a way that supports this idea: 'we can see that she has the kind of body that most men of colour fantasize about. Big hips and butt, slim waist and full, full breasts' (Kwei-Armah, 2009a, p. 17). The description that stresses her African physicality renders Anastasia as representative of an African 'Earth Mother Goddess' archetype. Anastasia has come to save Deli and his family. Yet for all the positive change she brings, her influence is destroyed by the jealous Clifton, who sees her as a threat to his ambitions for his son's attention and financial assistance. Clifton seduces her and then threatens to expose her unless she leaves Deli. Here, Kwei-Armah critiques a male-dominated culture that has lost respect for its women and any spiritual connection to their goddesses. Osborne criticises this particular stage direction as one among other examples of 'sexual denigration' of women within the play (2006b, p. 92). Kwei-Armah's intentions, however, seen through a non-Western value system, are in fact the reverse. Yet, as Osborne's critique reveals, the stage direction exposes the heterosexist and patriarchal values of a traditional African world-view and of the Black Power movement. The play, therefore, reflects a conservative world-view by dint of it being rooted in 1960s Black radical politics. An American reviewer noted that the play dealt with themes that may be new to a British audience, but to an American one, it trod upon familiar territory pioneered by the likes of Langston Hughes and Wilson (Marks, 2005).

Another archetypal figure emerges in *Statement of Regret* through the character of Soby. When Kwaku is desperate for money to keep the business afloat, it is Soby who offers to help him on the condition that he rejects his African name and takes on his Caribbean birth name, Derek, and that he stands up against the Africans and asserts Caribbean superiority. This separatist approach within the multicultural office ends up destroying the organisation and Kwaku loses everything. It is only at the end of the play that we discover Soby is the ghost of Kwaku's father. Soby's function is to demonstrate the dangers of a separatist approach. Had Kwaku not been tempted into following a path of ethnic particularism but instead embraced one of Black solidarity, and instilled these values in his organisation, then, Kwei-Armah suggests, the think-tank might have survived. Kwei-Armah provides two possible endings for the piece. In the first (the ending staged at the National Theatre), Kwaku is left alone and confused and unsure of what he has done. However, the alternate ending (used in his radio adaptation) provides redemption. Lola his wife comes back to him and they are reconciled:

LOLA: ... The battle had changed, Kwaku. Maybe it's time we rest.
    Maybe it's time we let the young ones make their mistakes.
KWAKU: Maybe. Take me home, Lola. (Kwei-Armah, 2009c, p. 255)

In the first ending, Kwaku remains deceived and his life is in shreds. In the second ending, Soby brings about an eventual self-awareness. Although the latter ends on a note of hope, both versions convey Kwei-Armah's message to the black audience: united we stand, divided we fall.

The inclusion of archetypal characters is in line with Kwei-Armah's approach, which seeks to root his drama beyond the purely social and place it within a larger mythological cosmos of the African diaspora. However, Kwei-Armah's route to these African cultural practices is mediated through African America. This explains the almost romantic and non-specific employment of African forms. Although it is possible that Kwei-Armah sourced these archetypes from West African culture directly, as he never references African writers, it is plausible, as seen with his other depictions of Africa such as the gurkel player, that he has accessed such knowledge from African America. And it is this cultural and political resource, not Africa, which informs his aesthetic. This is particularly striking through the use of music in the plays.

The blues features prominently in *Elmina's Kitchen* and in *Fix Up*. In the prologue to *Elmina's Kitchen*, the African griot is accompanied by music described as 'a slow lament-sounding concoction of American blues and traditional African music' (Kwei-Armah, 2009a, p. 5). The mixture of American blues and African music traces in sound the movement of slaves from Africa to the USA. As the scene is meant to contextualise the action of the rest of the play, set in Hackney, the mélange of musical styles seems oddly placed. The music of the blues is used a second time at the opening of the second act during the funeral of Deli's brother, when the cast sing *You Gotta Move*. Kwei-Armah also uses the blues in *Fix Up*. At the end of the play, Brother Kiyi cuts off his dreadlocks and sings the blues slave chant *Adam in the Garden*. Tellingly, Kwei-Armah signifies slavery and its impact on contemporary black Britishness in such a way that does not yield identification with the African Caribbean experience but rather locates it in an African American context.

The blues permeates beyond providing a soundtrack to the plays to influence their tone. Kwei-Armah's plays tend to end on a melancholic note. *Elmina's Kitchen* ends with Deli covering the body of his dead son, in *Fix Up* Brother Kiyi is forced to leave his shop and has been exposed as a father who abandoned his daughter and in *Statement of Regret* the positive work of the think-tank hangs in the balance after Kwaku's nervous breakdown. Nevertheless, juxtaposed with these endings the plays balance moments of light heartedness, songs and comic relief. The result is a bittersweet tone that epitomises the blues. Although this tradition has nothing to do with Africa or the Caribbean, it seems Kwei-

Armah uses the blues not to signify cultural specificity, but rather as a means to evoke an atmosphere of shared history. In this way, its use can be seen as a 'call and response' with not only a musical form, but with African American dramatists such as Baldwin, Baraka and Wilson, who are renowned for infusing their work with the spirit of the blues.

Kwei-Armah is one of a number of black British playwrights, and artists more generally, influenced by the USA. This suggests that when analysing black Britishness in general and black British theatre in particular, a broader model than the nation is sometimes required if we are to account for the multiple strands of influence that impact on the work beyond the limitations of more obvious shaping factors such as birthplace and ancestry. Kwei-Armah's plays may document the black British experience and its links to the Caribbean and Africa; however, thematically, dramaturgically and aesthetically, they demonstrate the important impact of African American artists, thinkers and popular culture on the black British experience. Thus, Kwei-Armah's perspective that stretches beyond the confines of the nation problematises assumptions that practitioners 'from a particular place by default situate their writing in an aesthetic tradition that derives foremost from their own or their parents' or their grandparents' birthplaces' (Stein, 2004, p. 16). Furthermore, it should not be assumed that influences and tradition are necessarily inherited from previous generations. As John McLeod points out: if we only regard black *British* art within the space of the nation, then there is the danger of 'falsifying the mechanics of black British creativity and tradition'; if analyses become 'spatially constricted', this will impact negatively upon the way an artist's work is 'mapped, remembered and read' (2006, p. 98). Kwei-Armah's works reveal the complex lines of influence and exchange that have developed over time between global black communities. They highlight how black British culture and politics is shaped by its specific local situation and yet, is part of a larger global tapestry encompassing the spaces of Africa, the Caribbean, the UK *and* the USA.

Notes

1. *Elmina's Kitchen* was adapted for television and broadcast on BBC Four in 2005, and *Statement of Regret* was broadcast as a radio play on BBC Radio 4 in 2009.
2. The only exception is *Big Nose*, which is a Caribbean take on Rostand's *Cyrano de Bergerac*. The play is set between the Caribbean and the UK during the late 1950s.
3. In 2002, *King Hedley II* premiered in Britain at London's Tricycle theatre.

4. The Upper and Lower Clapton Roads in Hackney earned the nickname at the start of the 2000s. For example, see the article in *The Independent*, 'Eight men shot dead in two years. Welcome to Britain's Murder Mile' (Mendick and Johnson, 2002).

5. Nevertheless, by portraying Alice as *'beautiful but troubled'* (Kwei-Armah, 2009a, p. 100) Kwei-Armah adheres to dominant representations of mixedness, stretching at least as far back as Charlotte Bronte's depiction of Bertha Mason in *Jane Eyre* (1847), that is, dual heritage manifests in confusion, unbelonging and, at worst, psychosis.

6. See Kasule (2006) and Goddard (2011b), who both highlight this key aspect of Kwei-Armah's dramaturgy.

Part III
Neo-Millennial

Part III

Neo-Millennial

9
The Social and Political Context of Black British Theatre: The 2000s

D. Keith Peacock

This chapter will centre on the interrogation of two assertions: Andrea Enisuoh's (2004) 'a lot of people are saying that there's a renaissance of black theatre. Certainly over the last year there's been a huge frenzy of activity' (*Daily Telegraph*, 4 December 2004) and Lindsay Johns' (2010) controversial accusation that black theatre is 'cruelly blighted by the ghetto mentality which passes for the only acceptable face of black British culture' (*London Evening Standard*, 9 February 2010). With the new millennium, black drama was beginning to infiltrate the mainstream and thereby receive national critical attention. As in the 1980s critics (usually white and male) and funding bodies attempted to define and categorise black theatre, but now in the new theatrical and multicultural context. Concurrently the Arts Council reviewed its policy of ethnic diversity and recognised the need for financial aid to promote black theatre and widen its audience base. It is, therefore, the aim of this chapter to explore these factors in relation to funding by Arts Council England, to debates among critics, practitioners and, with reference to Social Psychology, to the work of dramatists themselves during the first decade of the new millennium.

Enisuoh's enthusiastic comment concerning the renaissance of black theatre is drawn from an article, 'It's boom time for black theatre – but will it last?' (2004). She was a member of a panel of black theatre practitioners including Kwame Kwei-Armah, Paulette Randall and Steven Luckie, which was convened by a theatre critic, Dominic Cavendish, to discuss the apparently sudden rise to prominence and status of new black drama. Luckie noted that Kwame Kwei-Armah's *Elmina's Kitchen* (2003) had been produced at the Royal National Theatre, followed two weeks later by Roy Williams' *Fallout* (2003) at the Royal Court, whereas debbie tucker green's *born bad* (2003) had been produced at the Hampstead Theatre. Luckie also drew attention to the fact that the audience at the National Theatre for *Elmina's Kitchen* consisted of not only white middle class but also black people. This was, however, almost certainly partly the result of Kwei-Armah's celebrity resulting from his appearance as a major character in the television soap opera, *Casualty*. Nevertheless, he and the other speakers were cautious about claiming that this represented a renaissance; 'there's a shift' concluded Luckie, but 'I wouldn't really say a renaissance, because I think we have to wait and see. It takes time to create a renaissance, not just a year' (Enisuoh, 2004). Certainly, in addition to its promotion by the individual theatres cited earlier, the rise in the profile of black theatre from the late 1990s had increasingly been the result of evolving Arts Council England policy and its offers of financial incentives for theatres to programme black plays. Only two years after this article Arts Council England (ACE) funded the Sustained Theatre consultation which resulted in the *Whose Theatre Is It Anyway?* report, which was by no means sanguine about the state of black British theatre. It stated that 'Since 1948 Britain has attempted to come to terms with its changing demography in a variety of ways. The artistic landscape has been changed. ... But real embedded transformation has proved elusive' (ACE, 2006a, pp. 4–5).

Deirdre Osborne has suggested, however, that the increased visibility of black drama has also indicated a shift by theatre managements themselves 'towards perceiving Black British drama as commercially viable, moving away from traditional assumptions of its genesis and productions as residing primarily within community or non-mainstream theatre contexts' (Osborne, 2006b, pp. 82–3). Although undoubtedly the appearance of plays by black dramatists in major metropolitan theatres marked a significant recognition of black drama, in fact much of the work was performed in a small number of metropolitan venues and often initially in studios. Only one play, Kwame Kwei-Armah's *Elmina's Kitchen*, had appeared in the West End, at the Garrick Theatre in 2005. The Royal Court had long supported new and young writers and it consistently encouraged young black writers as part of its various writers' groups, such as the Unheard Voices group (Rachel De-lahay) and the Critical Mass initiative (Bola Agbaje and Levi David Addai), which was part of the Royal Court's Young Writers programme. The theatre also promoted access by non-theatre-going audiences with its 'Theatre Local' project with Addai's *Oxford Street* performed in an empty shopping unit in Elephant and Castle in 2008, followed by, among other plays, debbie tucker green's *random* in

2010. Her *truth and reconciliation* and Rachel De-lahay's *The Westbridge* were also performed in the Bussey Building, an old cricket bat factory in Peckham, in 2011. In addition, the new dramatist, Oladipo Agboluaje, was established as the Soho Theatre's Playwright in residence 2007 during which he wrote *The Christ of Coldharbour Lane*. In 2002, under Trevor Nunn's Artistic Directorship, the National Theatre produced the *Transformations* season in support of new writing directed particularly at young audiences. The season consisted of eight new plays by black and white dramatists including Roy Williams, Tanika Gupta and Richard Bean, albeit performed in a temporary studio space called The Loft. In 2009, the small Tricycle Theatre promoted a season of three plays by black writers, *Not Black & White*. Two of the dramatists, Roy Williams and Kwame Kwei-Armah, were already well established, but the group also included a relatively new writer, Bola Agbaje. Its director, Nicolas Kent, justified the season in terms of London's changing social demographic.

> As we approached the end of the first decade of the twenty-first century, and across London black and Asian children outnumber white British children by about six to four, I thought it important and challenging to look at the society in which we live from the perspective of black writers. (Kent, in Agbaje, Kwei-Armah & Williams, 2009, p. vii)

The ratio of this changing racial demographic had been increasing since the beginning of the 1990s. According to a BBC London programme, 'The Changing Demographic of London' (15 March 2010), in 1991, the ratio of ethnic diversity of London was 80% white and 20% other. By 2007, this had changed to 69%–31%. The programme projected that by 2031 this would alter further to 60%–40%. It would seem that, in Kent's opinion, the racial minority of marginalised writers, rather than those of the white majority, was best equipped to explore how Britain should respond to the evolution of racial diversity with its concomitant ambiguities and complexities. It would also appear that, certainly in mainstream venues, such as the National Theatre and the Royal Court, with their predominantly white audiences, it was now necessary for black plays not simply to reveal the cultural practices of a marginalised ethnic group but to encompass a multiracial society.

As Aleks Sierz has explained in some detail, the post-millennial increase in black writing should not be seen in isolation from general trends in British theatre. As he records in *Rewriting the Nation* (2011), 'According to the latest Arts Council statistics, which cover 2003–8, 42 per cent of plays in a sample of sixty-five English theatre companies were new, ... which means that "new writing has grown dramatically as a category since the mid-1990s"' (Sierz, 2011, pp. 15–16). He also notes that since 2000 'more than 300 playwrights have made their debuts' (Sierz, 2011, p. 16). He claims, however, that this did not produce a unified school, style or even sensibility but 'instead ... what you had was a flowering of various sensibilities, a whole variety of voices' (Sierz, 2011, p. 26) of which a black perspective on contemporary Britain was one. Although there was no unified school or style, Sierz notes that 'for sheer verbal energy, black playwrights are outstanding' (2011, p. 53). National recognition of black drama was also promoted by the increased publication by Oberon Books, Nick Hern Books and Methuen Drama, of individual editions of plays by black writers, rather than, as in the 1980s and 1990s, their anthologising in collections of black plays.

After the boom of black drama and theatre in the 1980s, by the end of the 1990s the only black theatre company to survive Arts Council cuts was Talawa Theatre. The feeling amongst many black practitioners was that theatre at all levels was still controlled by white people. Despite the attempts of companies such as the Temba Theatre Company (whose Arts Council funding was withdrawn in 1992) to employ black actors, writers, directors and technicians, non-whites were still being marginalised. An attempt to alleviate this situation appeared in 1998 in the form of the ACE's Cultural Diversity Action Plan. The fundamental stimulus for the plan was the recognition that Britain was now a racially and culturally diverse nation and its aim was to tackle what was perceived by non-white writers and theatre practitioners as cultural inequality. Its plan was not to offer financial support to individual writers, but to create bureaucratic structures which would 'encourage' mid-range theatres, by means of funding, to consider black and Asian plays in their programming and thereby introduce the work to a wider British public and bring black and Asian drama from the margins at least *towards* the centre of British theatre.

The concept of cultural diversity does not sit well with those of art and creativity in that it is defined by committees and applied to the cultural rather than aesthetic evaluation of an artist's work. However, to its credit the Arts Council has kept its Action Plan under review and, since its inception, it has been subject to various surveys which themselves have led to further reports and the adjustment of funding practice and goals. The Arts Council's response to changing societal views of the role and status of minority groups gradually moved the focus for black theatre from community arts to that of professional playwriting. The first review was Naseem Khan's *Towards a Greater Diversity* in 2002, which examined the effects of the cultural diversity action plan whose aims she had herself initially inspired in 1976 with her publication, *The Arts Britain Ignores*. She recognised that, from 1994, 'cultural diversity' had been by definition primarily ethnic and was applied to 'Black, Asian and Chinese arts', although the Chinese have little comparable representation in the theatre (Khan, 2002, p. 5). In 2001 a Lottery funded Arts Capital Programme had adopted 23 Black and Asian projects and 'earmarked a budget of £29 million for Black and Asian projects overall' (Khan, 2002, p. 5).

It is questionable how far second-generation, Caribbean British people could be categorised justifiably as ethnic. Compared to Asian groups who associated themselves more closely with South-East Asian cultural, artistic, linguistic (non-English) and religious roots, for Caribbean-heritage people, this would mean steel bands, calypso, dance and carnival. The latter were indeed seen in the Notting Hill carnival, which also established a presence for the Caribbean community. However ethnic arts could be viewed as hardly relevant to the young second and third generations whose sense of identity as black British needed to be represented in forms of expression that embodied a new cultural ethnicity that, although containing white British and American cultural reference in terms of dress and music and language, also embodied Caribbean elements relating to such things as family structures, the roles of men and women and non-Standard English usage. Lindsay Johns (more of whom later), considered that black patois, while asserting difference, could also isolate the speakers from mainstream society. In *The London Evening Standard* (16 August 2011), in the wake of the summer riots, Johns dismissed the street language in the following terms: 'Embracing street slang leads to disenfranchisement, marginalisation and ultimately the dole queue. Embracing "proper English" unlocks an intellectual feast.' His major concern here appears to have been to encourage assimilation. However, as the contrast between Asian and black post-millennial plays illustrates, unlike South-East Asians whose families may attempt to assert the religious and cultural values of their homeland, black British teenagers were less concerned with assimilation or with maintaining or opposing the religious or cultural identity of a diasporic ethnic community, than with asserting questions of individual identity and status within their own immediate communities.

Access by black dramatists to middle-scale, mainstream theatres outside London was addressed at the Eclipse Conference which took place at the Nottingham Playhouse in June 2001 and was instituted by the ACE, the East Midlands Arts Board, the Theatre Management Association and Nottingham Playhouse. The conference sought to formulate strategies to combat institutional racism in theatre. Its report recommended the setting up of regional training days with Credibility Ltd and the Theatrical Management Association that would be directed towards helping senior management and boards of theatre companies to form their own positive action plans and review equal opportunities policies' (Khan, 2002, p. 7). By funding the Black Regional Initiative in Theatre (BRIT) from 2002, Arts Council England focused on providing black dramatists access to mainstream theatres by creating a regional network of theatres whose aim would be to develop Black and Asian work and audiences. BRIT funding went to the Nottingham Playhouse, the Leicester Haymarket, the Derby Playhouse, the Hudawi Centre and the Lawrence Batley Theatre in Huddersfield, The Green Room, Manchester, The Oval House London, The Wolsey Theatre in Ipswich, Kuumba in Bristol (which had its ACE grant cut in March 2008) and the Bristol Old Vic. Other regional theatres producing black drama were the Birmingham Repertory Theatre, the West Yorkshire Playhouse and The Sheffield Crucible. In London, outside BRIT funding, were the Theatre Royal Stratford East, The Hampstead Theatre and the Soho Theatre. The Eclipse conference resulted, in 2003, in the ACE's formation of the Eclipse Theatre Company, which was charged with raising the profile of black work by commissioning and touring 'quality' work (however that might be defined), developing and sharing good practice in training and employment, marketing and new writing. It would initially tour productions to the Bristol Old Vic, the Nottingham Playhouse and the New Wolsey, Ipswich.

Since 2010 Eclipse Theatre has been based in Sheffield (in addition to those theatres identified by the Eclipse project) as a black-led company that tours work written from a black perspective to a consortium of middle-scale *regional* theatres, thereby extending contact with black drama beyond metropolitan confines. According to its website, Eclipse Theatre toured eight productions between 2003 and 2010, four of which were new black plays: *Little Sweet Thing* and *Angel House* by Roy Williams, Kester Aspden's *The Hounding of David Oluwale* adapted by Oladipo Agboluaje, and *Michael X* by Vanessa Walters. Eclipse claims that these productions were seen by nearly 100,000 people, with an average of 29% new audience bookings for each production. Undoubtedly, the company has widened access to black drama and theatre (and to a limited extent), to new work by black dramatists, particularly in English regions such as Leeds, Bristol, Nottingham and Manchester where there have been historically, large black populations.

In 2002, Khan concluded that the diversity action plan 'had made progress' (Khan, 2002, p. 12) but she also recorded a growing opinion, that, 'in the long term, the category cultural diversity should become redundant. To get there, we need to adopt the key concepts: inclusivity, cohesion and respect' (2002, p. 13). In the light of such opinion, in 2006 ACE chose to remove the term 'cultural diversity' from its lexicon and to broaden its work to include 'age, class, faith, gender and sexuality; working with refugees and asylum seekers; and ... issues around community development such as urban regeneration, anti-poverty initiatives and the whole rural agenda' (Arts Council England, 2006b, p. 209). By 2010, Appignanesi argued in *Beyond Cultural Diversity: The Case for Creativity* that the arts should not be categorised in terms of ethnicity but instead attention should to be given to how racial minorities could be represented as a significant sector of a *United* Kingdom. According to this policy document, emphasis should be placed on promoting equality of opportunity and encouragement of multiple artistic voices and perspectives, as well as acknowledging the role that recognising diversity has had, in driving innovation in British theatre. It advocated that the earlier goal of access should be replaced by the recognition of the range and excellence of black theatre. Evocative of 'quality' mentioned earlier in relation to Eclipse Theatre's remit, it should be noted that the term 'excellence' has, since the late 1960s, persistently dogged Arts Council funding terminology. Both dramatists and journalists have consistently questioned the basis for its application. Certainly, in the absence of agreed criteria of excellence, the term is meaningless.

With black plays appearing more frequently in the new millennium on metropolitan and regional stages and the accusation that the term 'cultural diversity' did not represent a United Kingdom, the nomenclature 'black theatre' might now seem less than appropriate. Some black dramatists, including Roy Williams, do not think it timely to abandon the identification, 'black' when he states, 'Personally, I love the phrase "black Theatre", and I think we need it to ensure we are heard. "Theatre" sounds so po-faced and white; "black theatre" sounds intriguing, daring' (2009). However, like 'feminist' and 'political' theatre, the term can become a thematic straitjacket for dramatists and encourage a ghettoisation of their work, so that black theatre can be seen as only relevant to black audiences. Dawn Walton, the current director of Eclipse Theatre (successor to Michael Buffong who became Artistic Director of Talawa in 2012), insisted that we should not waste energy trying to define black theatre.

To define black British theatre in terms of race alone is to miss the point. Black practitioners are uniquely placed to deliver an incisive view of Britain today because we view it from two perspectives – black and white. We ask more questions, we challenge perceptions, we stimulate more debate. And this approach can only enrich the canon of British theatre. (2008)

Indeed, as I shall now illustrate, the post-millennial focus of black drama has moved beyond primarily black immigrant issues of diaspora, race and identity politics in an alien culture, to individual and social concerns in contemporary multiracial Britain, and this exposes the limitations of the term 'black theatre'. Therefore, as Walton suggests, black theatre should no longer simply be associated with specifically black racial or community themes but with a broader cultural perspective.

As the definition and inclusiveness of cultural diversity has gradually expanded in arts funding, so also have the themes and racial scope of post-millennial dramas by black writers. Whereas in the new millennium black dramatists were proclaiming the health of black theatre, Johns, a mixed-heritage writer and broadcaster, offered a radically different opinion of its nature and quality.

> There is actually something rotten in the state of black British theatre. With the exception of Kwame Kwei Armah and one or two other playwrights, on closer inspection black British theatre is languishing in an intellectually vapid, almost pre-literate cacophony of expletives, incoherent street babble and plots which revolve around the clichéd staples of hoodies, guns and drugs. In short, it is cruelly blighted by the ghetto mentality which passes for the only acceptable face of black British culture. (2010)

Johns' confrontational claim provoked a considerable amount of discussion on the newspaper's website both in support and opposition to it. What was also revealed was that he had no understanding of the complexity of dramatic discourse and was able only to read the contextual surface of the play's setting, while ignoring the narrative contained within it. In part, this was because his assertion was inspired by the upcoming production of Bola Agbaje's *Off the Endz*, which he had not and did not want to see, as he had already made up his mind about it from the title. The play's identifiable fault was, for Johns, that 'the "z" replacing the "s" suggests to me that it's going to be yet another derivative black street play, probably set on a council estate, and probably with lots of patois and pimp-rolling protagonists to boot' (Johns, 2010). In fact the play is about moral choice, social aspiration, mobility and class. Johns claimed also that a further two plays, Levi David Addai's *93.2 FM* (2006) and debbie tucker green's *random* (2008), 'can be categorized as being about guns, drugs and council estates. In 2010, the London theatre-going public is still being presented with the Theatre of the Ghetto' (Johns, 2010).

Contrary to Johns' assertions, post-millennial black British drama has begun to deal with concerns common to young people of many of Britain's communities who are marginalised by class, race or poverty and who are attempting to establish an individual identity in the face of peer pressure or wider social stereotyping. Many of the plays now reflect issues of multiculturalism, individual aspiration, hybridity and social location beyond the ghetto in contemporary Britain. Most significantly they also reflect a wider racial demographic than that of the earlier diaspora drama. These themes are promoted not by directorial demands, current theatrical stereotypes or by the requirements of diversity funding, but by personal experience of negotiating a place within a multiracial society. Two plays that exemplify aspects of the nature and progression of this trend are: Roy Williams' *Sing Yer Heart Out for the Lads* (2002) and Bola Agbaje's *Gone too Far!* (2007) that will be discussed later.

The majority of post-millennial black British drama explicitly identifies itself with contemporary social and cultural concerns, with realism as the predominant dramatic form (with the notable exception of tucker green's plays). Diasporic criticism is, therefore, no longer widely applicable. In response to the realist aesthetic, post-millennial critical analysis has inevitably focused primarily not on form but on content and has referred to non-dramatic methodologies such as identity theory, cultural studies, ethnicity, multiculturalism, gender and feminism as a means of focusing on, and elucidating dramatic themes. Although a play should not be treated as a sociological thesis, a methodology that offers structure and focus to the systematic analysis of identity politics in the context of multiculturalism and hybridity is that of social psychology. As defined by Henri Tajfel and Colin Fraser, it explores individuals' senses of who they are based on their group membership(s). 'Whether a creator or a creature of society, a person will bring about change or be changed himself through contact with others. Thus social interaction provides the mediating link in the three-level analysis – individual: group: society – which should be characteristic of social psychology' (Tajfel & Fraser, 1978, p. 99). This theory posits that groups give us a social identity – a sense of belonging to the social world. In order to increase our self-image we enhance the status of the group to which we belong and divide the world into 'them' and 'us' through a process of social categorisation. The in-group (us) will then discriminate against the out-group (them) by stereotyping. Groups can embody, for example, social class, race, family, football team or gang membership. The theory further suggests that an individual's social behaviour varies according to the particular influence of interpersonal behaviour and intergroup behaviour. The former is determined by individual characteristics and interpersonal relationships and the latter by the social group with which the individual identifies. The methodological focus offered by such a theory is self-evidently applicable to the dramatic analysis of the individual as represented in relation to a racial and cultural group, a major feature of post-millennial black British drama.

In Roy Williams' *Sing Yer Heart Out for the Lads* the xenophobia of supporters watching the 2000 England versus Germany World Cup football qualifier offers an emotive context for the exploration of national identity in terms of social psychology. The symbolic setting of the play in the King George Public House (decorated with flags of St George) represents a microcosm of English society, an outpost of Englishness in a racially mixed urban area 'that is going nowhere' (Williams, 2004, p. 137). The constitution of this society is conveyed by the dominance of white characters. The characters are divided among three social and two racial groups representing a variety of attitudes to race – the white pub family – Gina, Jimmy and Glen; the two black adolescents, Bad T and Duane and Duane's mother; two black brothers, Mark and Barry; the white football team (for whom Barry plays) and the white racist British National Party members – Alan and Lawrie. As they watch the football match the personal and racial intergroup behaviour reveals a variety of racist attitudes ranging from ostensibly personal tolerance by the pub's landlady Gina, who has had a sexual relationship with Mark the black ex-soldier, to the racism of the representatives of the BNP. In between are Glen, white, and Barry, black, both of whom want to move along the social continuum from white to black or black to white. White Glen tries to speak black street talk and wants to be accepted into the black 'gang' of Bad T and Duane. The 'gang' is a figment of Bad T's imagination and is simply his adolescent attempt to establish individuality and 'respect' within his community. However, rather than merely portraying interaction between representative individuals and groups, characteristically Williams deconstructs the group stereotypes and undercuts audience expectations. Gina, the pub landlady, has ended her relationship with Mark. Because of his sensitivity to racism, he believes that this is because he is black. However, Gina informs him that in fact it was because he was boring.

The political racist, Alan, has stereotyped Mark as an uneducated black squaddie, an example of the white in-group discriminating against the black out-group. Williams challenges this stereotype, dumbfounding Alan with Mark's countering of his racist diatribes through lucid, historically knowledgeable argument. Mark is more intelligent and better read than Alan's other targets, Barry and Lawrie, and is able to respond in kind, by challenging his appropriation of 'Englishness'.

Mark: How English are you? Where do you draw the line as to who's English. I was born in this country. And my brother. You're white, your culture comes from northern Europe, Scandinavia, Denmark. Your people moved from there thousands of years ago, long before the Celtic people and the Beeker people what? You think cos I'm black, I don't read books. Where do you draw the line? (Williams, 2004, p. 218)

There is no such thing as racial or cultural purity. The play ends neither with one group dominant nor with a consensual multicultural respect for others' beliefs. Britain has not replaced racism with multiculturalism and, as the play implies, until a better way is found to accommodate the various groups that constitute Britain's multiracial society, dissent will repeatedly take the form of violence.

Another significant change in the black British demographic began in the 1980s, with the permanent migration of large numbers of Nigerians as a consequence of the collapse of the country's petroleum boom and peaked in 1995 as a result of the military dictatorship of Sani Abacha. There was now a black African presence that brought with it a first-generation ethnicity, which in some ways was alien not only to the white population, but also to the Caribbean community. Alongside these immigrants were numbers of migrants from Ghana. Racism now took a more complex form unrelated to white attitudes, emerging between those of Caribbean-heritage, Africans and, to a lesser extent, South-East Asians. As a result of this newer African presence in Britain, during the past decade there has not simply been an increase in new black British writing, but also a broadening of racial perspectives to reflect new forms of racial tensions, identity politics, assimilation and hybridity, and accompanying conflicts of similarity and difference, within an ethnically diverse British society.

In the light of her Nigerian background, Bola Agbaje's comedy drama, *Gone too Far* (2007), offers an even more complex opportunity for the application of social psychology to individual identity politics than *Sing Yer Heart Out for the Lads* – this time from an African British perspective and in the context of intraracial tensions, histories and cultural identities. The play was the outcome of the Royal Court's Young Writers Festival in 2007, and, like Williams, Agbaje interrogates the success of

British multiculturalism to reveal a disunited society. Agbaje extends the reference to racial groups from simply black and white to reveal tensions also within the black community between Africans, Caribbeans and Asians (whom Whites treat as one racial group). The play also illustrates what Stuart Hall has described as 'New Ethnicities'.

> If the black subject and black experience are not stabilized by Nature or by some other essential guarantee, then it must be the case that they are constructed historically, culturally, politically – and the concept which refers to this is 'ethnicity'. The term ethnicity acknowledges the place of history, language and culture in the construction of subjectivity and identity, as well as the fact that all discourse is placed, positioned, and situated and all knowledge is contextual. (Hall, 1992, p. 257)

The setting for the play is a racially mixed, council estate that is 'run-down, with graffiti all over the walls' (Agbaje, 2007, p. 7). Each scene of the play centres around the African British youth, Yemi's, conflict with characters from a variety of racial and social groups and reveals his and other's racial stereotyping. Central to the audience's reception of the play is Agbaje's use of language, which ranges from Nigerian Yoruba (which would be alien to both white and many black audience members), English spoken in a black urban street dialect, with pseudo American, Caribbean, African and Bangladeshi accents, officious English and parodies of street talk and Caribbean dialect. The auditory effect in itself conveys a multiracial and divided nation.

The play centres on two teenage Nigerian brothers. One of the brothers, Yemi, has a complex relationship to his social group. He was born in Britain and, while maintaining a separate identity from the local gang culture, he wants to identify with his black peers and to be liked by a local black girl, Paris. Yemi's brother, Ikudayisi, is a recent immigrant who has lived most of his life in Nigeria and attempts fiercely to maintain his cultural identity in terms of his indigenous language and history, but occasionally adopts an incongruous black American accent with the intention of conveying street awareness. He is nevertheless a cultural outsider in his brother's south-London estate and, indeed 'us' and 'them' is the basis for all the interactions and the phrase 'you people' is used both by Yemi and the mixed-race girl Armani.

The play's structure is that of a journey by the boys through the neighbourhood space, in order to buy milk. On the way, they meet various members of the community who serve to reveal a range of individual cultural and historical attitudes to racial identity. Each interaction contains a confrontation provoked by group stereotyping. Agbaje emphasises the prevalent racism that militates against the unity of any multicultural project. Yemi responds to a patriotic Bangladeshi British shopkeeper (who refuses him entry to his shop because of how he perceives Yemi's hoodie) with a familiar white racist tenet of 'Smelling of curry, coming over here, taking all the corner shops' followed by a patois-redolent, 'Dem people are racist, they don't like black people, and I don't like them either' (Agbaje, 2007, pp. 11–12).

The additional complexity of this non-white racism is revealed when the boys meet a group of Yemi's teenage acquaintances. In this key scene, Agbaje illustrates, through a step-by-step illustration of identity politics, the incongruities, contradictions and ignorance produced by racism. The most racist of the group is the mixed-race girl, Armani, whose view of Africans is that they are *black black* and have big lips and noses and were responsible for the slave trade. She is of Caribbean descent, her skin is light and she claims to be Jamaican but because her mother is white, refuses to acknowledge the seriousness of white people's contribution to slavery.

The message of the play is embodied in the gang leader Blazer's recommendation to Yemi 'to stand your ground, but keep it real at the same time. It's not a bad thing to be African. Be proud to be different' (p. 53). The play suggests that one's personal identity is formed by a combination of awareness of the positive psychological contribution of origin from one racial, cultural or social group, while privileging one's individuality in a current social group. Agbaje therefore constructs this 'New Ethnicity' in terms that echo Hall's definition, applying history, language, culture and contextuality 'in the construction of subjectivity and identity' (Hall, 1992, p. 257).

The social group and along with it, dramatic social realism, thematic and geographic parochialism, is abandoned by debbie tucker green. She instead explores, from a black women's perspective, universal social, sexual and domestic concerns and international conflict through poetic free-flowing dramatic structures in which the material environment plays no part and her characters' psychology dictates their behaviour. The dramatic structure informs and extends the content. During a performance, the audience inhabits the characters' minds rather than, as in the social realism, responds to their physical and environmental presence. In tucker green's plays the audience is required simply to observe behaviour and, in a post-modernist manner, to piece together the narrative and draw their own conclusions. In *dirty butterfly* (2003), during the first act of the play the characters sit on stools in a

Pinteresque limbo reminiscent of his *Silence* (1969), except that, where in the latter the actors are distanced on proscenium or end-stage, here they are surrounded by the audience. The audience can therefore see each other as well as the actors and are drawn into a sense of mutual implication in relation to the subject matter. Like Amelia and Jason, the audience is overhearing other's lives. It is positioned to decide if any one of the three characters is morally at fault – Jo who accepts her partner's violence, Amelia, who feels she cannot help and considers Jo an unwarranted intrusion into her life or Jason, who is sexually stimulated by the violence that he overhears from next door. The fact that Amelia and Jason are black and Jo is white does not imply a racial standpoint but universalises the topic. In the second act the play's setting transfers to the realistic context of the cafe that Amelia cleans. This both conveys her unwillingness to accommodate psychologically anything distasteful, and reveals the working-class social group to which Amelia belongs. Jo's intrusion and her 'soiling' of the cafe with her blood therefore assault not only Amelia's senses but also threaten her security of employment. Once again, it is left to the audience to decide whether Amelia's resentment of Jo is morally and socially justifiable.

In response to social and cultural changes within Britain in the new millennium the dramatic themes in black British plays have extended beyond social concerns within the black British community such as the drugs, gangs, knife and gun crime still seen in 2003 in Kwame Kwei-Armah's *Elmina's Kitchen* and Roy Williams' *Fallout*. They now encompass the politics of identity among young people within a range of racial groups, explore the possibility of transference from one social group to another and, particularly in the case of tucker green, examine universal human and social issues from a black female perspective. The predominant social and cultural concern for Britain in the New Millennium is not, as it was in the 1950s, 1960s and 1970s that of class politics, but an understanding of the evolution and nature of new ethnicities, which these and other black dramatists explore, and which white dramatists, for the most part, are still unwilling to contemplate.

10
Resisting the Standard and Displaying Her Colours: debbie tucker green at British Drama's Vanguard

Deirdre Osborne

Toril Moi identifies feminist semiotician Julia Kristeva's fundamental project as being 'the desire to produce a discourse which always confronts the *impasse* of language (as at once subject to and subversive of the rule of the Law), a discourse which in a final aporetic move dares to think language against itself' (Moi, 1986, p. 10). debbie tucker green's inimitable dramatic–poetics in many ways shares this impetus in her creation of a linguistic arsenal by which words seem to attack and counter-attack the bounds of syntax. At the same time, if not paradoxically, her technique renders the lines lyrical and articulable, in allowing threads of narrative meaning to emerge. The tension achieved between her writings' lyrical fluidity, and its dramatic realisation through discomposure (by grammatical disruption and uncompromising material), signals that she is creating a process of cultural innovation and renovation. Not only does her written play text serve as a precise roadmap of intra- and trans-linguistic directives for the actor to enunciate, it highlights as well its grapholectic strategies to the reader, a performativity distinct from its physical dramatisation possibilities.[1] Her plays consistently upend customary expectations in casting, acting, staging and reception within the contemporary British theatre complex.[2]

tucker green's playwriting career begins with her first play (unpublished), *She Three* (1999), short-listed for the Alfred Fagon Award. Its production genesis began as *Stratford* (2000), for the Paines Plough Wild Lunch IV series, inspired by the Jubilee line of the London Underground. Of nine playwrights, she and Amy Rosenthal were the only women, reflecting perhaps, the characteristic male dominance of British play-writing. Titled as *Two Women* (2000), this first play was directed by Rufus Norris (who directed her next play, *dirty butterfly*), for the Soho Theatre's Bloomberg Bites lunchtime programme. Such writer–director continuity, which is vital for a playwright's evolution (cf. Phillips, 2005, p. 16), is again noticeable in a longstanding collaboration with Sacha Wares, who has directed three of five plays, and with her radio production history with Mary Peate.[3] Her collaboration with Wares, a Royal Court Associate Director of many years' standing, is uncharacteristic. Typical theatre commissioning approaches towards black dramatists' work have been to use a white male director, or a black director contracted especially, with productions generally staged in a fringe or an off-West End venue. tucker green's developing international presence has seen *stoning mary* (2005), the most performed: across Europe, the USA, the Antipodes – perhaps due to its casting directive, 'The play is set in the country it is performed in. All the characters are white' (tucker green, 2005a, p. 2). *born bad* (2003) has garnered an OBIE Special Citation for its American premiere (SoHo Rep, New York, 2011) and a Best Director award for Leah C. Gardiner. tucker green has directed her latest plays, *truth and reconciliation* (2011) for the Royal Court Theatre and *nut* (2013), a Royal National Theatre commission where it was staged in the annex of The Shed rather than within the main theatre complex. Most recently, her move into television saw *random* (2008) as adapted and directed by her, receive a BAFTA award for Best Single Drama (2012). She has just completed her debut feature film *Second Coming* with Nadine Marshall who has starred in the majority of tucker green's work.

As a black female writer in a white-male-dominant artistic milieu, tucker green's aesthetic displays many characteristics that connect her to her women forebears, and a variety of socio-cultural legacies (understood here as the inter-relational matrix of race, sex-gender, nation and class categories). She acknowledges the influences of songwriters: Beverley Knight, Lauren Hill, Jill Scott; the impact of Ntozake Shange's choreo-poetics, Louise Bennett's dub poetry and Caryl Churchill's overlapping dialogue technique. Discernible too, are African American, Pulitzer Prize-winning, dramatist, Suzan-Lori Parks' dynamic silences and body–word synthesis, in which reading and writing are an inseparably and viscerally personified process. As Parks records, 'something that involves yr whole bod./ Write with yr whole bod./Read with yr whole bod' (Parks, 1995, p. 18).[4] Together with her British-born peers Kwame Kwei-Armah, Roy Williams and Bola Agbaje, tucker green has achieved certain permeation of the mainstream British theatre complex, although within a carapace of social realism, to which tucker green is arguably the only challenger, both experimentally and experientially.

This chapter places tucker green's work within traditions of women's experimental writing, where her intricate plaiting of African-diasporic and European-inflected inheritances charts a unique course beyond the confining theatrical and aesthetic parameters that Black British dramatists have faced in a white-hegemonic world. In order to navigate her story through the oceans of history, women writers' textual strategies have been both linguistically Luddite and ludic: in frame-breaking rebellion against the constrictions of linguistic structures that have reinforced patriarchal socio-cultural privilege, and in the playfulness of linguistic free-fall and rearrangements. In the same vein, the chapter distinguishes tucker green as the most stylistically innovative, and uncompromisingly poetic, dramatist in contemporary British theatre. Through analysing aspects of *dirty butterfly* (2003), the discussion will explore perspective and temporality through dramatic utterance. It considers, briefly, a theatrical ritualisation of death in relation to *generations* (2005) with reference to *random*, and monodrama as a form which interfaces techniques and traditions of performance poetry and drama in performance.

To purloin Marjorie Perloff's phrase 'radical artifice' (1991, p. 27), and apply it to tucker green's dramatic–poetics, addresses the tendency in critical reception to lace tucker green's work to social issues-based interpretations and contiguities. Such an approach curtails the epistemological restructuring process that playing and reading her lexis demands.[5] In terms of identity politics (which has historically dominated interpretive possibilities), tucker green's profile might elicit a wide range of inheritances from theatre and social and political heritages. She is a British woman playwright who inherits in-roads made by the late-twentieth-century coterie of Caryl Churchill, Pam Gems (1970s), Nell Dunn, Liz Lochead, Jacqueline Rudet, Winsome Pinnock (1980s), Sarah Kane, Rebecca Prichard (1990s) – to indicate a few key figures. tucker green is also a London-based writer in a theatrical context where, with only one exception (*White Open Spaces*, 2004), the dramatising of black people's experiences in Britain correlates primarily to urban spaces (and what have become negative associations of ghettoisation, socio-economic disenfranchisement and dysfunctionality). She can be located culturally as a Black British dramatist, one of a generation of writers born and raised in the UK, who have not lived directly the migratory dimension of diasporic identity, but are the consequences of settlement and are indigenes. She also writes informed by the spectre of socio-cultural derogation, namely, imperialism and – its foremost consequence – racism, which has variously effaced or distorted the historical existence of a black theatre legacy in Britain.

Nevertheless, tucker green's unique dramatic–poetic signature prevents the diminishment of her drama to identity politics – despite the best efforts of the white-male-dominant critical circles, or some emergent academic work.[6] As a means of charting social and political positions within contemporary culture from black citizens' perspectives, it must be remembered that identity politics is circumstantially specific rather than monolithic. This does not discount on-going and significant continuities in oppression and repression. It is to recognise that the tangle of generalisations, when teased apart, show differentiation, subtlety and nuance. Its use as a basis for creative work reflects the status of difference over time, raising questions about the primacy of black writers' experiences, their aesthetic rendering of these and the intellectual traditions by which their writing has been, and is critiqued. An identity politics focus has obstructed the recognition of contemporary texts' creative design in all its rewarding detail.

Before investigating the selected plays it is necessary to establish what it is about tucker green's aesthetic spectrum that implicitly contests the essentialism wrought by phrases such as 'the black community' or 'black aesthetics' and the ways in which her dramatic–poetic language registers the plurality and variegation of Black British writing. Although the projects of neo-millennial black writers differ to the previous generations', these earlier projects are frequently the measuring sticks designating success and failure, just as European aesthetic principles have been. Black indigenous British writers' progressive (in the sense of increasingly, *and* reforming *and* innovative) movement away from multicultural relentlessness, or, British identity reconfigurations as the main expressive preoccupation, finds its apotheosis in her dramatic corpus.

As Moi encapsulates Kristeva's semiotic investigations, tucker green's dramatic–poetic technique likewise alerts us to 'what it is that *resists* intelligibility and signification' (Moi, 1986, p. 90).[7] Resistance is always a productive route for artists as a means of generating generic and thematic boundary stretching. Testing the tensile strength of a creative idea, can be an (ir)resist(ible) impetus. Resistance can function as a rejection of categorisation or containment within prevailing socio-cultural labels, through an exertion of one's own terms. tucker green's artistic standpoints and practice support this duality, recalling Harryette Mullen's 'resistant orality', an articulatory strategy in African American women's enslavement narratives (1992, p. 244). Yet, as Mullen has oppositely also taken issue with black literary traditions which unilaterally privilege orality and a phonetically rendered black poetic diction on the page, so too do tucker green's printed texts exhibit a grapholectic performativity that embeds them within written heritages. The published text remains a decisive determiner of artistic longevity. Whereas her play text's live theatrical performance is ephemeral, her printed text remains for perpetuity, as written language. tucker green's poeticity hones its literary profile, while securing the promise of its dramatic durability.

Kathleen Crown makes the point that language writing actively disrupts the public performed, oral origins, common to both lyric and contemporary spoken word poetry (and by extension, to acted drama), which encourage conjuring the poet's voice as a representational self with whom the reader (or listener) can identify. Language writing, she expounds, 'complicates this identification between audience and speaker, deflecting the reader into language and away from the poet. In this way, language-based writing avoids the naïve assertion of "natural speech" as truth' (Crown, 2002, p. 216). tucker green's dramatic–poetics subtly evinces this displacement, deflection and estrangement from the veil of natural speech and biographical attribution. Her words urge an audience member and reader into unfamiliar ways of listening to dramatic text in performance *and* to the introspective reading voice of the page. She does not employ British Black Vernacular English (recalling African American Vernacular English) that her contemporaries Williams, Kwei-Armah and Agbaje have tended towards in their social–realist work. Nor does she employ a patois-esque stage idiom of Winsome Pinnock, Doña Daley or Courttia Newland, even though the pronunciation of her stage language by some actors can evoke this in response to the printed text's phonetic and contracted forms. A case in point, *truth and reconciliation* sees her distinctive dramatic–poetics rendered in print with conventional rather than phonetic spelling. A variety of trans-national accents might be decided upon to dramatise its characters from: Northern Ireland, Rwanda, Bosnia, Zimbabwe and black and white South Africans. However, even if shaped by actors' multi-accented distinctions, tucker green's dramatic–poetics as a stage lingua franca, remains noticeable – in a dimension of its own – as a poetically memorable score that conveys sonically, the play's performed national, political and personal identities, but is not subordinate to them.

Typographically, her use of lower-case lettering, sparse punctuation, end-dash or hyphenated sentences suggests a simultaneous pull between linguistic rules and their disruption. This implicit *a priori* critique or dissatisfaction with what standard grammar offers evokes Rosemarie

Waldrop's promotion of 'the liberating effects of constraints' (Waldrop, 1987, p. 197). The temporal and linguistic constraints that tucker green resists *and* creates – in returning to Waldrop's phrase – are locatable in this chapter's three sampled plays. Stylistic compression is evident through unity of time and place (one day, one afternoon or indeterminate time passing, one setting); non-straightforward structure (cyclical, sometimes chronological or anachronic); interrupted text (reinforcing the actors' responsibility as bearers of the lines, to make continuity from syntactical shards) and its delivery (conveyed by an economy of vocabulary and stage directions). In performance, orature dwarfs physical enactment. Actors' bodies are directed to be characteristically still in the majority of productions, her own direction of *truth and reconciliation* notwithstanding. The acting space is generally condensed even if it exists within a large playing area. Thus, tucker green's corpus utilises a less-is-more design, effected by working (mostly) with small casts, employing shorter than conventional running times, omitting intervals and in her use of pared-down language, single-set locations or minimal props. This minimalism, however, does not lessen her dramas' impact.

Through frequently mundane settings, tucker green's plays can portray extreme subject matter (murder, domestic violence, incest, genocide, civil war, epidemic), contained within the precision and concision of a spartan vocabulary signified (paradoxically) by endless multi-vocality. This is derived from repetition, internal echo, call and response; a rhythmic phonetics redolent of rap and ebonics; her collaging and sampling of the play's own text, as well as features identifiable by classical rhetoric's technical terminology (as component of the trivium of grammar, rhetoric and logic). Although beyond the remit of this chapter, analysis of any passage of tucker green's writing is fertile ground for discovering classical examples – intriguing given her counter-canonical impetus. Her stage language is grounded in a modest but pointedly powerful syntax that reinforces the emotional depth and complexity of her characters' communications, confirming that less *is* more.

This is evident in *dirty butterfly* and its graphic evocation of abjection, for which there is no rational discourse, in a context of domestic violence. tucker green employs a triologue form (until the Epilogue), to entwine three characters, Jo (white), with her (apparently co-habiting) neighbours Amelia and Jason (both black), into one consciousness. Although their speaking selves are split from each other by a physical wall between apartments, the characters cross porous borders of one another's perceptions, accessing each other's responses to Jo's nocturnal beatings from her nameless male partner. A catalyst and referent, he never appears on-stage.

Jo delineates the sadism to which she is subjected; Jason becomes increasingly obsessed with her nightly brutalising on which he eavesdrops addictively; Amelia sleeps downstairs to avoid it. The Epilogue (without Jason) relocates the action to the café where Amelia works as a cleaner, and is visited by Jo, injured to the point where she gruesomely expels blood and vomit on the clean floor.

Jo, Jason and Amelia's situation is marked by temporal changes between night (when Jo is attacked by her partner), and day (the Epilogue in the café), but it is non-chronological and non-linear. The audience are left uncertain of the sequence of events and this sharpens the focus on domestic violence as experienced as inexorable, reinforcing its nightmarish repetition. Only Jo's death would release all characters' entrapment within its certainty, as she will not leave the murderous perpetrator. tucker green creates an osmotic effect when characters access each other's perceptions. This aesthesis exploits both the suspension of belief theatre-going requires, and mirrors the convention of audiences' omniscient access to characters' thoughts and perceptions. Characters' interwoven thoughts ebb and flow in direct, yet, indirect conversation – a complex witnessing, confessional, eavesdropping – testifying to the successful baton passing required for performing as a triad, an experience from three perspectives. Such interlacing makes extracting quotations from the body of the play something of a mutilating manoeuvre, and difficult to effect concisely. The following excerpt confirms Kristeva's thesis of the dynamic and unrepresentable poetic aspect of language, which maintains a separate aesthetic identity, irreducible to the language of communication. The word, 'hear' considered as both poetically resonant, *and* as communication (when repeated throughout the passage), reveals breathtaking textual complexity (to perform it *and* to appreciate it grammatically). Hearing is the instructive sense in Aristotle's sensorial hierarchy. Hearing and listening are processes under scrutiny. The audience both hears and sees the play performed, Jason and Amelia overhear, Jo is hyper-aware of what her partner hears her doing. Each character's individual lines can stand alone monologically and yet, can be dialogic in differing combinations – depending on the weave. Overall, the effect of the triologic apportioning is to ramp up the intensity of their precipice-edge existence.

AMELIA: Jo
JO: And I look beside me to/check –
JASON: *Amelia*
JO: I take a peep, shift a touch, ease up –

JASON:	from under
JO:	Ease out
JASON:	from beside him
JO:	and creep out
JASON:	of their bed.
AMELIA:	Jason.
JASON:	She does –
JO:	I do, Amelia.
JASON:	I hear, Amelia.
JO:	I hear him hearing...
	...I hear him hearing me hear.
	And he knows it. (tucker green, 2003b, pp. 13–14)

Amelia has merely two utterances: 'Jo' and 'Jason', signalling her side-lining in what eventuates as their perverse eroticising of the situation. Jason's italicised '*Amelia*' alerts the actor or reader to an emphasis and a choice of selectable standpoints: irritation? exasperation? mollification? Simultaneously inside and outside each other's apartments via these furtive sensory perceptions, they are set on a heightened collision course. Such abstraction does not lessen its visceral impact. Reviewer Kate Bassett (who first extolled tucker green's virtuosity) notes of Norris' production, 'I left this play feeling as if I'd been punched in the throat' (2003, p. 251) while another advocate of tucker green's work, Lyn Gardner admits, 'I cannot say that I enjoyed it very much, but I liked it a great deal. And now I cannot get it out of my head' (2003, p. 252).

However, their propinquity does not extend to action, to prevent the abuse. Jo's and Jason's bodies might be a jumble of drives (pulsions) and states, almost undifferentiated psychically in their utterances, but the play never places them physically together. If communities function through interaction, this also involves 'the strain of dealing with other people, the effort of coping with the products of group activity, such as noise, trash, and the work necessary to make communication possible' (Jones, 2003, p. 662). Callous non-intervention is related to social disintegration. As the ability to act is at the root of power, the inability to act (in this instance due to the presence of another) appears to weaken learned social reflexes – of intervening to stop violence. Instead a bleak, urban dislocation and lack of community results. Its articulation occurs in an interlocked syntax, which requires exemplary interaction and ensemble-playing to achieve performable coherence and cohesion.

Jason and Amelia's inactivity parallels audience restraint (although an audience is a unique gathering, not daily neighbours), and spotlights the collective power to impose inaction upon individuals through psychological inhibition. A counter-pull persists between the staged social alienation of the characters and the impediment to communitas for its audience. tucker green's stage directions specify, 'The audience should surround the actors' (2003b, p. 2). Audience members are in view of each other watching the taboo material, aware of one another in proximity to the staged hyper-real, sensory interaction. Like Katrina Lindsay's vertiginously raked structure in Norris' production, in revival (Dir. Michael Longhurst, Young Vic, London, 2008), Garance Marneur's Stalinist-housing-block-evoking, halved, concrete, cuboid structure, was responsive to the precariousness conveyed by the play's representational elements. Longhurst's direction invited scrutiny of who is in the worst position. Until the Epilogue, all the characters' interactions were located on the concrete blocks. Audiences were boxed-in, inhabiting the periphery of the studio space. The set's grey impenetrability, its inferred inhospitable chill and the actors' minimal movement fortified the physical and psychological inertia, as contrasting to the buoyancy of the verbal and non-verbalised text. Actors' positions visually interrupted the straightforward grid perspective that cuboid forms invite and underscored the discomposure of moral norms.

Although negativistic, there are glimmers of salvation. Amelia's decisive 'No' truncates Jason's temptation in the opening, signalling her refusal to be drawn into the dysfunction.

JO: You ever –
JASON: found yourself doin something you can't help.
AMELIA: You ever –
JASON: gotcha self doin somethin you can't stop.
          Beat
          'Melia?
AMELIA: No. (tucker green, 2003b, p. 3)

Although she does not reject or repudiate Jo's dire situation, Amelia will not be edged out or dominated by abjection. She appears to offer audiences a more normal set of responses, a tempting identification as a point of relief from the perverse connection between Jason and Jo. However, tucker green undermines this with Amelia's desperation in inviting Jason (unsuccessfully) to her bed. It is never established whether or not Amelia and Jason are a couple, an estranged couple or simply flatmates, or that they even share the apartment, an ambiguity increased by Amelia's invitation to 'shut her out and sleep downstairs or come over and sleep downstairs with me on my sofa at mine' (tucker green, 2003b, p. 14). Ironically, her offer falls on deaf ears, ears singularly attuned with ever-increasing dedication to Jo's nightly abuse: 'Sitting up, back to the wall, ear to the glass – stayin in to listen – stayin up to listen – stayin up to listen in on her – and her man – from my side a the wall – again –' (tucker green, 2003b, p. 15). While Jason ignores Amelia's proposition, Jo cuttingly registers the rejection, to foreground a delusory tug-of-war over him.

Jo: A-melia
       A-lone
       A-gain (tucker green, 2003b, p. 16)

The typographically stylised and syllabically separated 'A' emphasises the different detail to be extracted from reading and performing its sonic and grapholect attributes, a discussion to develop beyond this chapter's parameters. Jo's provocative one-up-woman-ship is as hollow as her mockery (in the Epilogue) of Amelia's job. Amelia may be a cleaner but at least she is not in a murderous relationship. Yet, Jo's unkind fantasy of controlling what Jason hears complicates any straightforward sympathy for her, even though we can be shocked at her situation.

Jo: You never saw. You only *heard*. *You* don't know.
Jason: Know what I know you make me hear –
Jo: you hear what I wantcha to. (tucker green, 2003b, p. 31)

'Hear' used again points to Noam Chomsky's second-degree grammaticalness in relation to 'Know', which of course in performance, can be heard as 'no.' The play's multiples of lexical meaning (written and heard) can enhance the words (as figurative, evocative, strange). Jo's goading of Jason's (audio) scoptophiliac inadequacy affects Jason, as she becomes his alter ego in an ambiguous territory bounded by loathing. Kristeva notes of jouissance and affect, 'It follows that jouissance alone causes the abject to exist as such. One does not know it, one does not desire it, one joys in it [*on en juit*]. Violently and painfully. A passion' (Kristeva, 1982, p. 9). In making Jo (a white woman), and Jason (a black man) as the characters locked into the dysfunctional dynamic, what might tucker green be suggesting about supra-familial–racial associations? Violence as continuum: its gestation, incorporation of biological rhythms and drives; the *jouissance* it offers them is unrelenting. This is reinforced by language repetition (and its subtle reformations), which suspends audiences in a cyclical, unremitting dramatic temporality. Jo does not die but moves from one spatiality to another, to suggest futility or even nihilism as continuity. Reviewer Ian Shuttleworth complained that 'in offering no way out of the fundamental situation, it says nothing at all' (Shuttleworth, 2003, pp. 251–2), to confirm that being left to confront one's own response to *dirty butterfly*'s demands, perhaps runs counter to the distance-making, authoritative, evaluative judgements (derived from shared critical principles) upon which reviewers rely and perpetuate.

generations foregrounds a different kind of void to centralise black people in national mourning and remembrance (not of enslavement), but in contemporary South Africa. Like *random*, *generations* drama-tises the interruption of nature's expected progressive cycle – youth to old age – through a family's experience of unexpected death in their younger generation.[8] tucker green renders the shock, rupture and rituals that accompany human beings' processing of the unfathomable, but in contexts devoid of recognised institutional, religious, comfort. As Terry Eagleton notes, 'Liberal–capitalist societies, being by their nature divided, contentious places, are forever in search of a judicious dose of communitarianism to pin themselves together, and a secularised religion has long been one bogus solution on offer' (Eagleton, 2012, p. 8). *generations* gestures to spirituality and rituals for marking death beyond the monotheistic organised religions and hence, in the South African context, suggests the palimpsest of pre-colonial traditions. It joins *stoning mary* and *truth and reconciliation* in centralising Africa and the ways in which Europe's colonising legacy contours the continent's contemporary representations. This elicits how British theatre audiences (of all ethnicities) might encounter the representation of African soci-eties monolithically, or as culturally interchangeable, or as a form of idealised Pan-Africanism, by virtue of viewing from a British context.

Following its premiere in the National Theatre's Platform series (2005), Sacha Wares' revival at the Young Vic (2007) fostered a transformative sensory appeal through a dust-strewn floor and shabeen-evocative set. The audience sat on wooden crates surrounding a family meal in prepa-ration, with a continuous acoustic lamentation by the African Voices Choir. Letts describes, 'One minute you are in south London, the next, South Africa' (2007, p. 236). Halliburton records, 'the whole colour spec-trum has shifted [...] The dull greys of London's pavements are replaced with the red dust of a clay floor' (2007, p. 236). Visual, olfactory and audioscapes dominated the theatre space to convey a visceral rather than cerebral sensorium. The conviviality of greeting entering audi-ences created hospitality and inclusiveness, underscoring the present moment. It soon becomes apparent why this feature is necessary. The play's trajectory concerns passing from one state to another through the synecdoche of AIDS. Family members are called (die), and are lamented, from the opening choral dirge 'Another leaves us, another has gone' (tucker green, 2005b, p. 67) to the final surviving members, the Grandparents, who are left 'Looking for those that have gone' (tucker green, 2005b, p. 89) in a trajectory of cumulative bereavement. Thus audiences witness a distorted rites of passage, a frozen liminality of the undead and the soon-to-be so, 'at once no longer classified and not yet classified' (Turner, 1967, p. 96). Elders' authority (sustained by tradition) is broken by the epidemic just as the kinship structures are decimated. Youth's biological maturity is denied. The play's structure fits the components of *sacra*, which Turner derived and classified as '1. exhibitions, "what is shown"; 2. actions, "what is done"; and 3. instructions, "what is said"' (Turner, 1967, p. 102). If the audience occupy the role of neophyte, then they are similarly, 'alternately forced and encouraged to think about their society, their cosmos, and the powers that generate and sustain them. Liminality may be partly described as a stage of reflection' (Turner, 1967, p. 105). Remaining visible in the playing area's periphery, the actors are at a threshold, neither living characters, nor dead. Out of role they serve as a constant reminder that they were living characters in role. This indeterminateness functions as a gallery of remembrance in the eye line of the audience (and the remaining players), to implicate everyone in the process.

Although a eulogy to those killed by the AIDS pandemic, the term is never mentioned. Grandma in the penultimate scene says 'This big dying thing' (tucker green, 2005b, p. 87). This circumvents automatic generalisations about AIDS and Africa. Without the printed text, South Africa is only identified when the anthem is sung. Likewise, the use of a warm and charismatic family group with strong kinship values and history enables the consequences of a national tragedy to become intimate and affective. A series of steps from one state (a family group of seven), to its final group of two, without explanation from the characters, simply continues the dialogue between fewer people in the same setting. The characters' functioning as Everyman/woman, underlines the catastrophe's entrance at every level of society, tragically equalising, unlike socio-economic conditions. This representation resonates with the backdrop of Nelson Mandela's public testimony that his family has been decimated by AIDS, thus enmeshing him personally with the losses experienced by the general population.

Within its isocolonistic form, loops of dialogue relate complex interactions and subtle indications of familial heritage and behaviours through wordplay that celebrates language and its fluidity. The catalyst word 'cook' (contemporaneously communicative, poetic and thematic), conveys hierarchical jostling, seduction, double entendre, competitiveness, nostalgia, all the plural perspectives that characterise a family. Although unknown to an audience, Girlfriend and Boyfriend's dialogue is published in quotation marks, signalling self-awareness of roles to actor and reader, where the polysemy of 'cook' refers to anything but cooking.

GIRLFRIEND: '... I know I don't look
             like someone who couldn't ... '
BOYFRIEND: 'you look like someone who would ... '
MUM: oh God
BOYFRIEND: '– would cook. Who is able ... who has
             the talent ... ' (tucker green, 2005b, p. 74)

The humorousness creates an irrepressible and witty sympatico between the characters, and between the audiences and characters, who encounter many times over, the same vocal patternings, which may evoke an oft-repeated family myth. Shifting tense and pronouns pluralise possible addressees.

DAD is amused.
DAD: He has the mouth
GRANDMA: He has the mouth.
MUM: You had the mouth (tucker green, 2005b, p. 74)

The recycled vocabulary creates wholly new standpoints as family numbers diminish. As death eats family members, the futility of feeding becomes apparent – but continued – for what else is there to do in the face of such calamity?

generations uses little playing time but its impact Gardner felt 'will last you a lifetime' (2007, p. 235). For Halliburton it was 'Subtly devastating' (2007, p. 236). True to form, male critics (Nightingale, Macauley, Spencer) mentioned the play's performance duration (30 minutes), as self-justifying proof of insubstantiality. As audience members, critics form a specific demographic dominated until this decade by white, generally Oxbridge men. Reviews of tucker green's plays more often than not reveal the degree to which her work prevents their familiar position of authority towards what they see on-stage. Spencer declared of *generations* (capitalising her name as clearly he knows best), 'Debbie Tucker Green's stylised dialogue does no justice to her subject' and 'what might have been an overwhelming secular requiem for the dead is undermined by the triteness of the language' (2007a, p. 236). His resistance (ironically), recalls the blockage, Turner identifies in *rites de passage*: 'As members of society, most of us see only what we expect to see, and what we expect to see is what we are conditioned to see when we have learned the definitions and classifications of our culture' (Turner, 1967, p. 95).

In contrast to a family decreasing before our very eyes, the monodrama *random* begins with the smallest cast possible, one performer, from which a family grows. Multi-perspectives are achieved through the illusion of multiple conversations and interactions between characters, activated by one actor's vocal and physical performance repertoire. Ralph Berry has commented how 'An actor is his body. Whatever his acting skills, he is inescapably his physical self [...] Even a non-naturalistic play needs to be rooted in some kind of social reality' (Berry, 2000, p. 35). However, the parameters around zones of cultural citizenship and theatre casting remain racially encoded. As a counter-stance to this 'kind of social reality', tucker green asserts hers as a black-centred one in the trans-generational and trans-gendering stipulation, 'One Black actress plays all characters' (tucker green, 2008, p. 2). This cements black-centricity in a casting reality where parts are few. *random's* premiere in the Royal Court's main house employed a raw, cavernous stage space, stripped of its illusion-making façade (no props, set, lighting special effects or other actors) to augur its narrative arc of a family's experience of arbitrary homicide. While the staging compounded the actor Nadine Marshall's vulnerability and isolation, a contra-punctual intimacy was created by her complex self-intra-interactions where, as one character's voice comes to life, another is lost in a continual system of replacement. As no overlapping dialogue is physically possible, Marshall's seamless marking of one character from another gave the emotional sense of many people. Second, third or fourth ways of hearing and viewing were activated constantly and yet the physical conduit, one body and one voice, was an ever-present reminder of the performance's contrivance. Artifice co-exists with pseudo-seductive believability in a solo performer. Like the literary first-person singular pronoun, 'I' in live performance adds to the illusion of realness but not necessarily realism. In *random*, this single actor is split into a prism of a family's activities narratively bound by the character Sister's dominant focalisation and embodied by the sole actress. Beginning with the intimate ordinariness of a family getting ready to start their day through to the nadir (the effects of Brother's death upon the family) the play's formal unity is achieved through Sister. She remains the authoritative voice, while the actor is the conduit of differentiated voices and embodiments.

Her return home (or rather, when the actor transforms from Mum to Sister), to receive the news, occurs in the Front Room, a uniquely aestheticised domestic and social space for Britain's black population.[9] tucker green's gallows humour of Sister's innocent observations keeps a thread of connection to pre-murder normality. As a signal of dramatic irony, the audience (who already know what has happened as the actor has prior played Mum) now witness its disclosure to Sister. Sister's growing sense of unease, 'Su'un too quiet bout the house/su'un not right' (tucker green, 2010, p. 31) echoes her sensory processing of her environment in the play's opening scene: 'And the su'un in the air –' (tucker green, 2010, p. 3). Her registering of time (which has punctuated the play) occurs clinically like a medical professional recording the time of death, for the final time at '2.53' (tucker green, 2010, p. 32), the point when Mum transitions into Sister, underscoring that from this point time is suspended; from this moment onwards, life has changed forever. The play's final moments possess ecomiastic qualities (a Greek choral ode in praise of an athlete), capturing the sense of an elegiac eulogy to her brother. As Mum in *generations* must reconfigure her family numbers, 'I coached her to cook. Coached them to' (tucker green, 2005b, p. 77), so too, does the technique of elliptical writing in *random* signal the outer limits of verbal articulation as read or said. Sister must recalibrate her number of family members, and her pragmatic approach poignantly underscores her shock. The daily vitality of family interaction, previously, is replaced by stunned domestic separateness. Numbed, grief-stricken silence is marked by the Sister/actor's alliterative refrain as she charts her course through the house of mourning.

Pass the socked Supporting Officer
struggling –
in the best room
with our...
my
destroyed Mum. (tucker green, 2010, p. 50)

random is a familial love story, and a portrait of monumental family grief. An audience is shown the dimensions of human connection possible (amid a world of arbitrary cruelty) through the transference potential between actor and audience in marking the universality and magnitude of loss. This not incompatible with politics – and critical focus has been primarily upon its response to knife crime – (Goddard, 2009; Fragkou, 2010) – but it is also not circumscribed by it. tucker green lifts a topic that is too often a media and theatrical shorthand for negative stereotyping of black people into the realm of shared grief and loss that is not racially encoded but culturally distinctive, as it centralises the immediate consequences of murder for one family. As tucker green's stage language is a dismantling of standard grammar, the language spoken is not therefore a definitive indicator of characters' class, or educational, or socio-economic status, although according to an actor's performance choices, a chosen accent can resonate Caribbean diasporic heritage.

If tucker green's work is, as Elaine Aston decides, 'a *métissage* at the crossroads of poetry and theatre' (2011, p. 198) – in borrowing the term without acknowledging its complex sociological origins – then cross-referencing poetry and its influences upon contemporary drama articulates the scope of the phenomenon. To assert a black-centred trajectory of inspiration and influence does not exclude a Black British writer from also inheriting the white-writer-dominated canon, as long as there is room for multiple rather than singular attribution and recognition, as coupled with reference to writers' own standpoints. tucker green's unique aesthetic in relation to language and its performability on page and stage is combinational, investing writing for the theatre with polycultural and polygeneric intricacy. She has disarmingly confirmed such porosity, 'I didn't know whether it was a poem, the lyrics to a song or a play. It is all much of a muchness to me. It's all words, ain't it?' (Gardner, 2005, p. 13).

Notes

1. Ong (1982) employs Einar Haugen's 1964 coinage 'grapholect' to define established written language as an ever-increasing lexical repository, inclusive of the linguistic attributes of a creole spectrum (where the acrolect approximates most closely the Standard of a major language, whereas the basilect is the most remote from it).

2. Customary critical and receptive parameters for black British writers, playwrights notwithstanding, have connected the creative work to: the writer's (or perceived community's) cultural biography; negative media-driven reportage of social issues; as evidence of pre-existing prejudicial judgements about its quality – usually measured in terms of established Euro–US-centric aesthetic models. For elaboration upon these narratives of interference across humanities disciplines, see Arana (2007), for drama see Osborne (2011a).

3. See: Phillips (2005) for white writer–director pairings; Wu (2000), and Aragay et al. (2007) exclude women and Black or Asian writer–director examples.

4. What a playwright articulates, *as well as* the imprint of identifiable cultural inheritances, is requisite. Goddard notes the shortcoming where, 'assumptions of automatic feminist intentions and effect do not correlate with the practitioners' own sense of their work' (Goddard, 2007, p. 3). On tucker green see: (Sierz, 2003, p. 8), (Gardner, 2005, p. 13) and Young Writers Programme,

debbie tucker green, Educational Resources, *stoning mary* (www.royalcourtht-eatre.com/files/downloads/StoningMary.pdf).

5. Perloff's radical artifice is, 'less a matter of ingenuity and manner of elabora-tion and elegant subterfuge, than of recognition that a poem or a painting or a performance text is a made thing – contrived, constructed, chosen. At its best, such construction empowers the audience by altering its perceptions of how things happen' (1991, pp. 27–8).

6. The critical mass developing around Black British drama has been primarily one of survey, description, sex-gender or post-colonial (co-joined with British Asian drama) to the detriment of thorough aesthetic and theatrical analysis.

7. Both Kristeva and tucker green developed their ideas from positions outside the institutions in which they were to gain pre-eminence; Kristeva as a Bulgarian woman within the male French academy; tucker green as a black woman within white-male-dominated British theatre.

8. The monodrama *random*, where a black actress plays every role, dramatises one day in a nuclear black family's life, shattered by the son's murder during the school day.

9. See McMillan (2008), (2009), Goddard (2009) and Osborne (2011a).

11
Bola Agbaje: Voicing a New Africa on the British Stage

Ekua Ekumah

Bola Agbaje is considered 'one of Britain's most promising playwrights' (Walshe, *Coutts-Woman,* January 2012), given her rapid rise to critical acclaim in British theatre. Emerging onto the theatre scene during the 2000s decade and having four published plays to her name, winning an Olivier Award for Outstanding Achievement for her debut play *Gone Too Far!* (2007) and also being nominated for Most Promising Playwright at the *Evening Standard* Awards is a remarkable feat for a young playwright. These accolades and the many writing initiatives and commissions she has benefitted from indicate a level of recognition that suggests that Agbaje is making an impact on and bringing something new to the British cultural field. The British theatre industry has had to increasingly acknowledge and commit to the social inclusion of its multi-cultural constituency, which was made possible essentially through the rise of new writing particularly within the new millennium.

Commentary on Agbaje's career perceives her as a strong voice within black British theatre. Reviewers often compared her to her male contemporaries Roy Williams, Kwame Kwei-Armah and Oladipo Agboluaje who currently dominate the field, and their commentary is usually focused on Agbaje's black British identity. It is, however, the influences of her West African cultural heritage with which this chapter is concerned. Agbaje emphatically states 'My heritage has an effect on what I write about. I am proud to be Nigerian and my upbringing influences my work both consciously and subconsciously' (Personal Interview, 22 March 2011, London). For a young, second-generation diasporic African, born and bred in Britain, to identify as 'Nigerian' is significant. Having spent only a few years as a child in Nigeria, the majority of her African cultural experience is filtered through her British experience. Her African diasporic identity is largely informed by a collective sense of belonging to a specific cultural group as well as her personal relationship with her African history and ancestry, which she reinterprets to suit her current diasporic realities in Britain. She explains the impact of this heritage:

> Now I believe, and I have friends who believe the same too, the minute that we became more culturally aware and accepting of our culture, the more grounded we became as persons. I speak for myself, the minute that I accepted the fact that I was Nigerian and I was proud to be Nigerian, it didn't matter what anybody told me. Racism does not affect me; I don't sit there and think 'oh damn people are being racist to me and woe is me.' I just think I am Nigerian and I am proud. Part of it is making up for when I was younger, I wasn't proud and I was ashamed of my mother's accent. I was ashamed to wear the outfits, to have the accent. But now I am at this stage in my life, and when one day I go to the Oscars, I'm going with my African print, with the gele; my Mum is coming. I long for that to happen.[1] (Agbaje, Personal Interview, 22 March 2011, London)

The sense of pride in her newfound cultural heritage is unmistakable, especially in the way that it contradicts the commentary about her body of work. The commentary, awards and nominations say that she is a strong black British presence, helping to redefine the black community, when actually, Agbaje is consciously writing about 'home' – the possession of the idea of home – having only lived in Nigeria for two years when she was young. What is clear is the tension that exists between the world she is received by and the world that influences her. Together they create a dramatic tension evidenced in African diasporic identities in Britain.

Stuart Hall's approach to cultural identity provides a useful framework through which to analyse this hybrid postcolonial condition that embraces not one cultural heritage but the multiplicity of cultures and lived experiences that Africans in the diaspora inhabit. He argues that one way in which cultural identity can be viewed is through the idea of 'shared culture, a sort of collective, "one true self", hiding inside the many other, more superficial or artificially imposed "selves", which people with a shared history and ancestry hold in common. Within the terms of this definition, our cultural identities reflect the common historical experiences and shared cultural codes that make us into "one people", with stable, unchanging and continuous frames of reference and meaning, beneath the shifting divisions and vicissitudes of our actual history' (Hall, 1994, p. 393). This collective sense of identity also refers to the industry's perception that has been imposed on Agbaje, of an 'unchanging frame of reference' of black British theatrical history and representation that essentially informs critical commentary on her work.

Hall combines his first notion of cultural identity with a second position, which 'recognises that as well as the many points of similarity, there are also critical points of deep and significant difference, which constitute "what we really are," or rather – since history has intervened – "what we have become"' (1994, p. 394). Writing specifically on Caribbean cultural identity, the duality in how cultural identity can be viewed can also be applied to second-generation Africans born in Britain, like Agbaje, whose African cultural identity is a filtered, disrupted and fractured diasporic identity. Whether by coercion or choice, Africa has spawned a diasporic population who feel a collective sense of displacement regardless of their links to the continent, what Hall acknowledges as a shared 'experience of a profound discontinuity' (1994, p. 395) through slavery, colonisation and migration from Africa. Questions of identity and belonging in the context of Britain are important to all. For this reason, Hall suggests that '[w]e might think of the black Caribbean [and African] identities as "framed" by two axes or vectors, simultaneously operative: the vector of similarity and continuity; and the vector of difference and rupture' (1994, p. 395).

Agbaje is clearly motivated by the collective sense of an African community, evidenced in the positioning of Africa in her representation of her cultural identity on the British stage. She exhibits essentialist notions of African heritage, where fixed ideologies of traditional practices are held onto, with a strong sense of nostalgia, but she also manages to reinterpret them and adapt them to a British context. She shows an awareness of the complexities and contradictions of African diasporic identities in contemporary Britain, which results in the presentation of what I identify as a New Africa on the British stage. Agbaje's representation departs from a black British Caribbean aesthetic and represents an assertion of a distinctive cultural hybrid that is rooted in the African continent. In a black British theatre scene whose discourse is driven largely by a Caribbean hegemony, Agbaje places African-centred material within the larger theatrical landscape, thereby creating an intercultural engagement that brings a specific West African experience in Britain into the debate of what it means to be British.

Africa in Black British Theatre

The landscape of British theatre over the first decade of the twenty-first century has witnessed 'a unique situation develop in mainstream

London theatres (although not the West End) through the staging of a number of high-profile plays by Black British dramatists' (Osborne, 2005, p. 129). This new kind of British theatre, which emanates from the African diaspora, comments on the place of black communities within British society via multifarious forms and representations. It challenges long-established assumptions and ultimately complicates the notion of what it means to be British in the UK today. In an interview with Geoffrey Davis, Kwei-Armah explains his perception of the shift taking place within the arts in Britain: 'Right across the arts, there seems to be a new distinct black British voice that is coming out, that is...being very clear and true to its own cultural lens. I think that this is a cultural renaissance that, if chronicled properly, will equal that of the Harlem Renaissance' (Davis and Fuchs, 2006, p. 246).

Amidst this 'cultural renaissance', previously unheard voices from black British communities are beginning to surface. Of particular note is the emergence of stories of West African migration that are now being told on British stages. They highlight the presence of British-born artists with an inextricable link to Africa looking for expression of their distinct experiences in Britain. A much less visible African diasporic narrative in Britain is now beginning to counter the dominance of a discourse about the African Caribbean identity on the British stage. The fact that two African-centred theatre companies were created from the success of those productions – Collective Artistes founded by Chuck Mike and Tiata Fahodzi founded by Femi Elufowoju, Jr – attest to the fact that there was a demand for a broader definition of culturally specific black work on the British stage. Since 1997, Tiata Fahodzi's deliberate focus on producing African narratives through new texts, and reimagining and reinterpreting classical African texts, such as *The Gods Are Not To Blame* (2005), and making New Writing integral to their cultural product through its African writer's festival *Tiata Delights* (Arcola Theatre, 2004; Soho Theatre 2006 & 2007, Almeida Theatre, 2008) has not only created a gateway for British dramatists with an African heritage to come to the fore, but has also been directly instrumental in inspiring Agbaje to write.

> I saw a play called *The Gods Are Not To Blame* by a playwright called Ola Rotimi...I was blown away by the performance and by the fact that my culture was represented on stage and it wasn't watered down and there were no excuses, I just couldn't believe it...and when I watched that play I realised I wanted to celebrate my culture. (Fisher, 2012)

Staging the new Africa

The examination of the four plays addressed in this chapter is ordered around Agbaje's assertion that everything she writes is influenced by her notion of her Nigerian heritage, leading essentially to the presentation of a New Africa on the British stage. The analysis of characters, specific cultural nuances and strategic use of language will form the basis of the examination of her plays, which accumulatively read as a progression of her continued evolution and interaction with the continent and her lived experience in Britain. In *Gone Too Far!* Agbaje explores the matrix of identities in belonging to a black British urban youth culture in which cultural differences, perceptions of history and individual and group narratives play vital roles. The play was written in response to Agbaje's feeling that there was a lack of realistic reflection of her African cultural heritage and urban environment, in particular the perception of black youth culture, in dominant British society. Agbaje's play introduces a new element into the well-known formula of gun/knife crime and 'black on black violence' by providing an African diasporic cultural perspective on an often misunderstood, disenfranchised and under-represented minority.

Foregrounding racial and ethnic 'difference', Agbaje presents her young characters as they confront the tensions of diaspora, the impact and experience of being second-generation black immigrants in Britain, whose constantly shifting ideas on identity come from a variety of sources that they engage with at different levels. Agbaje uses this play to make a case for Nigerians in a Caribbean dominated arena, and she interrogates the difference in cultural identities, histories and geographical and current locations within what is viewed as a homogenised collective African diasporic community in Britain. Hall reflects on feeling puzzled 'by the fact that young black people in London today are marginalized, fragmented, unenfranchised, disadvantaged and dispersed. And yet, they look as if they own the place' (Hall, 1996a, p. 114), a scenario that is viewed through a Nigerian cultural lens in *Gone Too Far!* The posturing and bravado associated with African diasporic urban youth in their bid towards establishing a sense of place and belonging in Britain is rooted through their identification with a Nigerian cultural heritage.

The play is about two brothers, Ikudayisi, born and bred in Nigeria, and Yemi, his British-born younger brother. The simple task of going out to buy a bottle of milk on their South London estate opens up a complex debate on identity that finds the brothers involved in a number of confrontations. Through the portrayal of a Bangladeshi shopkeeper who will not allow Yemi into his shop unless he removes his controversial hoodie[2] to an elderly white woman, who is terrified that the brothers want to rob her, and two stereotypical police officers who provoke Yemi, we see a snapshot of contemporary Britain with all its multi-cultural prejudices highlighted. However, the encounter between the brothers and other black British second- and third-generation youths who live on the estate is where the dissecting of Britishness and ethnicity really takes place. On one level, this play demonstrates the interconnections that exist between different cultural traditions while focusing on the multiple identities of what Osborne defines as 'indigenous' black Britons, acknowledging an 'automatic constituency within British culture' (2011a, p. 185), which second- and third-generation African diasporic immigrants occupy, as well as their relationships to their other cultural heritages.

The idea of belonging to an 'automatic constituency' does not appear to resonate with Agbaje nor the characters she writes about. Agbaje's identification with her Nigerian cultural heritage reads as a rejection of the notion of a black British identification, which she confirms in an interview:

> After Nigerian, I consider myself a Londoner, before I will ever say I am British. British is what I would tick on a form; it is what is on the passport and if there was no Black British, I would tick London first because I feel comfortable identifying with that. I feel I can own being a Londoner; I can't own being British. (Personal Interview, 22 March 2011, London)

She rather engages with the tensions that exist in diasporic identities that feel the need to identify in varying degrees with another cultural space. This tension is evidenced in Yemi's battles to identify with his African heritage, personified by his mother and brother Ikudayisi, when he would prefer to fit into an urban black community that is dominated by a Caribbean streetwise culture. For example, when this 'street culture' in the form of Armani 'attacks' his African heritage, he is quick to defend it, and, yet, he later contradicts himself by stating: 'I was *born* here!' (Agbaje, 2007, p. 19), thereby distancing himself from any links with Africa when expected to understand and translate the Yoruba language Ikudayisi speaks. It is only through the subverted image and example of Blazer, the gang leader on the estate who has managed to reconcile his African heritage and his British experience, that Yemi begins to accept his multiple identities.

Armani, the mixed race character, embodies her own cultural inse-curities displayed in her ignorant and derogatory assault on Africans.

She states 'I'm from *yard* bruv', aligning herself to an imagined notion of a Jamaican cultural heritage she has not experienced from an absent father, to which Ikudayisi retorts 'D'backyard?' (Agbaje, 2007, p. 18), highlighting some of the cross-cultural differences attached to words and meaning and the lines of contention between Africans and Caribbeans. Blazer, whom Agbaje constructs as the contemporary African diasporic/ black British identity that functions and embraces both of his cultural heritages, dismantles her offensive and inaccurate historical accounts. As the leader of the area boys on the estate and the person everyone admires and wants to aspire to, he manages to command respect on the estate – an ability he equates to his Nigerian upbringing. As Lynette Goddard notes, '[h]is pride for his Nigerian heritage links an honouring of cultural traditions of respect that he learnt in the home to the status that he earns on the street' (Goddard, 2011a, p. xxiv). The linkage here of cultural roots to respect on the streets is problematic as Blazer essentially is a gang leader, hardly the kind of person you would associate with someone so proud of his roots. The contradiction of identifying with his cultural roots, and using this to justify his position on the estate, points to a cultural shift within African diasporic communities, where the dominant Caribbean hegemony is giving way to a new African experience. Blazer rationalises his position to Yemi this way:

> Blazer: When I was younger, people used to take the piss out of me cos I had an accent. And it used to get me *mad*, but I never used to say nothing. But then one day I had enough and every man who tried to take the piss – got knocked out straight! ... They can say what they want behind my back, but to my face, mans have to be careful what they say. And that's the way I like it. Gone are da days when mans take the piss out of this African! Cos I run this estate now. And you know, they don't like it. But what can they do? The roles have reversed now. (Agbaje, 2007, pp. 52–3)

Agbaje does engage with difference but focuses on the specifics within her personal cultural community. She positions Yemi, Ikudayisi and Blazer in central roles and explores how each of them negotiates the contradictions and the tensions of their culture and identities. The young men, particularly Yemi, find themselves caught in situations where they have to choose one identity and reject another. Agbaje unpicks the different dynamics of the diasporic condition of feeling the need to pick one side. She shows that accepting one does not necessarily mean the rejection of the other; rather, *Gone Too Far!* demonstrates what makes the diasporic individual complete: the adaptability of identity. This falls in line with Hall's explanation that 'identities are the names we give to the different ways we are positioned by and position ourselves within the narratives of the past' (1994, p. 394). I would suggest that Agbaje reflects her cultural identity through voicing the marginal histories of her heritage combined with British experiences, thereby creating new African diasporic identities. Through Blazer and Yemi, Agbaje presents the challenges young adults face in achieving self-determination. Blazer's identification with his roots is presented as one of the solutions to beginning to define one's self. Her final hopeful image of Yemi embracing both of his cultural experiences is the 'postmodern experience', where he appears to have started the journey to accept and integrate his hybrid identity into his psyche. Michael Billington comments on this:

> And her final image, in which Yemi dons traditional African attire while jauntily sporting a baseball-cap, implies that it (is) possible both to acknowledge one's origins and assimilate to urban, westernized culture. It is this notion of the potential for dual identity that gives the play its ray of hope. (2008)

The most revealing and intriguing aspect of Agbaje's display of identity is in her use of language across her plays. As Osita Okagbue identifies, 'Language is very central to the discourse and politics of identity within situations of enslavement, colonialism and post-colonialism which Africans and African Caribbean peoples have experienced over the past four hundred years' (2009, p. 203). Agbaje highlights the post-colonial realities of cultural hybridity in her handling of the language of the young black characters in *Gone Too Far!* An urban street talk heavily influenced by a Caribbean British culture dominates, especially the speech of the five youngsters that the two brothers encounter on the estate. The historical evolution of Creole, the contact language that has mutated on its journey from the African continent to the Caribbean and now in Britain, is effectively manipulated to suit the needs of a second and third-generation who use language as an identity signifier.[3] Agbaje's closely observed representation of urban youth culture is captured explicitly in the language and dialogue of her characters, which is often noted in the critical commentary of her work. The language has clearly been modified for clarity for the stage, but its strong urban flavour and different cultural strands remain. What is most interesting, however, is Agbaje's use of the indigenous Nigerian language of Yoruba in her plays,[4] for it suggests a deliberate construction of an African diasporic experience in Britain that is unapologetic about its cultural heritage. Ikudayisi, Mum and Blazer are the three characters that speak Yoruba. Their interjections in Yoruba are translated in the written text but not translated for performance, a deliberate choice by Agbaje, who is consciously making a statement about her Nigerian heritage by presenting it on her own terms. She places the majority of the audience in the position of having to grapple with not always having the privilege of knowledge by giving voice to her marginalised culture, without any mediation for a British audience's consumption. The insertion of the Yoruba language within the urban black British street talk through Ikudayisi, for instance, introduces a new level or system of constructing meaning through language, which is alien not only for most of the young people in the play but for a majority of the audience. This highlights the fragmentation and dislocation from the African continent within the diaspora, whilst emphasising a mixed hybridity, particularly through Blazer, and demonstrating Agbaje's subversion of the fixed ideology of black British identity. In her strategic bid to stage a West African worldview, Agbaje responds intelligently to her environment by portraying a different perspective of 'Black British culture' whilst dismantling the stereotypes within this popular culture. She is resisting the perpetuation of that stereotype by presenting alternative realities.

Alternative realities are the mainstay of Agbaje's second play, *Detaining Justice* (2009), which concerns itself with the controversial issue of Britain's immigration system. Through an almost exclusively black cast, Agbaje presents the multiple arguments about British immigration. The central plot is about Justice Ncube, a Zimbabwean political activist who tried to enter the UK on a false passport, was detained, and is now seeking asylum. His sister Grace has been successful in her application, and with the assistance of lawyers and the Home Office, Justice's appeal and his fate lie in the hands of immigration caseworkers.

Agbaje's deliberate positioning of Alfred, the black British caseworker, whose unsympathetic and resentful attitude towards Justice's plight critiques some of the tensions that exist within black communities now encountering the new, largely African migrant community. The complex nature of the negotiation of cultural identity and difference in Britain, where old and new 'migrants' converge, is a secondary theme, as demonstrated in the following scene where Alfred justifies his bigoted ideology to Ben, his laid-back Asian co-worker.

Ben: You take your job too seriously.

Alfred: *You* don't take it seriously enough. Watch when your daughter grows up and she need to look for a job. She is not going to stand a chance because all these damn immigrants would have come here and taken over. If it was up to you, these bloody lawyers and left-wing do-gooders, I bet you'd grant every asylum seeker not just leave to enter but free medical care and housing. Then when your daughter has no job, no house and has to queue for ten hours in the hospital you will only have yourself to blame with your soft approach and equal rights bullshit. (Agbaje, 2009, p. 220)

Aligning himself along national rather than racial lines, completely unaware of his prejudiced stance or the historical parallels of his own presence in Britain, it takes Grace to remind him what his parent's generation faced on their arrival in the 'motherland'.

Grace: And what were they invited here to do? Was it not to work in jobs that the immigrants you hate so much do right now?! The invitation was not limited to *your* people. (Agbaje, 2009, p. 242)

Agbaje points to the often understated fact that African colonies were also 'invited' and make up part of Britain's post-war migrant work force. Given the weighty subject matter and writing to a specific brief to fit the season, the impulsive nature of Agbaje's writing at times gets caught up in the explanation of the complexities of the machinery and management of the British immigration system, making her characters become the mouthpiece of the debates. But where she comes into her own is in the momentary shifts away from the central plot to the scenes involving the trio of illegal immigrant underground cleaners. The Nigerian Abeni, Ghanaian Pra and Jovan, of Eastern European extraction, represent a new generation of economic migration to Britain, providing a wider context to asylum seekers. Living in constant fear of being discovered by the authorities, this illegal group is united by difficult economic circumstances in their home nations, and most take up menial, difficult and dangerous jobs for lower wages in order to survive. Agbaje's ability to write such recognisable and comically perceived characters and at the same time portray their lives on the edge of British society, particularly in the case of Pra and Abeni, stems from the passing down and knowledge of her shared cultural heritage. The motifs of the rivalry that exists between the neighbouring West African nations of Nigeria and Ghana, such as the perpetual battle as to the provenance of the traditional West African dish of jollof rice, was a familiar nuance used to climax their numerous but harmless arguments and insults on one day, while the church, a rapidly growing phenomenon within African communities in Britain unified them on a Sunday.[5] Agbaje shows the church to be a source of enormous support to this new migrant community, which comes to function as and replace the extended family. Their working conditions are often found to be very poor, and as reported in Evan et al.'s study on underground cleaners, 'only a small minority (16%) were members of a trade union, (most of them with the RMT), but 58% reported they were active in faith organisations' (Evan et al., 2005). The contribution to the British economy made by this community is often unnoticed, and this play raises the question of what Britain would be like without its services.

Agbaje boldly rose to the challenge of placing her voice amongst the canon that the Tricycle's 'Not Black and White' season was exploring. Nicolas Kent, the then artistic director, programmed the season as a way of chronicling black British experience in Britain. Kent commissioned Kwei-Armah, Williams and Agbaje to write on the issues of British life that summed up the last decade. Once again, by drawing the focus to her West African heritage, Agbaje shows the direct impact of history through its most recent migration from the continent, through the hardships of illegal life in Britain and the communal spirit that somehow underlies it all.

Having taken on this challenge, Agbaje's next play, the controversial *Off the Endz,* is a return to more familiar territory. As *Gone Too Far!* moved the debate about black culture out of its victimised position, presenting an insider's take on estate culture, *Off the Endz,* also situated on an estate, explores the notion of choice. The factors that make Sharon and Kojo, the working black professionals, decide to leave the estate and make a new start are countered by David's choices; recently released from prison and out of touch with the shifts in his community and society at large, David's attitude to success is an out-dated, 'get rich quick' scheme involving the selling of drugs. Without an obvious reference to her West African cultural heritage, apart from the names of Kojo and David's surname, the play is firmly situated within the realms of 'indigenous black Britons' and the impact of their environment on their future choices. Agbaje normalises 'Africa' in this production through Kojo and David, both African, but not wholly defined by it. She presents a second-generation black British citizenry open to make the choice of partaking in mainstream society by conforming to the society's 'rules of engagement', illustrated in the consumerist culture adopted by Kojo and his partner Sharon.

Writing from personal experience, Agbaje revealed to me a more significant motivation behind her writing *Off the Endz;* she has a brother in the prison system and the impact of that fact on her family and her frustrations at not being able to see him drove her to write this play (Personal Interview, 22 March 2011, London). David represents her brother, choosing to function outside the structures of society. Like the youth scrutinised in Hall's 'Minimal Selves' essay, who are marginalised yet paradoxically 'centred' in the postmodern experience, David's character operates in the manner described by Hall as 'the long discovery–rediscovery of identity among blacks in this migrant situation which allows them to lay a kind of claim to certain parts of the earth, which aren't theirs' (Hall, 1996a, pp. 114–15). This 'centring' of difference puts the spotlight on black youth as they search for a sense of place and recognition, in spite of their dispossessions, by actively 'owning' the space they occupy. David behaves as if everyone owes him something because he views himself as a victim. Agbaje, however, shows how young black professionals like Kojo and Sharon have moved on from that one-time essential affirmation of identity and the archetypal image of disenfranchised black youth to which David still clings. This is illustrated in David's encounter with Keisha, the secretary at Kojo's workplace. When his inappropriate macho posturing, stereotypically connecting his race and sexuality, fails to impress the young lady, the encounter quickly degenerates into abusive insults. Further examples of David's inability to recognise the changes within his community are displayed in the following conversation between the two friends.

David: [...] What's the latest on the endz?
Kojo: What?
David: Fill me in. Who got shot, stabbed, killed!
Kojo: Recently? No one.
David: No one?
Kojo: Yeah, things have calmed down nowadays.
David: ON THE ENDZ!
Kojo: Yeah... the ting dat happened to Jerome was the last big thing. It kinda caused people to stand up and take notice. His death affected people real bad, man. I don't think I've seen people come together like that. (Agbaje, 2010, p. 18)

Agbaje subtly links David's out-dated attitude with the increasingly predominant image of young African men involved either as perpetrators or victims in gun and knife crime in London. *Citizens Report UK,* an online organisation set up to empower local communities to address crimes in their area, draws some attention to this fact when it reports on 'black on black' crime:

When I talk about young Black men this includes those of both Black African AND Black Caribbean heritage. I emphasize this as the greatest number of those teenagers murdered in London over the last 6 years have been from a recent African heritage. ... yet much of the discourse in this area seems to be focused on Caribbean issues or heritage. Like London's demographic it is time to move these discussions on so they truly reflect the changing cultures and communities within the capital. (2011)

Agbaje certainly moves the discussion on in the ways that she distinguishes different black British identities in her work. Even though the African distinction is subtle in *Off the Endz*, she affirms her intentions for writing this play.

> David was a Nigerian, his surname is Nigerian. He was to represent the second generation who are not necessarily defined by their parents' history. And I also wanted to dispel the myth that Nigerian and Ghanaian children are never in trouble. (Personal Interview, 22 March 2011, London)

The disconnection of culture evidenced in *Off the Endz* is an indication of the control Agbaje now has in how she engages with her Nigerian culture. She is in a position to see the effects of those who are removed from it, like David, who stands in contrast to Blazer in *Gone Too Far!*

Her next play, *Belong*, displays Agbaje perhaps at her most essentialist, in terms of her relationship with her African culture. It interweaves living in Britain as immigrants with returning to Nigeria, something she has expressed the desire to do in the future. *Belong*, commissioned by Tiata Fahodzi, examines the broad issues of national identity, the notion of home and politics as the action moves between Britain and Nigeria. Beginning to acknowledge all the dimensions of her diasporic identity, Agbaje deepens and broadens her subject matter by engaging as a diasporic identity with the African continent. Hall reminds us that 'The diaspora experience [...] is defined, not by essence or purity, but by the recognition of a necessary heterogeneity and diversity; by a conception of "identity", which lives with and through, not despite, difference; by *hybridity*' (Hall, 1994, pp. 401–2). *Belong* is Agbaje's exploration into what Hall defines as a 'diasporic aesthetic and its formations in the postcolonial experience' (1994, p. 402).

Having lost the local elections in London, Kayode, a Nigerian who has acquired British citizenship, returns to Africa to recover from his defeat. His British-born wife Rita has no inclination to visit or live in Nigeria. She states resolutely when her Nigerian friend Fola confers the Nigerian tag on her: 'No, my grandparents were and I never met them, so I'm not

Nigerian! My mother and my father were born here and they have never been to Nigeria in their whole lives' (Agbaje, 2012, p. 49).

This time, Agbaje's representation of the complexities that exist within black British communities through her exploration of first, second and third generations of African diasporic people shifts from urban youth to a more professionally established black British community. She juxtaposes this community with a modern West African politically aware urban society, where endemic corruption and opportunity operate side by side. Through her portrayal of the corrupt Chief Olowolaye, who has the local community under his control, the young idealistic Kunle, a former 'area boy'[6] who is being 'groomed' by the chief, and Kayode's well-to-do mother, we are presented with the matrices of the realities of modern-day Nigeria.

Further, we are offered multiple perspectives on the notion of belonging. Kayode's Black British experience involves him working his way into British citizenship and feeling let down because of his cultural heritage. He proclaims the reason for his failure. 'My crime was being Nigerian. I am being chastised for being an African!' (Agbaje, 2012, p. 12). His escape to Nigeria nods towards a current phenomenon of second-generation diasporic Africans returning to the continent, often seduced by the predictions in economic growth and the chance to take their place as part of Africa's new elite. Afua Hirsch's article on Africa's 'returnee' population reports: 'The facts about Africa's change in fortunes are dazzling. Dubbed the "next Asia" for its rapid growth, the IMF forecasts that seven of the world's fastest-growing economies over the next five years will be in Africa; Ethiopia, Mozambique, Tanzania, Congo, Ghana, Zambia and Nigeria are expected to expand by more than 6% a year until 2015' (Hirsch, 2012). Kayode soon becomes embroiled in Nigerian politics through his discussions with Kunle, who swiftly reminds him 'All you foreigners think and act like a white pesin.. What you fail to realise is that, this is not the white man's land' (Agbaje, 2012, p. 23). From the outset, Kayode is viewed as an outsider, often referred to as 'white', an absolute stance that conflicts with his own notion of himself. He proclaims his 'Nigerianness', but it is denied him at every turn. He is not perceived to be Nigerian because he does not eat with his fingers, which is viewed as a betrayal of his cultural heritage. This obvious display of African essentialism is a naïve interpretation of the African continent. Kayode is only Nigerian when the chief thinks that he will invest in his political campaign, but quickly becomes 'white' when Kayode refuses. The traces of his British identity, which are traces of a colonial legacy of superiority, appear at odds with his African identity.

Agbaje displays a Nigerian environment that cannot accept Kayode's hybrid condition, nor can he bring himself to understand the post-colonial Nigeria. Kayode is portrayed as the one who is perhaps being more realistic compared to the essentialist Rita, who belongs to the third-generation, and who has a very different black British experience. Where she lives has little to do with her heritage, and it does not inform her sense of identity. She accepts London as her home. Rita's experience of Nigeria is a negative one because she does not know it intimately. She does not speak the language or understand the nuances of the culture, as this experience was never passed down from her parents. Hence, Nigerian culture became a filtered, alien reality that isolated her. At the brutal ending of *Belong*, when Kayode is confronted with the harsh realities of the consequences of his actions, he quickly realises that he is out of his depth. His lack of understanding of the complex dynamics of a political system established during colonialism, resulting in a failed political state, cannot be compared to the opinion polls based on something you might have 'tweeted'[7] back in Britain. Kayode's inability to function during the crisis makes one question where he really belongs. Kayode has grown up knowing he was Nigerian first, despite his British passport, but he clearly feels a sense of displacement. In this sense, Agbaje touches on the realities of immigrants in Britain who are constantly reminded of their difference. Fola presents this notion explicitly to Rita, who resists the fixed identity of her cultural heritage by maintaining a strong sense of her Britishness.

> The colour of your skin automatically tells the world you are not from this land. Keep fooling yourself, just know that everyone you meet, everywhere you go, people will ask you where you are from. Even if they won't know straight away because of your accent, they will still ask where your parents are from, and if you tell them British, next question will always be where are your grandparents from, and will never be satisfied till you say Nigeria. (Agbaje, 2012, pp. 49–50)

The tension between defining one's self and how one is placed by the dominant culture is a continuing battle and a recurring theme in Agbaje's plays. Agbaje's sense of authenticity in her writing comes I believe from her performing her life through her plays. Agbaje uses her plays to find a way to make her African identity more visible within British society. Her plays address issues that are particular to the diasporic experience within Britain. She explores complex ideas of a 'British black community' that are informed by the specifics of her West African heritage, making a shift to move away from the generalised collapsing of Black British culture as representative of only an African Caribbean experience, by making clear distinctions between African and African Caribbean heritages in her work. Agbaje's theatre says something about herself and the tensions of diaspora. Her personal experience and environment have been inspirations for her writings. As she negotiates her identity in this space, so too will her work evolve.

Notes

1. 'Gele' is a traditional hand loomed cloth called 'Aso Oke', woven by the Yoruba people to tie a head wrap that accompanies a traditional Nigerian outfit worn by women to special occasions. The stiff fabric is manipulated to create an elaborate headpiece.
2. A hoodie refers to a sweatshirt with a hood that has become associated with antisocial behaviour to the point where some shopping centres in the UK had a policy to ban the wearing of the garment.
3. See Okagbue, 2009, p. 205 and Dabydeen et al., 2007, p. 48 for further discussions of language and identity.
4. This is certainly not the first time this has occurred on a London stage. Oladipo Agboluaje introduces Yoruba phrases in most of his plays with a Nigerian setting or subject matter, such as *The Estate* (2006), Ola Rotimi's *The God's Are Not To Blame* (2005) as performed by Tiata Fahodzi is laced with Yoruba songs as was the case with Soyinka's *Lion and the Jewel* (1966) produced at the Royal Court.
5. Jollof rice is said to originate from Gambia but has spread to most nations along the West African coast, especially to Ghana and Nigeria. The dish consists of rice, cooked in a tomato and onion sauce, to which meat and vegetables can be added.
6. An area boy is a particular term used to describe a homeless street rogue in Lagos. They make their living running all manner of dubious errands or extorting money from the public.
7. A 'Tweet' is a type of short electronic message sent out from a social network called Twitter on a device, such as a mobile phone or computer.

12
Witnessing to, in, and from the Centre: Oladipo Agboluaje's Theatre of Dialogic Centrism

Victor Ukaegbu

Oladipo Agboluaje made his debut on the UK stage in 2003 with the political satire *Early Morning* and he has since written over 20 plays. *The Wish Collector*, in *Class Acts: New Plays for Children to Act* (2010), *The Hounding of David Oluwale* (2009), *The Christ of Coldharbour Lane* (2007), and *The Estate* (2006) have been published, and like his unpublished adaptation of Bertolt Brecht's *Mother Courage and Her Children*, have been staged in the UK, France, Germany and the USA. An appraisal of his plays reveals a dramaturgy that subsumes centrifugal relationships and binaries and, more importantly, relegates the 'us–them' and 'two worlds' (Sierz, 2000) of post-colonial othering to dialogic centrism. Centrism is used here to refer to a political philosophy that avoids the extremes of left and right, instead taking a moderate position or course of action, in this case a dramaturgical style that is neither marked by ideological radicalisms of the left, such as relying exclusively on socialist–Marxist dialectics, nor by right-wing views such as cultural revisionism, racial bigotry, hegemonic relations and social conservatism. Agboluaje's work reveals a broad thematic and stylistic freedom that can neither be categorised as exclusively African in orientation nor defined by rejection of West-European dramatic conventions.

In a paper delivered at the 'New Directions in African Theatre and Performance' Conference titled 'Writing for Whom? Fields of Contest in Writing Africa in Britain' (2009), he discusses otherness and the double-consciousness he feels as a British-born Nigerian playwright in his attempts to locate his work within African diasporic and black British theatre contexts.[1] In the paper Agboluaje interrogates marginalisation in sections of Nigerian and British societies and raises questions about the authenticity of his work as a playwright writing for Nigerian and diasporic audiences:

Questions arise about authenticity, otherness and who can speak for whom but from which position do these questions arise? ... My plays tend to be from a particular Nigerian perspective, which is of course inflected by my own experiences, education and social class. Thus my position as a writer writing about Nigeria in Britain for a British audience raises several of the noted issues for me. (Agboluaje, 2009)

Like Frederic Jameson (1991), the Marxist literary theorist that he cites in the presentation above and who draws from many theoretical positions from structuralism to post-modernism and dialectic criticism in his writings on culture, society, gender, race and myth, Agboluaje draws from several theoretical and dramatic influences for his subjects such as negotiating socio-cultural dislocations and sense of place and identity in the diaspora, and tackling post-colonial and post-modern angst. In the conference paper mentioned earlier, Agboluaje also refers to his place in UK theatre and the politics in programming black plays by mainstream theatres. His search for a dramaturgy for communicating his understanding of minority experiences in the black diaspora has evolved into a writing style that other than satisfying the aesthetic and thematic concerns of Black British theatres for authentic representation of black peoples' cultural and historical experiences (McMillan, 2006) is, in my view, defined by an ideological centrist stance that avoids divisive cultural nationalisms but privileges dialogue between sections of society. This frames his plays as platforms for inclusive debates, and contextualising his audiences as witnesses to incidents that are themselves parts of a bigger picture.

The plays discussed in this chapter reveal the playwright's undeniable interest in transnational dialogues across cultures, a feature that has influenced his dramaturgy. For example, he combines African presentational staging and episodic plots, Western realism and aspects of Brechtian epic theatre conventions, such as symbolic props and representative characters, in the creation of an inclusive dialogic framework that also renders the boundaries between mainstream and margin redundant. Here, I draw on several related positions for my definition of otherness and othering and how both are used in Agboluaje's dramaturgy. Firstly is Theodore Shank's (1996) observation that otherness and othering are consequences of cultural and socio-political settings in which there are 'people who are perceived as having political and economic power and there are other cultures existing alongside the dominant one' (1996, p. 3). Secondly is Hingorani's use of the term to describe Tara Arts' journey 'from the margins of British theatre to the centre' (2010, p. 69). Otherness and othering are more than ideological terms for defining socio-political relations between social and racial groups; they are also spatial constructs, a relationship and condition that Ashcroft et al. (pp. 8–9; 12) also highlight when they use 'centre-periphery' to describe cultural relations in post-colonial discourse in *The Empire Writes Back* (1989). Whereas these sources see centre–margin as an inevitable consequence of multi-cultural relations or differences, Agboluaje rejects this view. Operating instead on C. W. E. Bigsby's thesis that 'boundaries exist to be violated and it is through this violation that meaning is generated' (1982, p. 68), Agboluaje contextualises his theatre as an interface or site for disrupting hegemonic relations, a feature mirrored aptly in his handling of character, class and cultural relations. The disruption of normative boundaries, culturally and theatrically, frees the dramatic space for Agboluaje to locate his plays within the wider spectrum of British theatre and a black British theatre aesthetic characterised by the 'reimagining of the self in a cultural and political context, where identities are continuously fragmented and hybridised' (McMillan, 2006, p. 60). The diasporic audience Agboluaje writes for is heterogenous and includes people whose life experiences have been defined by colonialism, post-colonialism and post-modernism, and whose identities are neither fixed nor based on cultural purity but are instead, constantly shifting and in flux.

By the 2010s, the theatrical experiment and quest for a theatre that reflects Nigerian British sensitivities that Agboluaje started in 2003 with *Early Morning* had led to two important developments. The first is a theatre of dialogic centrism that witnesses to local and diasporic audiences to and from the core rather than from the margins. This led to his development of a writing style that is best described as witnessing drama, a term used in the 1990s by Martin Orkin (1991) and Dennis Walder (1992) to describe the dramaturgical features of Athol Fugard's apartheid-period plays. According to Orkin, Fugard's witnessing plays 'address directly, represent or fictively interact with the social order from which they' derive and 'provide a glimpse of' this social order (1991, p. 252). Although the cultural tensions in British society are a far cry from the racist ideological extremities of apartheid-era South Africa, Agboluaje's plays, like the notable examples of Fugard's *People Are Living There* (1970), Fugard et al.'s *Sizwe Banzi Is Dead* (1973), *The Island* (1974) [2] and Percy Mtwa et al.'s *Woza Albert!* (1983), do not simply authenticate and historicise group and individual experiences of events, but rather they 'bear witness' (Walder, 1992, p. 347) to them. Walder elaborates that 'the idea of bearing witness offers something to cling to across the boundaries of class, race, gender, and nation state' (1992, p. 347). The second and most crucial factor in Agboluaje's dialogic centrist, witnessing dramaturgy is the conception of his drama as a critical facility for historicising and interrogating individual and group interactions and the politicising of characters as frameworks for addressing 'the wider issues of how people either become agents in the process of making history or function as subjects under the weight of oppressions and exploitation within the various linguistic and institutional boundaries that produce dominant and subordinate cultures in any given society' (Giroux, 1992, p. 256).

This chapter uses three of Agboluaje's plays set in the UK, *The Hounding of David Oluwale* (Eclipse Theatre, 2009), *The Christ of Coldharbour Lane* (Soho Theatre, 2007) and *Early Morning* (Futuretense/Oval House Theatre, 2003) to interrogate his concepts of dialogic centrist witnessing theatre and its contributions to an ever-expanding black British theatre aesthetics.

Agboluaje's text as socio-cultural interaction

The Christ of Coldharbour Lane (referred to from hereafter as *Coldharbour Lane*) is set in the late-twentieth century in Brixton, London, an area associated with deprivation and disenfranchisement. The Brixton of the play is a place of unrealistic visions and fading dreams, a veritable marketplace and *pot-pourri* of religious activities, where every religion from Paganism and spirit worship to Christianity, Islam and New Age are peddled. In the words of one of the main characters, Dona, Brixton is more than a tense shifting space populated by an amalgam of confused characters jostling for position; it is the one place where people face a daily barrage from different proselytising *acts*:

> Our survey shows that Brixtonians are preached to on average twelve times a day. They learn of a new religion twice a month. And they hear preaching from six denominations every day. And that's just between Coldharbour Lane and Electric Avenue. (Agboluaje, 2007, pp. 22–3)

In the play, characters of African and Caribbean descent face a life of aimless drift, bamboozled by competing cultural, religious and

ideological agendas and trapped in a socio-economic climate of exploitation, desperation, inequality and anguish. This is the setting in which
Omotunde (Omo), a deluded schizophrenic, ex-prisoner and new
convert to the art of proselytising, unleashes a hybrid religion derived
from combining aspects of Yoruba Shango worship, Celestial Church
of Nigeria, Bahia of Brazil, Islam and American-style television evangelism. The mélange of cultural and religious groups jostling for space and
visibility in Brixton may have been viewed by the then Conservative
(1970–4, 1979–83) and Labour (1974–9) governments as evidence of
successful multi-culturalism and gentrification of the commoners but
not so to Agboluaje, for whom the purported integration of different
cultural backgrounds and classes masks race and class tensions between
whites and non-whites, the wealthy and struggling poor. Although
multi-culturalism makes it possible for people and religions of African,
European, Brazilian and Middle-Eastern origins to interact and co-habit,
in Agboluaje's reading at least, the resulting social tensions and fragmentation of identities and communities are undeniable. To him the
hybridisation and cultural eclecticism that Omo resorts to is also no
viable solution to marginalisation and angst.

At the end of the play, Omo dies attempting to transform himself and
Brixton, trapped between shifting identities as no form of worship that
he propagates could save him. Agboluaje problematises the character
and his situation as well as questioning the homogenising conformity
that Dona pushes for the Mission. Dona, for example, cajoles Omo, and
resorts to threats of expulsion and bribery when the first tactic fails, but
Omo rejects her prescription for 'transformation', insisting on a hybridised identity and simultaneous celebration of his difference. This affront
is Omo's undoing, but through his death Agboluaje proffers an ironic
post-modernist deconstruction of multi-culturalism and the social
engineering attempted in the Brixton of the play as problematic spaces
where centre–margin binaries, cultural hegemonies and intra- and intergroup tensions persist. Despite his marginalisation Omo attempts to
transform himself and the space he operates in; his transgressive actions
are in effect driven by a socio-cultural imperative to *perform* his *presence*
or what Joseph Chaikin (1972) refers to as a manifestation. Agboluaje
presents Omo's performance of his presence visually and symbolically
in a long process of hybridisation across three pages of dialogue and
stage directions:

> DONA: ... (*She ... brings out the chain around Omo's neck. The pendant is a
> piece of rock.*) I thought you'd done away with all this.

OMO: I have. I have kept it to remind me of my past. ...
DONA: What about your crucifix?
Omo brings out a crucifix from his pocket
DONA: Brother Omo!
OMO: (*Puts it around his neck*) The rock is around my neck but the
 cross is always on my mind. ...
He [Omo] takes off the crucifix and puts it back in his pocket and puts the
rock pendant back around his neck. ... He puts the Prayer Request Live DVD
on. As the DVD plays, Omo changes his top. On his chest is a marking,
resembling the cross. ... Omo goes down on his knees. He mimics Reverend
Williams: ... sways as he feels himself being pulled one way and then
another. He reaches for the bracelet of cowries and puts it around his ankle.
(Agboluaje, 2007, pp. 25–7)

Omo is a product of confusing messages from various religions and
cultures that compete for his attention, and though his choices may
appear assured on the surface, they reveal the fragmentation, indetermi-
nacy, unpredictability and pessimism that characterised some individuals
and groups in 1970s Brixton. Here Agboluaje resorts to what Hutcheon
(1985, 1994) describes as post-modernist appropriation of parody in the
sense that Omo's choices and death parody the very freedom, stability
and peace that the different religions fail to deliver. In this ironic swipe
at religion, multi-culturalism, hybridity and gentrification, Agboluaje
signals cultural pluralism rather than homogenisation as the proper and
main function of multi-culturalism.

 The Hounding of David Oluwale (*Hounding* hereafter) is a documen-
tary-style stage adaptation of Kester Aspden's novel by the same title,
which deconstructs and gives an ideologised reading of the discovery in
River Aire in Leeds on 4 May 1969 of the battered body of 38-year-old
David Oluwale.[3] In this large cast play (38 in all), David Oluwale's ghost
guides DCS John Perkins and the audience through a forensic inquiry
into the circumstances of his death. The dramatised inquiry overturns
the result of 'death by misadventure' that was returned by the internal
police inquiry into David's death. By historicising the experiences and
actions of the characters, the play implicates official and public apathy
in the actions of the police officers, Sergeant Ken Kitching and Inspector
Geoffrey Ellerker, and for the *othering* and stereotyping that paved the
way for the two officers to hound David to death. The play's reading
of relations between margin and centre, *other* and mainstream, victim
and victimiser does not only reveal the destructive prejudices beneath
the actions of some public functionaries, however. Through Perkins

and David, Agboluaje links past and present acts of *othering*, discrimination and marginalisation into an unbroken historical sequence. In the process, David's racial othering and marginalisation by Kitching and Ellerker are given the political voice and significance they deserve and, without which, the discrimination and violence perpetrated against him by the two police officers would have, if nothing else, been overlooked.

Dramaturgically, it is important for the playwright as well as for audiences that David *performs* his presence visually and vocally. His voice is important as his story is the signpost DCS John Perkins requires to recreate the circumstances surrounding his death rather than rely on official records (and histories) produced by the officers responsible for his death. His well-documented, appalling treatment was glossed over in the internal report but is later recalled on the witness stand by Meg, the unsung heroine of the play. Meg's testimony is not only important in revealing the bureaucratic and systematic failings and concealments that led to David's death, it enables the *ghost* to take centre-stage to give his version of the incident as both witness and victim:

> Meg:...It were unbearable to see him treated that way....But that day he gave up. Like there was nothing left in him....That day were no different....I can hear his screams. There were times when I made myself believe it was his fault...the new initiatives were supposed to have stopped things like this from happening but it were the same old Millgarth. See all, hear all, say nowt. (*exits*). (Agboluaje, 2009, pp. 95–6)

Together David, speaking through his ghost, and Meg through her testimony, provide a fuller account of systemic and policy failings that make it possible for some people to abuse the system. The play exposes the racial tensions, public silences, stereotypes, judicial delays and lapses that undermine social cohesion and multi-culturalism. Agboluaje is usually critical of his characters and their motives, and although David receives posthumous justice, he is no saint. David's censure by the judge highlighted the victim's own faults, and although it mitigates the weight of the legal condemnation Kitching and Ellerker deserved and received, Agboluaje indicts this type of censure for mitigating the justice the victim receives by simultaneously granting the guilty officers a cause-and-effect escape route:

> Judge:...No doubt David Oluwale was an undesirable character...a repeat offender beyond the pale of civilised society....But under the

law he was entitled to your protection. By your wicked misbehaviour you have brought disgrace to our noble force and given ammunition to those who are critical of the police. (Agboluaje, 2009, p. 109)

Despite David's tragic death and pillory by the Judge, *Hounding* is still a redemptive play with respect to the victim and the British judicial system. It restores David's selfhood, and, more importantly, Agboluaje avoids the simplistic temptation to condemn all UK institutions as racist and prejudiced. Instead, he distinguishes the statutory instruments of law and society and public institutions such as the police and judiciary from the actions of misguided functionaries like Ellerker and Kitching.

The third play, *Early Morning*, explores the motives and actions of three Nigeria-born office cleaners who question their rationales for leaving better-paid jobs and lifestyles in Nigeria for menial jobs in the UK. In the face of a strict but frequently improvised work regime enforced by their white, inexperienced supervisor Mike, the three office cleaners Mama Paul, Kola and Ojo reveal the undoubted failings on the part of the citizenry in Nigeria in the rampant corruption of public office and civil society that precipitated their migration to the UK. The work ethics of the three workers shocks their supervisor whose position and authority they question constantly, a ruse used by Agboluaje to interrogate some of the *myth* and outrageous dreams the migrants have about the UK and the complex but differing natures of work and nepotism in Nigeria and UK. Their response and strategies are self-serving, for rather than adjust to their new environment and combating Mike's purported racism collectively, each tries to outwit the others to impress Mike in order to be assigned to less demanding tasks. Disappointed by their tantrums, Mike asserts his authority and confronts the workers with their unrealistic expectations:

Mike: Here we go again. So what if you used to be a high-ranking civil servant? This ain't Nigeria. You've come here to work, we've given you a job so do it! People like you don't get plum jobs so get used to it! People like you don't get plum jobs. Get used to it! (Agboluaje, 2013, p. 30)

Exasperated by what he considers to be the brutality of the workplace and the apathy of his colleagues, Kola launches an imaginary revolution that temporarily overthrows Mike in a move reminiscent of the violence and excesses of Africa's military dictators. In the resulting crude, putative symbolic game of military machismo that has no room for success, Mama Paul, Ojo and Mike switch sides under the threat of Kola's gun. As in the plays discussed earlier, Agboluaje has no sympathies for the workers. His condemnation of the immigrant workers for their poor work ethos and vacuous polemics extends to a deconstruction of marginalisation and othering:

> Kola: Gone now the shackles of neocolonialism and capitalist captivity. Dead now the theories of postmodern otherness and decentring of the subject, for we are now the centre! No more the trawl of Bus 133 early in the morning, ferrying our brothers and sisters to the City to do degrading work. (Agboluaje, 2013, p. 50)

Early Morning satirises capitalism, but it also challenges the immigrant workers to examine the severe personal and collective social and cultural deficits that undermine their engagement and understanding of the harsh contours of UK work places and ethics.

Style and dramaturgy

In a conversation in May 2011, Agboluaje stated: 'my work may appeal to several sections of a multi-cultural society or at least that's my intention but I'm not conscious of writing to any specific group or audience. I believe I write for a diverse audience, not a particular audience. Critics may see my plays as witnessing to my Nigerian, African and black British constituencies but I don't think that is a criticism. Writing from my own cultural background does not make me less British or exclude anyone' (Ukaegbu, Telephone Conversation, 2011). This statement more than reinforces the syncretic dramaturgy and polyphonic audiences for which Agboluage writes. His plays have been performed in Germany, France, Nigeria and Britain to good reviews. *For One Night Only* was described by Siobhan Murphy as a 'warm-hearted knockabout' with 'an inventive set, plenty of clowning and some smart one-liners' (2008). Philip Fisher commends *Coldharbour Lane* on 'the setting of few props', 'a potentially blasphemous dance pole' and 'open setting' that 'easily adapts to become Tube train and nightclub, as well as bed-sit and street' (2007a). Fisher concludes that the play has 'its faults' but 'cannot be too highly recommended' for offering 'a deeper understanding of London life'. On his part, Alfred Hickling describes *The Hounding of David Oluwale* as 'a powerfully imagined, theatrically fluid reconstruction' in which 'Agboluaje makes Oluwale a vivid presence by conceiving the narrative as an imagined dialogue between the dead man and the Scotland Yard inspector charged with leading the investigation' (2009). These observations highlight three other important features of Agboluaje's dramaturgy: minimalism and flexibility of staging, capturing the pulsating rhythms of his characters' experiences and their socio-cultural settings and lastly, a penchant for strong narratives and storylines.

Agboluaje uses a form of episodic storytelling in which actions and settings are shaped by theme and character rather than by plot development. The result is a loosely structured storyline in which dramatic action flows from one episode to another without the need for chronological sequencing or for cause-and-effect plot development. His syncretic style re-configures African performance aesthetics such as flashbacks, play-within-play, stage–audience interaction, symbolic characterisation and European forms of language, plot devices, unities and epic staging into an episodic form that privileges African aesthetics whilst speaking simultaneously to global audiences. His characters resist othering and exclusion while his subjects explore relationships at micro and macro levels. As we see in the three plays analysed in this chapter, Agboluaje uses Omo, David and Kola to disrupt socio-cultural boundaries and spaces, thus, achieving by their presence or manifestation (Chaikin, 1972) what Gomez-Pena describes in post-colonial terms as the 'colonised cultures sliding into the space of the coloniser' (1989, p. 20). Redefining socio-cultural relations and boundaries is one of the central thrusts of Agboluaje's witnessing and dialogic centrism, the other being the historicisation of human experiences as in *Hounding* that sets out specifically to 'rediscover David, to recuperate him as a person' (Agboluaje, 2009, p. 17). The documentary approach and courtroom setting of *Hounding* bear the hallmarks of witnessing and presenting facts in their authentic locations and contexts. This writing style is essentially metatheatrical in its combination of different generic features, the humourous and serious, self-criticism, destabilisation of norms and references to its own fictive materiality. Agboluaje's plays interrogate 'the process through which constructed subjectivities are performed for an audience which, moreover, has also become more conscious of its individual and social "constructedness"' (Jernignan, 2008, p. 62) as mainstream or as *other*. In addition to their episodic structures and complex theatricality, the plays contain evocative visual imageries and the kind of presentational performativity found mostly in live art in which stage picture evolves incrementally with unfolding action.

Theatrically *Coldharbour* and *Hounding* call for minimalist, representational staging and levels, symbolic props, flashbacks and trance scenes that break sequences of events and actions into non-chronological time frames. These features make for a variety of theatrical renditions from expressionism and symbolism to realist and naturalistic staging styles. Spatially Agboluaje signposts locations and settings as more than mere stage décor, a scheme that extends and increases the socio-cultural significance of the offices, dancehalls, tube stations, open spaces and bed-sits inhabited by his characters. With a writing style that re-packages African and Western theatrical sensibilities into an inclusive syncretic aesthetic, Agboluaje's dialogic centrist drama is not simply a response to artistic and historical necessities to stage Nigeria and its diaspora; rather, his plays belong, arguably, to the category of black British playwriting that 'challenges the critical, orthodoxy and paradigmatic discourse of black theatre, and complicates the term by bringing within its compass a heterogenous range of practices and aesthetic desires in the twenty-first century' (McMillan, 2006, p. 60). His subjects and themes conform to those described by Geoffrey Davis and Anne Fuchs as the focus of Black British playwriting: 'migration, the diaspora, ethnicity, gender, marginalisation, urban violence etc. from a particular focus' (2006, p. 16) but they do this with a mixture of critical self-examination, irony, satire, sardonic humour and sometimes, tragedy.

Character as politicised site

Agboluaje deploys characters on three levels, firstly as vehicles for communicating experiences and ideas, secondly, as politicised sites for critical self-examination, and, thirdly, for contesting homogenising stereotypes about black people and cultures. He achieves these objectives because, as Elam re-visiting and citing Petr Bogatyrev's (1938) essay on folk theatre rightly argues, 'the stage radically transforms all objects and bodies defined within it, bestowing upon them an overriding signifying power which they lack – or which at least is less evident – in their normal social function: "on the stage things that play the part, the theatrical signs ... acquire special features, qualities and attributes that they do not have in real life"' (Qtd in Elam, 2002, p. 6). The characters' presences challenge on-stage orthodoxy as David does in resisting all attempts by Kitching and Ellerker to marginalise and keep him out of the city-centre in Leeds because they consider him an affront and negation of their stereotypes about black people and white racial superiority. These characters politicise the stage and re-map the theatrical canvas with their actions, whether conforming to or contesting stereotypes. For example, the religious orthodoxy in *Coldharbour* and its socio-political counterpart in *Hounding* stereotype Omo and David respectively as incompetent acolyte and troublemaker, whose personalities would not make a good impression in court: as Kitching points out, 'You should have seen him when he took the stand. Magistrate didn't have a clue what he was on about' (Agboluaje, 2009, p. 90). In their actions, though, the two characters come across as more complex and rounded than as stereotyped by their detractors.

On a second level, the characters are supposed *outsiders* intent on accessing the centre, even if that quest for the centre, as in Omo and David's cases, leads to tragedy. In this regard, many of Agboluaje's characters, Omo, Dona, David, Kola and Perkins, are symbols with multiple significations. They are neither flat nor fully developed, neither social archetypes nor one-dimensional entities. Their presences counter hegemonic narratives about race and culture – for example, Omo, who learnt all he needed for proselytising from Shango, Islam, Celestial Church and American Television evangelism and not from Dona, David whose 'ghost' refuses to accept culpability for his death, and Kola who *overthrows* his supervisor. All three destabilise the status quo that is founded on cultural stereotypes, and, in the process, achieve what Ian Steadman describes as the production of complex meanings that 'subvert the meanings intended' (1990, p. 208). At a third level, the characters negotiate race and class relations, and their attempts to transcend race and class polarisation reveal the tensions and contradictions in homogenising a race or society and in multi-culturalism as an antidote to racism and sectional nationalisms.

The characters defy cultural fixity and are written much like narratives, as complex codes of meanings even when they are silent. Their speeches are socialised gestures and their actions are codified with live 'theatrical verbal and non-verbal components' (Irobi, 2007, p. 270) of physicality that are difficult to overlook as identity markers. Omo, for example, looks and acts differently from what Dona and the Mission expect and sees neither conflict nor dysfunction in combining different religions and cultural artefacts. He is content to mirror the eccentricities of different religions and cultures in order to redefine and negotiate his several shifting identities. His physical display of faith, among his other activities, ruptures spatial and religious conventions; his actions are neither contrived nor affected despite accusations to the contrary. He and David are the most politicised *bodies* in their respective plays, and both meet tragic ends – Omo at the hands of unwilling convert Jason whereas David is hounded to death by those who, in the words of the judge, should have protected him. Their deaths, which result from resisting pigeon-holing and their opposition to religious and cultural institutions, show that resistance against powerful orthodoxies is not without political and personal dangers. However, the violence to which orthodoxies would resort in order to enforce the status quo are lessons Omo and David ignore to their cost. In death, the two characters remained centre-stage in their respective spaces and universes. All efforts by agents of orthodoxy, Jason, Ellerker and Dona, to erase their political capital and agency fail, the bodies still achieve public prominence, a task Agboluaje accomplishes through Omo's translation to sainthood and Inspector Perkins' new inquiry that exculpates David.

David's body in *Hounding* frames an overdue post-mortem and leads the audience through a painful self-examination of its complicity in the actions of its functionaries. Perkins' investigation follows the journalistic writing style popularised by The Presnyakov Brothers in *Playing the Victim* (2003), in which society and its functionaries are on trial. The result is an ideologically astute implication of the judiciary and political establishment in David's death. Agboluaje's recourse to the aesthetics of Boal's Legislative Theatre, such as the 'destabilisation of detachment', and the incorporation of participation, acting out and performing as a prelude to action that happens in the overturned verdict by the internal inquiry, is very effective. This technique is more successful in *Hounding* than in *Coldharbour* and *Early Morning* for three reasons: firstly, the dramatic technique of making David an active player and accessory to the facts of his own narrative denies the corrupt policemen the *silence* and official protection they sought. Secondly, the re-staging of events transforms David's body into a powerful symbol and canvas upon which the jury (the public) can make the necessary connections between the psychological and physical hounding David suffered and his battered body. Thirdly, bodies serve as critical space and metaphor in the sense that characters re-live and articulate their experiences in their own terms. In the process, David and Omo's dead bodies, and the roundly harassed Ojo in *Early Morning* to a limited extent, acquire the political voice without which the discriminations and violence they suffered would have, if nothing else, wrongly acquired the status of legality.

In general, Agboluaje's characters resist 'the "fixedness" of stereotypes' (Ravengai, 2010, p. 63) about race and class. Like David in *Hounding* who ruptures space by entering the City Centre, Omo and the office cleaners resist the impositions of social space and their presence in it as migrants and outsiders with 'socialized gesture', a physical vocabulary that includes what Meg Mumford describes as 'the moulded and sometimes sub-conscious body language of a person from a particular social class or workplace' (2009, p. 53). Mumford's 'sub-conscious body' can be likened to Brecht's *gestus*, a physical vocabulary for communicating a character's experience and social history. The result is characters imbued with socialised physical and gestic languages whose actions, directly and indirectly, tend towards socio-cultural and ideological assertion of their presences. On stage, their actions are similar to those of young black people in London in the 1980s and 1990s, who in the words of Beth-Sarah Wright, used poetry to notate their 'sense of place and belonging' and 'to increase visibility and recognition, by delineating boundaries and carving spaces' for themselves 'in spite of their obvious dispossession' (2000, p. 275). Agboluaje's characters are in effect engaged in what Stuart Hall describes as 'a complex historical process of appropriation, compromise, subversion, masking, invention and revival' and 'a complex structure of diverse and contradictory, yet connected relations' (1994, p. 401). Their actions do not only resist *othering*, but also transgress normative boundaries, spatial and otherwise, and render their perceived 'otherness' unstable as a social and analytical category.

Agboluaje's *Dialogic Centrist Witnessing* theatre

Agboluaje's theatre earns witnessing and dialogic labels on its presentation of contents, images and metaphors like a legal submission before a jury. His dramatic and theatrical styles corroborate Walder's notion of witnessing in the sense that it is 'a means of providing some kind of focus within the swirling uncertainties of contested discourse generated by the large historic changes which everyone can see happening' (1992, p. 347). The characters in the three plays analysed in this chapter bear witness to the social circumstances that shaped them rather than explaining themselves or justifying their places in post-colonial and diasporean subjects and contexts such as race relations, questions of identity, belonging and place. Agboluaje's dramatic space is more social than political. His theatre rejects polemics and Sierzian 'in yer-face' aesthetic radicalism combining, instead, indigenous African and Brechtian dialogic staging conventions. In dramaturgical terms, the result is a theatre that advocates dialogue and centrism, a politicised space that bears witness to 'the battles for truth, value and power' (Taylor, 1998, p. 162) in relations between different sections of UK society, the diaspora and the world.

Agboluaje's theatre of witnessing and dialogic centrism transforms events in the plays into a visual historical collage and suggests that the story of David Oluwale and similar events ought to be viewed from several angles. His questioning of centre–margin dichotomy by turning the spotlight on a centre-facing margin is an ideological stance that has since gained some ground, as demonstrated by the documentary, *Margins to Mainstream: The Story of Black Theatre in Britain* (2012) by Nu Century Arts, Birmingham, and The Octavia Foundation. A similar sentiment, 'Mainstreaming from the Margins' has been used by the All Wales Ethnic Minorities Association (AWEMA) to describe the association's interest in cross cultural dialogue. Despite the continuing engagement with margin–centre discourses by artists and by arts and cultural organisations in various fora, the significance of Agboluaje's dramaturgy stems from the centrist approach he first announced in *Early Morning*, in which Kola pronounces death on 'the theories of postmodern otherness and decentring of the subject, for we are now the centre!' (2013, p. 50). The imaginative reversal of relations between 'centre' and 'margin' was strategic and the first step towards the development of his witnessing dialogic centrist theatre as an inclusive space, one defined not by exclusion or by binaries and polarisations but by the multifarious expressions of diversity and differences operating simultaneously towards rather than against or in opposition to the centre.

Conclusion

Agboluaje is part of the 'second-generation Black and Asian playwrights' born in the UK 'that reject the second class citizenship of their parents' (Mercer, 1994, p. 79), and who use the evocative voices of victims as powerful witnesses to the problems of their societies. His witnessing draws from physical images that require no embellishing in order to achieve their purpose as counter-narratives. The dialogic, centrist notes he strikes in his texts and stagecraft do not only mitigate racial and cultural polarisations, but also tend towards a non-hegemonic performance space of multiple, oscillating narratives and identities. Theatre of dialogic centrism is not designed to debate taboo subjects or shock audiences; to the contrary, the dignified tone of Agboluaje's witnessing reveals shocking truths about events and people and provokes discomforting self-examination in his unsuspecting audiences, local and diasporic. Agboluaje's plays witness a particular socio-cultural experience to a polyphonic multi-cultural world of multiple, oscillating narratives and identities. His theatre is a space for multiple voices to, for and from the centre, a platform for 'alternative ways of thinking, remembering and imagining action, and a wholescale stretching out of what a society', in this case one of its sections, 'thinks might be possible' (Pilkington, 2010, p. 10). The way in which Agboluaje's theatre witnesses to national, transnational and diasporic audiences, and abjures centre–margin binaries, distinguishes him from other black British playwrights. His drama of social witnessing is beginning to occupy a unique place on the British stage in what Procter describes with regards to fiction, as 'writing Black Britain' (Procter, 2000), itself part of the bigger project of writing multicultural Britain.

Notes

1. Hosted by the University of Northampton, 31 July 2009.
2. *Sizwe Banzi* was collaboratively devised and scripted, whereas *The Island* was the product of a collaboration with John Kani and Winston Ntshona.
3. The events surrounding the second inquiry into the discovery of Oluwale's body and the public inquiry of 1998 into the racist killing of 18-year-old black teenager, Stephen Lawrence, in 1993 in Eltham, south-east London, 24 years apart, reveal the historical pattern of racial prejudice and stereotyping in race-motivated crimes. The fact that the two incidents are linked to centre–margin dichotomy, to multi-culturalism, and the search for equality in cross-cultural relations, highlights the significance of all three facets of Agboluaje's dialogic centrist witnessing theatre.

Bibliography

Primary Texts: Plays

Addai, L. D. (2006) *93.2 FM*. (London: Methuen).
Agbaje, B. (2007) *Gone Too Far!* (London: Methuen).
—— (2009) *Detaining Justice*, in Agbaje, B., K. Kwei-Armah and R. Williams, *Not Black & White*. (London: Methuen), 184–269.
—— (2010) *Off the Endz*. (London: Methuen).
—— (2012) *Belong*. (London: Methuen).
Agboluaje, O. (2006) *The Estate*. (London: Oberon).
—— (2007) *The Christ of Coldharbour Lane*. (London: Oberon).
—— (2009) (adapt.) *The Hounding of David Oluwale*. (London: Oberon).
—— (2013) *Early Morning*, in *Plays One*. (London: Oberon).
Beckett, S. (1955) *Waiting for Godot*. (London: Samuel French).
Ellis, M. (1987) *Chameleon*, in Brewster, Y. (ed.) *Black Plays*. (London: Methuen).
Green, D. (2000) *Two Women*. MS.9391 British Library, London.
Fugard, A. (1970) *People Are Living There: A Drama in Two Acts*. (London: Samuel French Ltd).
Fugard, A., J. Kani and N. Winston [1973] (1993) *Sizwe Banzi Is Dead*, in *Athol Fugard: Township Plays*. (Oxford: Oxford University Press), 147–92.
—— [1974] (1993) *The Island*, in *Athol Fugard: Township Plays*. (Oxford: Oxford University Press), 193–227.
Hansberry, L. (1959) *A Raisin in the Sun*. (New York: Random House).
Ikoli, T. (2013) *Scrape off the Black*. (London: Oberon).
Kay, J. (1985) *Chiaroscuro*, in Goddard, L. (ed.) (2011) *The Methuen Drama Book of Plays by Black British Writers*. (London: Methuen), 59–118.
Kwei-Armah, K. (2009a) *Elmina's Kitchen*, in Kwei-Armah, K., *Kwame Kwei-Armah: Plays 1*. (London: Methuen).
—— (2009b) *Fix Up*, in Kwei-Armah, K. (ed.) *Kwame Kwei-Armah: Plays 1*. (London: Methuen).
—— (2009c) *Statement of Regret*, in *Kwame Kwei-Armah: Plays 1*. (London: Methuen).
—— (2010) *Seize the Day*, in Agbaje, B., K. Kwei-Armah and R. Williams, *Not Black & White*. (London: Methuen), 103–83.
Matura, M. (1980) *Rum an' Coca Cola*, in *Nice, Rum an' Coca Cola & Welcome Home Jacko: Three Plays by Mustapha Matura*. (London: Methuen), 13–31.
—— (1991) *The Coup – A Play of Revolutionary Dreams*. (London: Methuen).
—— (1992a) *As Time Goes By*, in *Matura: Six Plays*. (London: Methuen), 1–66.
—— (1992b) *Play Mas*, in *Matura: Six Plays*. (London: Methuen), 83–170.
—— (1992c) *Welcome Home Jacko*, in *Matura: Six Plays*. (London: Methuen), 237–93.
—— (1992d) *Independence*, in *Matura: Six Plays*. (London: Methuen), 171–236.
—— (1992e) *Meetings*, in *Matura: Six Plays*. (London: Methuen), 295–374.
—— (2006) *Three Sisters*. (London: Oberon).

—— (2010) *The Playboy of the West Indies*. (London: Oberon).

Mtwa, P., N. Mbongeni and B. Simon (1983) *Woza Albert!* (London: Methuen).

Norris, B. (2010) *Clybourne Park*. (London: Nick Hern).

Phillips, C. (1981) *Strange Fruit*. (London: Amber Lane).

—— (1982) *Where There Is Darkness*. (London: Amber Lane).

—— (1984a) *The Shelter*. (London: Amber Lane).

—— (1984b) *The Wasted Years*, in *Best Radio Plays of 1984* (London: Methuen).

—— (1985) *Crossing the River*. (unpublished) BBC Radio 3, 7 September.

—— (1987) *The Prince of Africa*. (unpublished) BBC Radio 3, 3 March.

—— (2007) *Rough Crossings*. By Simon Schama Adapted for the Stage by Caryl Phillips. (London: Oberon).

Pinnock, W. (1989) *Leave Taking*, in Harwood, K. (ed.) *First Run: New Plays by New Writers*. (London: Nick Hern), 139–89.

—— (1993) *A Hero's Welcome*, in George, K. (ed.) *Six Plays for Black and Asian Women Writers*. (London: Aurora Metro), 21–55.

—— (1995) *Talking in Tongues*, in Brewster, Y. (ed.) *Black Plays: Three*. (London: Methuen), 172–227.

Reckord, B. (2010a) *Flesh to a Tiger*, in Brewster, Y. (ed.) *For the Reckord: A Collection of Three Plays by Barry Reckord*. (London: Oberon), 17–69.

—— (2010b) *White Witch*, in Brewster, Y. (ed.) *For the Reckord: A Collection of Three Plays by Barry Reckord*. (London: Oberon), 161–242.

—— (2010c) *Skyvers*, in Brewster, Y. (ed.) *For the Reckord: A Collection of Three Plays byBarry Reckord*. (London: Oberon), 74–153.

tucker green, d. (2003a) *born bad*. (London: Nick Hern).

—— (2003b) *dirty butterfly*. (London: Nick Hern).

—— (2005a) *stoning mary*. (London: Nick Hern).

—— (2005b) *trade and generations: Two Plays by debbie tucker green*. (London: Nick Hern).

—— (2008) *random*. (London: Nick Hern).

—— (2006) *Handprint*, BBC Radio 3, directed by Mary Peate. Sunday, 26 March.

—— (2011) *truth and reconciliation*. (London: Nick Hern).

—— (2013) *nut*. (London: Nick Hern).

White, E. N. (1983) (1985) *Redemption Song and Other Plays*. (London: Marion Boyars).

Williams, R. (2002) *Sing Yer Heart Out For The Lads*. (London: Methuen).

—— (2003) *Fallout*. (London: Methuen).

—— (2004) *Roy Williams: Plays Two*. (London: Methuen), 129–235.

—— (2007) *Joe Guy*. (London: Methuen).

—— (2010) *Sucker Punch*. (London: Methuen).

Wilson, A. (1986) *Fences*. (New York: Plume).

—— (1988) *Joe Turner's Come and Gone*. (New York: Plume).

—— (1990) *The Piano Lesson*. (New York: Plume).

—— (1992) *Two Trains Running*. (New York: Plume).

—— (2005) *King Hedley II*. (New York: Theatre Communications).

—— (2006) *Gem of The Ocean*. (New York: Theatre Communications).

Secondary Works Cited

Adeleke, T. (2009) *The Case Against Afrocentrism*. (Jackson, MS: University Press of Mississippi).

Agbaje, B. (2011) 'Personal Interview with Ekua Ekumah'. 22 March, London.

Agboluaje, O. (2009) 'Writing for Whom? Fields of Contest in Writing Africa in Britain'. Unpublished Conference Paper: African Theatre Association (AfTA); New Directions in African Theatre and Performance', University of Northampton. 30 July–2 August.

—— (2011) 25 May. Telephone conversation with Victor Ukaegbu.

Akwagyiram, A. (2011) 'Did the New Cross Fire Create a Black British Identity?' BBC News Caribbean.com Archive. 18 January 2011. http://www.bbc.co.uk/caribbean/news/story/2011/01/110118_birth_black_britain.shtml (Accessed 13 December 2013).

Amos, V., G. Lewis, A. Mama and P. Parmar (eds) (1984) 'Many Voices, One Chant: Black Feminist Perspectives', Special Issue *Feminist Review*, 17.

Anon. (1958) 'Flesh to a Tiger', in *Punch*, 4 June, Victoria and Albert Museum, Department of Theatre and Performance Core Collection: Production File: Reckord: *Flesh to a Tiger*.

Anon. (1963a) Untitled Review, in *The Sunday Telegraph*. Victoria and Albert Museum, Department of Theatre and Performance Core Collection: Production File: Royal Court, *Skyvers*.

Anon. (1963b) Untitled Review, in *The Observer*. Victoria and Albert Museum, Department of Theatre and Performance Core Collection: Production File: Royal Court, *Skyvers*.

Anon. (1963c) 'An Outsider in Search of Identity', in *The Times*. Victoria and Albert Museum, Department of Theatre and Performance Core Collection: Production File: Royal Court, *Skyvers*.

Anon. (1971) 'Review of *Skyvers*', in Victoria and Albert Museum, Department of Theatre and Performance Core Collection: Production File: Royal Court, *Skyvers*.

Anon. (1987) *Evening Standard*, in Miscellaneous Black Theatre File, Victoria and Albert Museum, Theatre Collection, London, 29 Jan., n.p.

Appignanesi, R. (ed.) (2010) *Beyond Cultural Diversity: The Case for Creativity*. (London: Third Text).

Aragay, M., H. Klein, E. Monforte and P. Zozaya (eds) (2007) *British Theatre of the 1990s: Interviews with Directors, Playwrights, Critics and Academics*. (Basingstoke: Palgrave Macmillan).

Arana, R. V. (2005) 'The 1980s: Retheorising and Refashioning British Identity', in Sesay, K. (ed.) *Write Black, Write British: From Post Colonial to Black British Literature*. (Hertford: Hansib Publications), 230–40.

—— (ed.) (2007) 'Black' British Aesthetics Today. (Newcastle-Upon-Tyne: Cambridge Scholars Press).

—— and L. Ramey (eds) (2004) *Black British Writing*. (Basingstoke: Palgrave Macmillan).

Armitstead, C. (1989) 'Review of *A Hero's Welcome*'. The Financial Times. 23 February. Reprinted in *London Theatre Record*, IX: 4, 12–25 February, 208.

Arnott, P. (1989) 'Review of *A Hero's Welcome*'. The Independent. 23 February. Reprinted in *London Theatre Record*, IX: 4, 12–25 February, 207.

Arts Council England (2002) *Eclipse Report: Developing Strategies to Combat Racism in Theatre*. http://www.artscouncil.org.uk/media/uploads/documents/publications/308.pdf (Accessed 12 December 2013).

—— (2006a) *Whose Theatre? Report on the Sustained Theatre Consultation.* http://www.artscouncil.org.uk/publication_archive/whose-theatre-report-on-the-sustained-theatre-consultation/ (Accessed 12 December 2013).

—— (2006b) *Navigating Difference: Cultural Diversity and Audience Development.* http://www.artscouncil.org.uk/publication_archive/navigating-difference-cultural-diversity-and-audience-development/ (Accessed 12 December 2013).

Ashcroft, B., G. Griffiths and H. Tiffin (1989) 'Introduction', in Ashcroft, B., G. Griffiths and H. Tiffin (eds) *The Postcolonial Studies Reader.* (London: Routledge), 1–13.

—— [1989] (2002) *The Empire Writes Back: Theory and Practice in Post-Colonial Literatures.* 2nd edition. (London: Routledge).

Aston, F. (ed.) (1997) *Feminist Theatre Voices.* (Loughborough: Loughborough Theatre Texts).

—— (2011) 'debbie tucker green', in Middeke, M., P. P. Schnierer and A. Sierz (eds) *The Methuen Drama Guide to Contemporary British Playwrights* (London: Methuen), 183–202.

Back L., T. Crabbe and J. Solomos (1998) 'Racism in Football: Patterns of Continuity and Change', in Brown, A. (ed.) *Fanatics! Power, Identity and Fandom in Football.* (London: Routledge), 71–87.

Bakhtin, M. M. (1981) 'Discourse in the Novel', in Holquist, M. (ed.), C. Emerson and M. Holquist (trans.) *The Dialogic Imagination: Four Essays.* (Austin: University of Texas Press).

Barber, J. (1983) 'Review of *The Shelter*'. *Daily Telegraph.* 5 September. Reprinted in *London Theatre Record,* III: 18. 27 August–9 September, 699.

Barry, E., and W. Boles (2006) 'Beyond Victimhood: Agency and Identity in the Theatre of Roy Williams', in Godiwala, D. (ed.) *Alternatives Within the Mainstream: British Black and Asian Theatres* (Newcastle: Cambridge Scholars), 297–313.

Barthelemy, A. G. (1987) *Black Face, Maligned Race: The Representation of Blacks in English Drama from Shakespeare to Southerne.* (Baton Rouge: Louisiana State University Press).

Bassett, K. (2003) 'Review of *dirty butterfly*'. *The Independent on Sunday.* 16 March. Reprinted in *Theatre Record,* XXIII: 5, 26 February–11 March, 251.

Bayley, C. (1991) 'Cultural Dispatches', *What's On,* 21 August, 29, Theatre & Performance Collections, London, MS THM/273/7/2/708.

Beard, F., S. Bhattacharyya, I. Marchant, K. Miller, C. Newland, R. O'Neill and R. Smith (2006) *White Open Spaces: Seven Plays about Race and Belonging in the Countryside* (London: Oberon).

Bell, C. R. (1991) 'Worlds Within: An Interview with Caryl Phillips'. *Callaloo,* 14.3, 578–606.

Benedict, D. (2002) 'Review of *Sing Yer Heart Out for the Lads*'. *The Observer.* 5 May. Reprinted in *Theatre Record,* XXII: 9, 2–15 May, 556.

Bennett, L. (1966) 'Colonization in Reverse'. *Jamaican Labrish.* (Jamaica: Sangster's Bookstores). 179–80.

Benson, E. and L. W. Conolly (2005) 'Reckord, Barrington (Barry) (1926–)', in Benson, E. and L. W. Conolly (ed.) *Routledge Encyclopaedia of Post-Colonial Literatures in English,* 2nd Edition. http://gateway.proquest.com/openurl?ctx_ver=Z39.88–2003&xri:pqil:res_ver=0.2&res_id=xri:lion&rft_id=xri:lion:rec:ref:R04297279, (Accessed 28 September 2012).

Berry, R. (2000) 'Shakespeare and Integrated Casting'. *Contemporary Review*, 285.1662, 35–39.

Bewes, T. (2006) 'Shame, Ventriloquy and the Problem of the Cliché in Caryl Phillips'. *Cultural Critique*, 63, 33–60.

Bigsby, C. W. E. (1982) *Joe Orton: Contemporary Writers*. (London: Methuen).

Billington, M. (1974) 'Review of *Play Mas*'. *The Guardian*. 17 July. http://arts.guardian.co.uk (Accessed 9 April 2013).

—— (2006) 'All Our Yesterdays'. http://www.guardian.co.uk/stage/2006/aug/03/theater.politicaltheater (Accessed 8 March 2012).

—— (2008) 'Review of *Gone Too Far*'. *The Guardian*. 29 July. http://www.guardian.co.uk/culture/2008/jul/29/gonetoofar (Accessed 12 May 2012).

Boal, A. (1998) *Legislative Theatre: Using Performance to Make Theatre*. (London: Routledge).

Brathwaite, E. K. (1971) *The Development of Creole Society in Jamaica, 1770–1820*. (Oxford: Clarendon).

—— (1984) *History of the Voice: The Development of Nation Language in Anglophone Caribbean Poetry*. (London: New Beacon Books Ltd).

Breslin, P. (2001) *Nobody's Nation: Reading Derek Walcott*. (Chicago: University of Chicago Press).

Brewer, M. F. (1999) *'Race', Sex and Gender in Contemporary Women's Theatre: The Construction of Woman*. (Brighton: Sussex Academic Press).

—— (2005) *Staging Whiteness*. (Middletown,CT: Wesleyan University Press).

Brewster, Y. (1987) 'Introduction', in Brewster, Y. (ed.) *Black Plays: One*. (London: Methuen), 7–8.

—— (1989) *Black Plays: Two*. (London: Methuen)

—— (1995) *Black Plays: Three*. (London: Methuen)

—— (2010) 'Introduction', in Brewster, Y. (ed.) *For the Reckord: A Collection of Three Plays by Barry Reckord*. (London: Oberon), 11–15.

Brighton, P. (2010) 'Skyvers: An Appreciation', in Brewster, Y. (ed.) *For the Reckord: A Collection of Three Plays by Barry Reckord*. (London: Oberon), 72–3.

Brown, G. (2010) 'Review of *Sucker Punch*'. *The Mail on Sunday*. 27 June. Reprinted in *Theatre Record*, XXX.13, 18 June–1 July, 699.

Brown, I. (1993) Letter to F. Housley, 11 August, Theatre & Performance Collections, London, MS ACGB/34/157.

Brownmiller, S. (1975) *Against Our Will: Men, Women and Rape*. (London: Secker & Warburg).

Bryan, B., S. Dadzie and S. Scafe (eds) (1985) *The Heart of the Race: Black Women's Lives in Britain*. (London, Virago).

Bryden, R. (1963) 'Theater'. Victoria and Albert Museum, Department of Theatre and Performance Core Collection: Production File: Royal Court, *Skyvers*.

Burns, G. (1978) 'Interview: World in Action'. 27 January http://www.margaret-thatcher.org/document/103485 (Accessed 19 December 2013).

Busby, M. 'Barry Reckord Obituary'. http://www.guardian.co.uk/stage/2012/jan/16/barry-reckord. (Accessed 21 August 2012).

Carne, R. (1982) 'Review of *Where There Is Darkness*'. *Financial Times*. n.d. Reprinted in *London Theatre Record*. II.3. 28 January–10 February, 70.

Carrington, B. (1998) '"Football's Coming Home" But Whose Home? And Do We Want It?: Nation, Football and the Politics of Exclusion', in Brown, A. (ed.) *Fanatics! Power, Identity and Fandom in Football*. (London: Routledge), 101–23.

—— (2000) 'Double Consciousness and the Black British Athlete', in Owusu, K. (ed.) *Black British Culture and Society: A Text Reader.* (London and New York: Routledge), 133–56.

—— (2002)'*Race'*, *Representation and the Sporting Body.* Critical Urban Studies: Occasional Papers, Centre for Urban and Community Research, Goldsmiths, University of London.

—— (2010) *Race, Sport and Politics: The Sporting Black Diaspora.* (London: Sage).

Casey, M. (2004) *Creating Frames: Contemporary Indigenous Theatre 1967–1990.* (St. Lucia: University of Queensland Press).

Cavendish, D. (2004) 'It's Boom Time for Black Theatre – But Will It Last?' *The Daily Telegraph* 4 December. http://www.telegraph.co.uk/culture/theatre/drama/3632809/Its-boom-time-for-black-theatre-but-will-it-last.html (Accessed 3 March 2013).

Cazeaux, C. (2005) 'Phenomenology and Radio Drama'. *British Journal of Aesthetics*, 45.2, 157–74.

Chaikin, J. (1972) *The Presence of the Actor.* (New York: Atheneum).

Chambers, C. (1989) *The Story of Unity Theatre.* (London: Lawrence and Wishart).

—— (2002) *The Continuum Companion to Twentieth Century Theatre.* (London: Continuum).

—— (2011) *Black and Asian Theatre in Britain: A History.* (London: Routledge).

Choudhury, M. S. (2000) *Interculturalism and Resistance in the London Theatre, 1600–1800: Identity, Performance, Empire.* (London: Associated University Press).

CitizensReport (2011) 'Black on Black Serious Violence and Murder'. *Citizens Report UK.* http://www.citizensreportuk.org/news/2011/05/07/black-on-black-serious-violence-and murder/ (Accessed 3 September 2013).

Clifford, J. (2000) 'Taking Identity Politics Seriously: "The Contradictory, Stony Ground"', in Gilroy, P., L. Grossberg and A. McRobbie (eds) *Without Guarantees: Essays in Honour of Stuart Hall.* (London: Verso), 94–112.

Cochrane, C. (2011) *Twentieth-Century British Theatre: Industry, Art and Empire.* (Cambridge: Cambridge University Press).

Colley, L. (2009) *Britons: Forging the Nation: 1707–1837.* (New Haven: Yale University Press).

Considine, A. and R. Slovo (eds) (1987) *Dead Proud: From Second Wave Young Women Playwrights.* (London: The Women's Press Ltd).

Constantine, L. (1954) *The Colour Bar.* (Essex: Anchor).

Coveney, M. (1991a) 'Review of *The Coup*'. *The Observer.* 21 July. http://arts.observer.co.uk. (Accessed 9 April 2013).

—— (1991b) 'Review of *Talking in Tongues*'. *The Observer.* 1 September 1991. Reprinted in *Theatre Record*, XI.18, 27 August–9 September, 1045.

Crabbe, H. (1989) 'Review of *A Hero's Welcome*'. *What's On.* 1 March. *London Theatre Record*, IX.4, 12–25 February, 207–8.

Croft, S., S. Bourne and A. Terracciano (eds) (2003) *Black and Asian Performance at the Theatre Museum: A User's Guide.* (London: Victoria and Albert Theatre Museum).

Crown, K. (2002) '"Sonic Revolutionaries": Voice and Experiment in the Spoken Word Poetry of Tracie Morris', in Hinton, L. and C. Hogue (eds) *We Who Love to be Astonished: Experimental Women's Writing and Performance Poetics.* (Tuscaloosa: The University of Alabama Press), 213–26.

Cushman, R. (1983) 'Review of *The Shelter*'. *The Observer*. n.d. Reprinted in *London Theatre Record*, III.18. 27 August–9 September, 700.

Dabydeen, D., J. Gilmore and C. Jones (eds) (2007) *The Oxford Companion to Black British History*. (Oxford: Oxford University Press)

Darlington, W. A. (1963) 'Salvation of a Rebel Schoolboy'. Victoria and Albert Museum, Department of Theatre and Performance Core Collection: Production File, Royal Court, *Skyvers*.

Davis, G. V. (2006) '"This is a Cultural Renaissance": An Interview with Kwame-Kwei Armah' in Davis, G. V. and A. Fuchs (eds) *Staging New Britain: Aspects of South Asian British Theatre Practice*. (Brussels: Peter Lang), 239–52.

Davis, G. V. and A. Fuchs (2006) "Introduction", in G. V. Davis and A. Fuchs (eds) *Staging New Britain: Aspects of South Asian British Theatre Practice*. (Brussels: Peter Lang), 15–34.

DeGruy-Leary, J. (2005) *Post Traumatic Slave Syndrome: America's Legacy of Enduring Injury and Healing* (Milwaukie, OR: Uptone).

de Jongh, N. (1971) '*Skyvers*'. Victoria and Albert Museum, Department of Theatre and Performance Core Collection: Production File: Royal Court, *Skyvers*.

—— (1989) 'Review of *A Hero's Welcome*'. *The Guardian*. 23 February. Reprinted in *London Theatre Record*, IX: 4, 12–25 February, 209.

—— (1991) 'Review of *Meetings*'. *The Guardian*. 19 March, p. A14. .

Dennis, F. (1983) 'Review of *The Shelter*'. *City Limits*. n.d. Reprinted in *London Theatre Record*, III.18. 27 August–9 September, 700.

Derbyshire, H. (2007) 'Roy Williams: Representing Multicultural Britain in *Fallout*'. *Modern Drama*, 50.3, Fall, 414–34.

Desani, G. V. (2007) *All About H. Hatter*. (New York: New York Review Books).

Deslandes, C. V. (1963) 'Hamilton House Notes: The Royal Court Theater'. *The London Teacher*, June, 155.

Donnell, A. (ed.) (2002) *Companion to Contemporary Black British Culture*. (London, Routledge).

Eagleton, T. (2012) 'Review'. *The Guardian*. 14 January, 8.

Eboda, M. (2004) 'What I Said Was Racist – But I'm Not A Racist. I Am An Idiot'. *The Guardian*. 25 April. http://www.guardian.co.uk/uk/2004/apr/25/race.football (Accessed 24 September 2012).

Eckstein, L. (2006) *Re-Membering the Black Atlantic: On the Poetics and Politics of Literary Memory*. (Amsterdam: Rodopi).

Edwardes, J. (1989) 'Review of *A Hero's Welcome*'. *Time Out*. 1 March. Reprinted in *London Theatre Record*, IX.4, 12–25 February, 207.

—— (2006) 'Racing Through History'. *Time Out*, 4 January, 120.

Elam, H. J. (2004) *The Past as Present in the Drama of August Wilson*. (Ann Arbor, MI: University of Michigan Press).

Elam, K. (1995) 'Tempo's Sickle: Rapping, Zapping, Toasting, and Trekking Through History in Black British Drama'. *The Yearbook of English Studies*, 25, 173–98.

—— (2002) *The Semiotics of Theatre and Drama*, 2nd Edition. (London: Routledge).

Enisuoh, A. (2004) 'Debate: State of Black Theatre'. Transcribed in Cavendish D. 'It's Boom Time for Black Theatre – But Will It Last?' *The Daily Telegraph*, 4 December. http://www.telegraph.co.uk/culture/theatre/drama/3632809/Its-boom-time-for-black-theatre-but-will-it-last.html (Accessed 3 March 2013).

Esslin, M. (1971) 'The Mind as Stage'. *Theatre Quarterly*, 1.3, 5–11.

Eugenics Society (1958) 'Statement and Aims'. *The Eugenics Review*, April. http://www.ncbi.nlm.nih.gov/pmc/articles/PMC2974469/?page=1

Evan, Y., J. Herbert, K. Datta, C. McIlwain and J. Wills (2005) 'Making the City Work: Low Paid Employment in London.' Department of Geography, Queen Mary University of London. http://swslim.org.uk/downloads/sl2266.pdf (Accessed 20 August 2012).

Fisher, P. (2007a) 'Review of *The Christ of Coldharbour Lane*'. *British Theatre Guide*. http://www.britishtheatreguide.info/reviews/christcoldharbour-rev (Accessed 19 December 2013).

—— (2007b) 'Review of *Rough Crossings. British Theatre Guide*'. http://www.britishtheatreguide.info/reviews/roughcrossings-rev (Accessed 21 July 2014).

Fisher, G. (2012) 'Agbaje, Bola-Belong'. http://www.afridiziak.com/theatrenews/interviews/april2012/bola-agbaje-belong.html (Accessed 3 September 2013).

Fragkou, M. (2010) 'Intercultural Encounters in debbie tucker green's *random*', in Huber, W., M. Rubik and J. Novak (eds), *Contemporary Drama in English*, 17, 75–87.

Fryer, P. (1984) *Staying Power: The History of Black People in Britain*. (London: Pluto).

Gainor, E. J. (ed.) (1995) *Imperialism and Theatre: Essays on World Theatre, Drama and Performance 1795–1995*. (London: Routledge).

Gardner, L. (2003) 'Review of *dirty butterfly*'. *The Guardian*. 3 March. Reprinted in *Theatre Record*, XXIII.5, 26 February–11 March, 252.

—— (2005) '"I Was Messing About"'. *G2: Arts. The Guardian*. 30 March, 13.

—— (2007) 'Review of *generations*'. *The Guardian*. 1 March. Reprinted in *Theatre Record* XXVII.5, 25 February–11 March, 235.

Gates Jnr, H. L. (1984) *Black Literature and Literary Theory*. (London: Methuen).

—— (1988) *The Signifying Monkey: A Theory of African-American Literary Criticism*. (Oxford: Oxford University Press).

—— (1997) 'A Reporter at Large: Black London', in Owusu, K. (2000) (ed.) *Black British Culture and Society: A Text Reader*. (London: Routledge), 169–80.

George, K. (ed.) (1993) *Six Plays by Black and Asian Women Writers*. (London: Aurora Metro Press).

Gibbs, P. (1958) 'Review of *Flesh to a Tiger*'. *Daily Telegraph*. 22 May, Victoria and Albert Museum, Department of Theatre and Performance Core Collection: Production File: Reckord, *Flesh to a Tiger*.

Gilroy, P. (1987) *There Ain't No Black in the Union Jack: The Cultural Politics of Race and Nation*. (London: Unwin Hyman).

—— (1993) *The Black Atlantic: Modernity and Double Consciousness*. (London: Verso).

—— (2001) 'Foreword', in Carrington, B. and I. McDonald (eds) *'Race', Sport and British Society*. (London: Routledge), xi–xvii.

Giroux, H. (1992) *Border Crossings: Cultural Workers and the Politics of Education*. (London: Routledge).

Goddard, L. (2005) 'Back pages'. *Contemporary Theatre Review*, 15.3, 369–86.

—— (2007) *Staging Black Feminisms: Identity, Politics, Performance*. (Basingstoke: Palgrave Macmillan).

—— (ed.) (2008) 'Mojisola Adebayo in Conversation with Lynette Goddard', in Osborne, D. (ed.) *Hidden Gems*. (London: Oberon Books), 142–8.

—— (2009) 'Death Never Used to Be for the Young', in Osborne, D. (ed.) 'Contemporary Black British Women's Writing', Special Issue, *Women: A Cultural Review*, 20.3, 299–309.

—— (2011a) *The Methuen Drama Book of Plays by Black British Writers*. (London: Methuen).

—— (2011b) 'Kwame Kwei-Armah', in Middeke, M., P. P. Schnierer and A. Sierz (eds) *The Methuen Drama Guide to Contemporary British Playwrights*. (London: Methuen), 323–4?

—— (n.d.) 'Cultural Diversity and Black British Playwriting on the Mainstream, 2000–2012.' National Theatre Black Plays Archive. http://www.blackplaysarchive.org.uk/featured-content/essays/lynette-goddard-rennaisance-black-british-drama-1990s (Accessed 11 December 2013).

Godiwala, D. (ed.) (2006) *Alternatives Within the Mainstream: British Black and Asian Theatres*. (Newcastle: Cambridge Scholars).

Gomez-Pena, G. (1989) 'The Multicultural Paradigm: An Open Letter to the National Arts Community High Performance'. *High Performance Quarterly Magazine*, 47, 20–27.

Goodman, L. and J. de Gay (1996) 'Yvonne Brewster', in L. Goodman with J. de Gay (eds) *Feminist Stages: Interviews with Women in Contemporary British Theater*. (Amsterdam: Harwood), 121–27.

Goyal, Y. (2003) 'Theorizing Africa in Black Diaspora Studies: Caryl Phillips' Crossing the River'. *Diaspora*, 12.1, 5–38.

Gramsci, A. (1988) 'Common Sense', in Forgacs, D. (ed.) *A Gramsci Reader: Selected Writings 1916–1935*. (London: Lawrence & Wishart), 421.

Gray, F. (ed.) (1990) *Second Wave Plays: Women at the Albany Empire*. (Sheffield: Sheffield Academic Press).

Griffin, G. (2003) *Contemporary Black and Asian Women Playwrights in Britain*. (Cambridge: Cambridge University Press).

—— (2006a) 'Theatres of Difference: The Politics of "Redistribution and Recognition", in the Plays of Contemporary Black and Asian Women Playwrights in Britain'. *Feminist Review* 84, 10–28.

—— (2006b) 'The Remains of the British Empire: The Plays of Winsome Pinnock', in M. Luckhurst (ed.) *A Companion to Modern British and Irish Drama 1880–2005*. (Oxford, Blackwell), 198–210.

Griffin, G. and Aston, E. (eds) (1991) *Herstory Volume One: Plays by Women For Women*. (Sheffield: Sheffield Academic Press).

Gunning, D. and Ward, A. (2009) 'Tracing Black America in Black British Culture', in *Atlantic Studies: Literary, Cultural and Historical Perspectives on Europe, Africa and the Americas*. 6.2, 149–58.

Haley, A. (1976) *Roots: The Saga of an American Family*. (New York: Doubleday).

Haley, A. and X, M. (1965) *The Autobiography of Malcolm X*. (New York: Grove).

Hall, S. (1987) 'Minimal Selves', in *Identity: The Real Me*. London: Institute for Contemporary Arts, Document 6, 44–6.

—— (1988) 'New Ethnicities'. Reprinted in Kobena Mercer (ed.) *Black Film/British Cinema*. Institute for Contemporary Arts, Document 6. Reprinted in Baker, H. A., M. Diawara and R. H. Lindeborg (eds) *Black British Cultural Studies: A Reader*. (Chicago, University of Chicago Press), 163–72.

—— (1992) 'New Ethnicities'. Reprinted in Donald, J. and A. Rattansi (eds) *'Race', Culture and Difference*. (London: Sage Publications), 252–59.

—— (1994) 'Cultural Identity and Diaspora', in Williams, P. and L. Chrisman (eds) *Colonial Discourse and Post-colonial Theory: A Reader*. (London: Harvester Wheatsheaf), 392–401.

—— (1996a) 'Minimal Selves'. Reprinted in Baker, H. A. Jr., M. Diawara and R. H. Lindeborg (eds) *Black British Cultural Studies: A Reader*. (Chicago University of Chicago Press), 114–19.

—— (1996b) 'New Ethnicities'. Reprinted in Morley, D. and K-H. Chen. *Stuart Hall: Critical Dialogues in Cultural Studies* (eds) (London: Routledge), 441–49.

—— (1998) 'Frontlines and Backyards: The Terms of Change', in Owusu, K. (ed.) *Black British Culture and Society: A Text Reader*. (London: Routledge), 127–29.

—— (2003a) 'New Ethnicities'. Reprinted in Ashcroft, B., H. Tiffin and G. Griffiths (eds) *The Postcolonial Reader*. (London: Routledge), 223–27.

—— (2003b) 'Cultural Identity and Diaspora'. Reprinted in Braziel, J. Evans and A. Mannur (eds) *Theorizing Diaspora*. (Oxford: Blackwell), 233–46.

Harrison, P. C. (2002) 'Praise/Word', in Harrison, P. C., V. L. Walker II and G. Edwards (eds) *Black Theatre: Ritual Performance in the African Diaspora*. (Philadelphia, PA: Temple University Press), 1–10.

Halliburton, R. (2007) 'Review of *generations*'. *Time Out*. 7 March. Reprinted in *Theatre Record* XXVII.5, 26 February–11 March 2007, 236.

Hattenstone, S. (2010) 'Confessions of an Uncool Kid'. *The Guardian*, June 19 http://www.guardian.co.uk/stage/2010/jun/07/roy-williams-sucker-punch-interview (Accessed 18 August 2011).

Hickling, A. (2009) 'Review of *The Hounding of David Oluwale*'. *The Guardian*, 6 February. http://www.theguardian.com/stage/2009/feb/06/review-david-oluwale-leeds (Accessed 17 December 2013).

Hiley, J. (1989) 'Review of *A Hero's Welcome*'. *Listener*. 2 March 1989. Reprinted in *London Theatre Record*, IX:4, 12–25 Februrary, 208–9.

Hill, E. (1997) *The Trinidad Carnival: Mandate for a National Theatre*. (London: New Beacon).

Hingorani, D. (2010) *British Asian Theatre: Dramaturgy, Process and Performance*. (Basingstoke: Palgrave Macmillan).

Hirsch, A. (2012) 'Our Parents Left Africa – Now We Are Coming Back'. *The Guardian*, 26 August. http://www.theguardian.com/world/2012/aug/26/ghana-returnees-afua-hirsch-africa (Accessed 3 September 2013).

Hope-Wallace, P. (1963) 'Theater', Victoria and Albert Museum, Department of Theatre and Performance Core Collection: Production File, Royal Court, *Skyvers*.

Howe, S. (1998) *Afrocentrism: Mythical Pasts and Imagined Homes*. (London: Verso).

Hudson, C. (1983) 'Review of *The Shelter*'. *Standard*. n.d. Reprinted in *London Theatre Record*, III.18, 27 August–9 September, 699.

Hughes-Tafen, D. (2006) 'Women, Theatre and Calypso in the English-Speaking Caribbean'. *Feminist Review*, 84, 48–66.

Hutcheon, L. (1985) *A Theory of Parody: The Teachings of Twentieth-Century Art Forms*. (London: Methuen).

—— (1994) *Irony's Edge: The Theory and Politics of Irony*. (London: Routledge).

Hutner, H. (2004) *Colonial Women: Race and Culture in Stuart Drama*. (Oxford: Oxford University Press)

Hylton, K. (2010) 'The Black Family and Sport: It's All Good … Right?', in Ochieng B. and C. Hylton (eds) *Black Families in Britain as the Site of Struggle*. (Manchester: Manchester University Press), 234–57.

Irobi, E. (2007) 'What They Came With: Carnival and Persistence of African Performance Aesthetics in the Diaspora'. *Journal of Black Studies*, 37.6, 896–913.

Jaggi, M. (2001) 'Rites of Passage'. *The Guardian* Profile: Caryl Phillips. *The Guardian*, 2 November. http://www.theguardian.com/books/2001/nov/03/fiction.artsandhumanities. (Accessed 13 December 2013).

Jameson, F. (1991) *Postmodernism, or the Cultural Logic of Late Capitalism*. (Durham: Duke University Press).

Jeyifo, B. (2004) *Wole Soyinka: Politics, Poetics and Postcolonialism*. (Cambridge: Cambridge University Press).

Jernignan, F. K. (2008) *Drama and the Postmodern: Assessing the Limits of Metatheatre*. (Amherst, Massachussetts: Cambria).

Johns, L. (2010) 'Black Theatre Is Blighted by Its Ghetto Mentality'. *The London Evening Standard*, 9 February. http://www.standard.co.uk/news/black-theatre-is-blighted-by-its-ghetto-mentality-6709941.html (Accessed 3 March 2013).

—— (2011) 'Ghetto Grammar Robs the Young of A Proper Voice'. *The London Evening Standard*. http://www.standard.co.uk/news/ghetto-grammar-robs-the-young-of-a-proper-voice-6433284.html (Accessed 21 July 2014)

Jones, C. (1964) 'The Caribbean Community in Britain'. *Freedomways*, 4, 341–57.

Jones, E. D. (1965) *Othello's Countrymen: The African in English Renaissance Drama*. (Oxford: Oxford University Press).

Jones, Q. (2003) 'Information Communities', in Christensen K. and D. Levenson (eds) *Encyclopaedia of Community: From Village to the Virtual World Vol. I*. (Thousand Oaks, California: Sage), 657–63.

Joseph, M. (1998) 'Bodies Outside the State: Black British Women Playwrights and the Limits of Citizenship', in Phelan P. and J. Lane (eds) *The Ends of Performance*. (New York: New York University Press), 197–213.

—— (1999) *Nomadic Identities: The Performance of Citizenship*. (Minneapolis: University of Minnesota).

Kamali, L. (2009) 'The Sweet Part and the Sad Part: Black Power and the Memory of Africa in African–American and British Literature'. *Atlantic Studies*, 6.2, 207–21.

Kasule, S. (2006) 'Aspects of Madness and Theatricality in Kwame Kwei-Armah's Drama', in D. Godiwala (ed.) *Alternatives within the Mainstream: British Black and Asian Theatres*. (Newcastle: Cambridge Scholars), 314–28.

Kellaway, K. (1991) 'Coup for Trinidad's Acting Ambassador'. *The Observer*, 14 July, 55.

Kennedy, H. (2004) '20 Questions with ... Roy Williams'. *What's On Stage.Com*. 10 May http://www.whatsonstage.com/interviews/theatre/london/E8821083945389/20+Questions+With...Roy+Williams.html (Accessed 18 August 2011).

Kent, N. (2009) 'Introduction', in Agbaje, B., K. Kwei-Armah and R. Williams (eds) *Not Black and White*. (London: Methuen), vii–viii.

Khan, N. (1976) *The Arts Britain Ignores: The Arts of Ethnic Minorities in Britain*. (London: Community Relations Commission).

—— (2002) *Towards a Greater Diversity: Results and Legacy of the Arts Council of England's Cultural Diversity Action*. http://www.artscouncil.org.uk/media/uploads/documents/publications/354.pdf (Accessed 3 September 2013).

King, B. (2004) *The Internationalization of English Literature*. (Oxford: Oxford University Press).

Kretzmer, H. (1963) 'Cockney Kids in a Glass Jungle'. Victoria and Albert Museum, Department of Theatre and Performance Core Collection: Production File, Royal Court, *Skyvers.*

Kristeva, J. (1982) *Powers of Horror: An Essay on Abjection.* Trans. L. S. Roudiez (New York: Columbia University Press).

Kwei-Armah, K. (2007) 'Interview with Dr Joy DeGruy-Leary', in *'Statement of Regret* Production Programme'. (London: National Theatre Archive).

—— (2009) 'Sixty Years of Forgotten Treasures', 27 September http://www.theguardian.com/stage/2009/sep/27/black-theatre-archive-kwei-armah (Accessed 13 December 2013).

—— M. Norfolk and C. Newland (2003) 'Our Job Is to Write About What Is in Our Hearts'. *The Guardian,* 6 October. http://www.theguardian.com/stage/2003/oct/06/theatre.race (Accessed 13 December 2013).

Lacey, S. (1995) *British Realist Theater: The New Wave in Its Context 1956–1965.* (London: Routledge).

Ledent, B. (2006) 'Caryl Phillips' Drama: A Blueprint for A New Britishness', in Davis, G. V. and A. Fuchs (eds) *Staging New Britain: Aspects of South Asian British Theatre Practice.* (Brussels: P.I.E.- Peter Lang), 189–201.

Letts, Q. (2007) 'Review of *generations'. The Daily Mail.* 2 March. Reprinted in *Theatre Record,* XXVII.5, 26 February–11 March, 236.

Lewis, J. (1963) 'The Happiest Days …' Victoria and Albert Museum, Department of Theatre and Performance Core Collection: Production File: Royal Court, *Skyvers.*

Lhamon, W. T. (1998) *Raising Cain: Blackface Performance from Jim Crow to Hip Hop.* (Cambridge, MA: Harvard University Press).

Loomba, A. (1998) *Colonialism/Postcolonialism.* (London: Routledge).

Low, G. and M. Wynne-Davies (eds) (2006) *A Black British Canon?* (Basingstoke: Palgrave Macmillan).

Macauley, A. (2007) 'Review of *generations'. The Financial Times.* 2 March Reprinted in *Theatre Record,* XXVII.5, 26 February–11 March, 235.

Macdonald, J. G. (ed.) (1997) *Race, Ethnicity, and Power in the Renaissance.* (London: Associated University Press).

Macpherson, Sir W. (1999) *The Stephen Lawrence Inquiry: Report of an Inquiry by Sir William Macpherson of Cluny.* (Norwich: The Stationery Office Limited).

Malchow, H. (2011) *Special Relations: The Americanization of Britain?* (Stanford, CA: Stanford University Press).

Malik, K. (1996) *The Meaning of Race: Race, History, and Culture in Western Society.* (New York: New York University Press).

—— (2010) *From Fatwa to Jihad: The Rushdie Affair and Its Aftermath.* (New York, Melville House).

Malik, S. (2002) *Representing Black Britain: Black and Asian Images on Television.* (London: Sage Publications).

Mama, A. (1992) 'Black Women and the British State: Race, Class and Gender Analysis for the 1990s', in Braham, P., A. Rattansi and R. Skellington (eds) *Racism and Anti-Racism: Inequalities, Opportunities and Policies.* (London: Sage), 79–104.

—— (1995) *Beyond the Masks: Race, Gender and Subjectivity.* (London: Routedge).

Marks, P. (2005) 'Melting Pot Stew: Hearty Ingredients of "Elmina's Kitchen"'. *The Washington Post.* 6 January. http://www.washingtonpost.com/wp-dyn/articles/A51954-2005Jan5.html (Accessed 8 December 2013).

Marqusee, M. (1995) 'Sport and Stereotype: From Role Model to Muhammad Ali', in *Race and Class: All in the Game? Sport, Race and Politics*. Special Issue, 36:4, April–June, 1–29.

Mason-John, V. (ed.) (1995) *Talking Black: Lesbians of African and Asian Descent Speak Out* (London: Cassell).

—— (1999) *Brown Girl in the Ring: Plays, Prose and Poems*. (London: Get a Grip).

—— and Khambatta, A. (eds) (1993) *Lesbians Talk. Making Black Waves*. (London: Scarlet Press).

Maynard, J. A. (1996) 'Trends in Black Writing for Theatre'. *Performing Arts International*, 1.1, 53–5.

McLeod, J. (2004) *Postcolonial London: Rewriting the Metropolis*. (London, Routledge).

—— (2006) 'Fantasy Relationships: Black British Canons in a Transnational World', in Low G. and M. Wynne-Davies (eds) *A Black British Canon?* (Basingstoke: Palgrave Macmillan), 93–104.

—— (2009) 'British Freedoms: Caryl Phillips's Transatlanticism and the Staging of Rough Crossings'. *Atlantic Studies*, 6.2, 191–206.

McMillan, M. (2000) '"Ter Speak in Yer Mudder Tongue": An Interview with Playwright Mustapha Matura', in Owusu, K. (ed.) *Black British Culture and Society: A Text Reader*. (London: Routledge), 255–64.

—— (2006) 'Rebaptizing the World in Our Terms: Black Theatre and Live Arts in Britain', in Davis, G. V. and A. Fuchs (eds) *Staging New Britain: Aspects of South Asian British Theatre Practice*. (Brussels: Peter Lang), 47–64.

—— (2007) 'Aesthetics of the West Indian Front Room', in Arana, R. V. (ed.) *'Black' British Aesthetics Today*. (Newcastle-Upon-Tyne: Cambridge Scholars), 297–312.

—— (2008) 'Ah Room Fe She Self.' *SABLE*, Spring/Summer, 42–9.

—— (2009) *The Front Room; Migrant Aesthetics in the Home*. (London: Black Dog).

Mendick, R. and A. Johnson (2002) 'Eight Men Shot Dead in Two Years. Welcome to Britain's Murder Mile'. *The Independent*. 6 January. http://www.independent.co.uk/news/uk/this-britain/eight-men-shot-dead-in-two-years-welcome-to-britains-murder-mile-662314.html (Accessed 8 December 2013).

Mercer, K. (1994) *Welcome to the Jungle: New Positions in Black Cultural Studies*. (London: Routledge).

—— (2007) '"Diaspora Didn't Happen in a Day": Reflections on Aesthetics and Time', in Arana, R. V. (ed.) *'Black' British Aesthetics Today*. (Newcastle-Upon-Tyne: Cambridge Scholars), 66–78.

Mill, J. S. (1859) *Utilitarianism* 1975. 12th impression. Warnock, M. (ed). (Glasgow: William Collins Sons).

Miller, M. (2013) http://www.politics.co.uk/comment_analysis/2013/04/24.culture-secretary-maria-miller-s-arts-speech-in-full (Accessed 12 December 2013).

Mirza, H. S. (ed.) (1997) 'Introduction.' *Black British Feminism: A Reader*. (London: Routledge), 1–28.

Moi, T. (1986) 'Revolution in Poetic Language', in Moi, T. (ed.) *The Kristeva Reader*. (New York: Columbia University Press), 89–136.

Morris, M. (2010) 'White Witch' in Brewster, Y. (ed.) (2010) *For the Reckord: A Collection of Three Plays by Barry Reckord*. (London: Oberon), 156–60.

Mullen, H. (1992) 'Runaway Tongue: Resistant Orality in Uncle Tom's Cabin, Incidents in the Life of a Slave Girl, Our Nig and Beloved', in Samuels, S. (ed.) *The Culture of Sentiment*. (Oxford: Oxford University Press), 244–64.

Mumford, M. (2009) *Bertolt Brecht*. (London: Routledge).

Murphy, S. (2007) 'Review of *Rough Crossings*'. *Metro*. 2 October. Reprinted in *Theatre Record*, XXVII, 24 September–7 October. 1108.

—— (2008) *Evening Standard*. 21 April. http://www.standard.co.uk/goingout/theatre/double-the-fun-7405863.html (Accessed 17 December 2013).

Nasta, S. (1995) 'Setting Up Home in a City of Words', in Lee, R. (ed.) *Other Britain, Other British: Contemporary Multicultural Fiction*. (London: Pluto), 48–68.

Ngcobo, L. (ed.) (1988) *Let It Be Told: Black Women Writers in Britain*. (London, Virago).

Nightingale, B. (2007) 'Review of *generations*'. *The Times*. 28 February Reprinted in *Theatre Record*, XXVII.5, 26 February–11 March, 235.

Noble, P. (ed.) (1946) *British Theatre*. (London: British Yearbook).

Nu Century Arts and Octavia Foundation (2012) 'Margins to Mainstream: The Story of Black Theatre in Britain', premiered Birmingham, 11 May, 2012.

Okagbue, O. (2009) *Culture and Identity in African and Caribbean Theatre*. (London: Adonis and Abbey).

Ong, W. J. (1982) *Orality and Literacy*. (London: Routledge).

Orkin, M. (1991) *Drama and the South African State*. (Manchester: Manchester University Press).

Orr, B. (2001) *Empire on the Stage 1660–1714*. (Cambridge: Cambridge University Press)

Osborne D. (2005) 'The State of the Nation: Contemporary Black British Theatre and the Staging of the UK', in Houswitschka, C. and A. Muller (eds) *Staging Displacement, Exile and Diaspora, Contemporary Drama in English* 12. (Dusseldorf, Germany: Wissenschaftlicher Verlag Trier), 129–47.

—— (2006a) 'Writing Black Back: An Overview of Black Theater and Performance in Britain', in Godiwala, D. (ed.) *Alternatives Within the Mainstream: British Black and Asian Theatres*. (Newcastle: Cambridge Scholars), 61–81.

—— (2006b) 'The State of the Nation: Contemporary Black British Theatre and the Staging of the UK', in Godiwala, D. (ed.) *Alternatives within the Mainstream: British Black and Asian Theatres*. (Newcastle: Cambridge Scholars), 82–100.

—— (2007a) '"Know Whence You Came": Dramatic Art and Black British Identity.' *New Theatre Quarterly*, 23.3, 253–63.

—— (2007b) 'Not "in-yer-face" But What Lies Beneath: Experiential and Aesthetic Inroads in the Drama of debbie tucker green and Dona Daley', in Arana, R.V. (ed.) *"Black" British Aesthetics Today* (Newcastle: Cambridge Scholars Press), 222–42.

—— (ed.) (2008) *Hidden Gems*. (London: Oberon Books).

—— (2009) 'No Straight Answers: Writing on the Margins, Reclaiming Heroes'. *New Theatre Quarterly*, 25.1, 6–21.

—— (2010) '"I ain't British though / Yes you are. You're as English as I am": Belonging and Unbelonging in Black British Drama', in Lindner, U., M. Mohring, M. Stein and S. Strothe (eds) *Hybrid Cultures, Nervous States: Britain and Germany in a (Post)Colonial World*. (Amsterdam & New York: Rodopi), 203–27.

—— (2011a) '"How Do We Get the Whole Story?" Contra-dictions and Counter-narratives in debbie tucker green's Dramatic Poetics', in Tönnies, M. and C. Flotmann (eds) *Contemporary Drama in English*, 18 (Trier: Wissenschaftlicher Verlag Trier), 181–206.

—— (2011b) 'Roy Williams', in Middeke, M., P. P. Schnierer and A. Sierz (eds) *The Methuen Drama Guide to Contemporary British Playwrights*. (London: Methuen), 487–509.

—— (2011c) 'Black British Drama', in Baumbach, S., B. Neumann and A. Nünning (eds) *A History of British Drama: Developments, Interpretations*. (Trier: Wissenschaftlicher Verlag Trier), 429–49.

—— (ed.) (2012) *Hidden Gems Vol.II*. (London: Oberon Books).

Owusu, K. (2000) 'Introduction', in Owusu, K. (ed.) *Black British Culture and Society: A Text Reader* (London: Routledge), 1–18.

—— (2000) 'The Struggle for a Radical Black Political Culture: An Interview with A. Sivanandan', in Owusu, K. (ed.) *Black British Culture and Society: A Text Reader* (London: Routledge), 453–62.

Parks, S-L. (1995) 'An Equation for Black People Onstage', in *The America Play and Other Works*. (New York: Theatre Communications Group), 19–22.

Parmar, P. (1997) 'Other Kinds of Dreams', in Mirza, H. S. (ed.) *Black British Feminism: A Reader* (London: Routledge), 67–69.

Paton, D. and M. Forde (eds) (2012) *Obeah and Other Powers: The Politics of Caribbean Religion and Healing* (Durham, N.C.: Duke University Press).

Peacock, D. K. (2006a) 'Home Thoughts from Abroad: Mustapha Matura', in Luckhurst, M. (ed.) *A Companion to Modern British and Irish Drama 1880–2005*. (Oxford: Blackwell), 188–97.

—— (2006b) 'The Question of Multiculturalism: The Plays of Roy Williams', in Luckhurst, M. (ed.) *A Companion to Modern British and Irish Drama 1880–2005*. (Oxford: Blackwell), 530–40.

—— (2008) 'Black British Drama and the Politics of Identity', in Holdsworth, N. and M. Luckhurst (eds) *A Concise Companion to Contemporary British and Irish Drama*. (London: Blackwell), 48–65.

Perloff, M. (1991) *Radical Artifice: Writing Poetry in the Age of Media*. (Chicago: University of Chicago Press).

Phillips, C. (1984c) 'The Black British Experience: A Dramatist's Viewpoint'. Unpublished Lecture, American Theatre Critics Association Conference, *Literature Across Cultures*. Providence, Rhode Island, 13 March.

—— (1984d) 'Introduction'. *The Shelter*. (Oxford: Amber Lane Press), 7–12.

—— (2004a) *A Kind of Home: James Baldwin in Paris*. (Unpublished). BBC Radio 4. 9 January.

—— (2005) 'Lost Generation'. *The Guardian*, 23 April, 16.

—— (2006) 'I Could Have Been a Playwright', in Davis, G. V. and A. Fuchs (eds) *Staging New Britain: Aspects of South Asian British Theatre Practice*. (Brussels: Peter Lang), 37–46.

—— (2011) *Colour Me English: Selected Essays*. (London: Harvill Secker).

Philip, F. (2007) 'Review of *Rough Crossings*'. *The British Theatre Guide*, 12 September. http://www.britishtheatreguide.info/reviews/roughcrossings-rev (Accessed 19 May 2014).

Phillips, M. (1981) 'Black Theatre in Britain'. *Platform*, 3, 3–6.

Pinnock, W. (1991) 'Letter'. *The Evening Standard*. 4 September, n.p., Theatre Performance Collections, London, MS THM/273/7/2/708.

—— (1997) 'Winsome Pinnock Interview', in Stephenson, H. and N. Langridge (eds) *Rage and Reason: Women Playwrights on Playwriting*. (London: Methuen), 45–53.

—— (1999) 'Breaking Down the Door', in Gottlieb, V. and C. Chambers (eds) *Theatre in a Cool Climate* (Oxford: Amber Lane), 27–38.

—— (2012) 'Laying Ghosts to Rest', in Osborne, D. (ed.) *Hidden Gems Vol. II*. (London: Oberon), 95–99.

Pilkington, L. (2010) *Theatre and Ireland*. (Basingstoke: Palgrave Macmillan).

Polley, M. (2004) 'Sport and National Identity in Contemporary England', in Smith, A. and D. Porter (eds) *Sport and National Identity in the Post-War World.* (London: Routledge), 10–30.

Ponnuswami, M. (2000) 'Small Island People: Black British Women Playwrights', in Aston, E. and J. Reinelt (eds) *The Cambridge Companion to Modern British Women Playwrights,* (Cambridge: Cambridge University Press), 217–34.

—— (2007) 'Alienation and Alienation Effects in Winsome Pinnock's Talking in Tongues', in Arana, R. V. (ed) *'Black' British Aesthetics Today* (Newcastle: Cambridge Scholars Press), 206–21.

Prior, I. (2004) 'TV Pundit Ron Atkinson Sacked For Racist Remark'. *The Guardian.* 22 April. http://www.theguardian.com/media/2004/apr/22/football. raccintheuk (Accessed 6 May 2014).

Procter, J. (ed.) (2000) *Writing Black Britain 1948–1988: An Interdisciplinary Anthology.* (Manchester: Manchester University Press).

Programme (1963) 'Skyvers' Royal Court Theatre, Victoria and Albert Museum, Department of Theatre and Performance Core Collection: Production File: *Skyvers.*

Puwar, N. (2004) *Space Invaders: Race, Gender and Bodies Out of Place.* (Oxford: Berg).

Rahbek, U. (2001) '"I am 200 Years Old Now, and Getting Older": Blackness in Caryl Phillips's Plays from *Strange Fruit* to *The Shelter'*, in Ulf, L. and A. Holden Rønning (eds) *Dialoguing on Genres* (Oslo: Novus Press, 2001), 113–25.

Ramdin, R. (1999) *Reimagining Britain: 500 Years of Black and Asian History.* (London: Pluto).

Ravengai, S. (2010) 'Contesting Constructions of Cultural Production in and Through Urban Theatre in Rhodesia, c. 1890–1950'. *African Theatre 9: Histories 1850–1950,* 53–71.

Reckord, B. (1971) *Does Fidel Eat More Than Your Father?* (London, Andre Deutsch).

—— (2003) 'I Should Have Studied Science, Says Playwright'. *The Gleaner.* 17 August. http://jamaica-gleaner.com/gleaner/library/archives.html (Accessed 18 December 2013).

—— (2010d) 'Preface', in Brewster, Y. (ed.) *For the Reckord: A Collection of Three Plays by Barry Reckord.* (London: Oberon), 77–78.

Reckord, M. (2009) 'Jamaica's Gifts to British Theater.' http://jamaica-gleaner. com/gleaner/20090315/ent/ent1.html (Accessed 21 August 2012).

Rees, R. (1992) *Fringe First: Pioneers of Fringe Theatre on Record* (London: Oberon Books).

Reynolds, H. (1928) *Minstrel Memories: The Story of Burnt Cork Minstrelsy in Great Britain from 1836–1927.* (London: Alston Rivers).

Riggio, M. C. (ed.) (2004) *Carnival: Culture in Action – The Trinidad Experience.* (London: Routledge).

Rommel-Ruiz, B. W. (2006) 'Crossing the Black Atlantic: The African Colonization Movements in Postwar Rhode Island and Nova Scotia'. *Slavery and Abolition,* 27.3, 349–65.

Runnymede Trust (2000) *The Future of Multi-Ethnic Britain: The Parekh Report.* (London: Profile Books).

Said, E. W. (1993) *Culture and Imperialism.* (London: Chatto &Windus).

Sawyer, M. (2008) 'Taking the Stage'. *The Observer.* 10 February. http://www. guardian.co.uk/stage/2008/feb/10/theatre1 (Accessed 18 August 2011).

Scafe, S. (2007) 'Displacing the Centre: Home and Belonging in the Drama of Roy Williams', in Anim-Addo, J. and S. Scafe (eds) *I Am Black/White/Yellow: An Introduction to the Black Body in Europe*. (London: Mango Publishing), 71–87.

—— (2011) 'Personal Interview with Caryl Phillips'. 29 November.

Scarman Report, The (1981) http: www.peoplecan.org.uk/media/.../1981scarman-report_summary.pdf. (Accessed 13 December 2013).

Schäffner, R. (1999) 'Assimilation, Separatism and Multiculturalism in Mustapha Matura's Welcome Home Jacko and Caryl Phillips's Strange Fruit'. *Wasafiri*, 29, 65–70.

Schama, S. (2005) *Rough Crossings: Britain, the Slaves and the American Revolution*. (London: BBC Books).

Scott, D. (1991) 'Review of *Talking in Tongues*'. *Plays & Players*. November, 32.

Shank, T. (1996) 'The Multiplicity of British Theater', in T. Shank (ed.) *Contemporary British Theatre*. (Basingstoke: Macmillan), 3–18.

Shellard, D. (1999) *British Theatre since the War*. (New Haven: Yale University Press).

Shepherd, S. (2009) *Cambridge Introduction to Modern British Theatre*. (Cambridge: Cambridge University Press).

Shulman, M. (1958) 'Mr. Reckord's Phrases Can't Hide the Flaws'. *Evening Standard*. 27 May, Victoria and Albert Museum, Department of Theatre and Performance Core Collection: Production File: Reckord: *Flesh to a Tiger*.

Shuttleworth, I. (2003) 'Review of *dirty butterfly*'. *The Financial Times*. 4 March. Reprinted in *Theatre Record*, XX.III, 26 February–11 March, 251–2.

Sierz, A. (2000) *In-Yer-Face Theatre: British Drama Today*. (London: Faber and Faber).

—— (2003) 'Debbie Tucker Green: "If You Hate the Show at Least You Have Passion"'. *The Independent on Sunday*. 27 April, 8.

—— (2006a) '"What Kind of England Do We Want?"' *New Theatre Quarterly*, 22.2, 113–21.

—— (2006b) 'Two Worlds Fighting Each Other: Roy Williams and Contemporary Black British Theatre', in Davis, G. V. and A. Fuchs (eds) *Staging New Britain: Aspects of South Asian British Theatre Practice*. (Brussels: Peter Lang), 177–88.

—— (2011) *Rewriting the Nation*. (London: Methuen).

Sivanandan, A. (1976) 'Race and Class and the State: The Black Experience in Britain'. *Race and Class*, 17, 347–68.

—— (1982) *A Different Hunger: Writings on Racism and Resistance*. (London: Pluto).

Smith, D. J. (1977) *Racial Disadvantage in Britain: The PEP Report*. (Harmondsworth: Penguin Books).

Smith, A. and D. Porter (eds) (2004) 'Introduction'. *Sport and National Identity in the Post-War World*. (London: Routledge), 1–9.

Spencer, C. (2007a) 'Review of *generations*'. *The Daily Telegraph*. 3 March. Reprinted in *Theatre Record*, XXVII.5, 26 February–11 March, 236.

—— (2007b) 'Review of *Rough Crossings*'. *The Daily Telegraph*. 1 October. Reprinted in *Theatre Record*, XXVII, 24 September–7 October, 1107.

Stafford-Clark, M. (2012) 'Reckord Celebrations'. Bush Theatre, London. 23 September.

Stanton, W. (2004) 'The Invisible Theatre of Radio Drama'. *Critical Quarterly*, 46.4, 94–107.

Steadman, I. (1990) 'Towards Popular Theatre in South Africa'. *Journal of South African Studies: Performance and Popular Culture*, 16.2, 207–28.

Stein, M. (2004) *Black British Literature: Novels of Transformation*. (Columbus: Ohio State University Press).

Storry, M. and P. Childs (1997) *British Cultural Identities*. (London, Routledge).

Tajfel, H. and C. Fraser (1978) 'Social Interaction: Introduction', in Tajfel, H. and C. Fraser (eds) *Introducing Social Psychology*. (Harmondsworth: Penguin), 99–103.

Taylor, D. (1998) 'A Savage Performance: Guillermo Gomez-Pena and Coco Fusco's "Couple in the Cage"'. *The Drama Review*, 42:2, 160–75.

Thomas, H. (2006) *Caryl Phillips*. (Tavistock, London: Northcote Press).

Thompson, A. (2008) *Performing Race and Torture on the Early Modern Stage*. (London: Routledge).

Thornber, R. (1963) 'Awkward Stage'. Victoria and Albert Museum, Department of Theatre and Performance Core Collection: Production File: Royal Court, *Skyvers*.

Tokson, E. H. (1982) *The Popular Image of the Black Man in English Drama, 1550–1688*. (Boston, Mass: G. K. Hall and Co).

Travis, A. (2002) 'Blunkett Deeper in "Swamp" Row'. *The Guardian*. 26 April. www.theguardian.com/politics/2002/apr/26/immigrationandpublicservices. immigration.

Tunstall, K. E. (2004) 'Border/Crossings'. Oxford Amnesty Lecture, in Tunstall, K. E. (ed.) *Displacement, Asylum, Migration*. (Oxford: Oxford University Press), 210–25.

Turner, V. (1967) 'Betwixt and Between: The Liminal Period in Rites de Passage', in Turner, V. (ed.) *The Forest of Symbols: Aspects of Ndembu Ritual*. (Ithaca: Cornell University Press), 93–111.

Ugwu, C. (1995) *Let's Get It On: The Politics of Black Performance*. (London: Institute of Contemporary Arts).

Vaughan, V. M. (2005) *Performing Blackness on English Stages 1500–1800*. (Cambridge: Cambridge University Press)

Vivan, I. (2008) 'The Iconic Ship in the Atlantic Dialogue of Black Britain', in Oboe, A. and A. Scacchi (eds) *Recharting the Black Atlantic: Modern Cultures, Local Communities, Global Connections*. (London: Routledge), 225–37.

Waldrop, R. (1987) 'Poem', in Lehman, D. (ed.) *Ecstatic Occassions, Expedient Forms: 65 Leading Poets Select and Comment on their Poems*. (New York: Macmillan), 97.

Walder, D. (1992) 'Resituating Fugard: South African Drama as Witness'. *New Theatre Quarterly*, VIII.32, 343–62.

Walshe, B. (2012) 'Bola Agbaje – Risky Business'. http://www.coutts.com/news-and insights/coutts-woman/2012/january/features/bola-agbaje/ (Accessed 3 September 2013).

Walton, D. (2008) 'Stop Trying to Define Black Theatre'. *The Guardian*. 29 October. http://www.guardian.co.uk/stage/theatreblog/2008/oct/29/black-theatre-dawn-walton-eclipse (Accessed 3 March 2013).

Wandor, M. (ed.) (1985) *Plays by Women*. Vol. IV. (London: Methuen).

Warrington, D. (2010) 'Meetings with Barry Reckord', in Brewster, Y. (ed.) *For the Reckord: A Collection of Three Plays by Barry Reckord*. (London: Oberon), 245–48.

—— (2012) 'Reckord Celebrations'. The Bush Theatre, London, 23 September.

Waters, H. (2007) *Racism on the Victorian Stage: Representation of Slavery and the Black Character.* (Cambridge: Cambridge University Press).

West, N. (2008) 'The World of Kwame Kwei-Armah'. *The Daily Telegraph.* 19 January. http://www.telegraph.co.uk/culture/theatre/3670618/The-world-of-Kwame-Kwei-Armah.html (Accessed 8 December 2013).

Wild, R. (2008) *Black Was the Colour of Our Fight: Black Power in Britain, 1955– 1976.* (Unpublished PhD Thesis: University of Sheffield)

Williams, R. (2004) 'Foreword'. *Roy Williams: Plays Two.* (London: Methuen), ix–xlll.

—— (2009) 'Black Theatre's Big Breakout'. *The Guardian.* 27 September. http://www.theguardian.com/stage/2009/sep/27/black-theatre-roy-williams (Accessed 11 December 2013).

Wittig, M. (1992) *The Straight Mind and Other Essays.* (New York: Harvester Wheatsheaf).

Wolf, M. (2005) 'He Talks of Black Britain, and the West End Listens'. *New York Times.* 1 June. http://www.nytimes.com/2005/06/01/theater/newsandfeatures/01kwam.html (Accessed 8 December 2013).

—— (n.d.) 'Tear Down the Wall'. *Theatre News Online.* http://theaternewsonline.com/LondonTheatreReviews/Teardownthewall.cfm (Accessed 8 December 2013).

Worrall, D. (2007) *Harlequin Empire: Race, Ethnicity, and the Drama of Popular Entertainment.* (London: Pickering and Chatto).

Worthen, W. B. (1994) 'Of Actors and Automata: Hieroglyphics of Modernism'. *Journal of Dramatic Theory and Criticism*, IX.1, 3–19.

Wright, B. S. (2000) 'Dub Poet Lekka Mi', in Owusu, K. (ed.) *Black British Culture and Society: A Text Reader.* (London: Routledge), 271–88.

Wu, D. (2000) *Making Plays: Interviews with Contemporary British Dramatists and Their Directors.* (Basingstoke: Macmillan).

Young, R. (1995) *Colonial Desire: Hybridity in Theory, Culture and Race.* (London: Routledge).

Index